THE LONDON
VOLVO B7TL

THE LONDON VOLVO B7TL

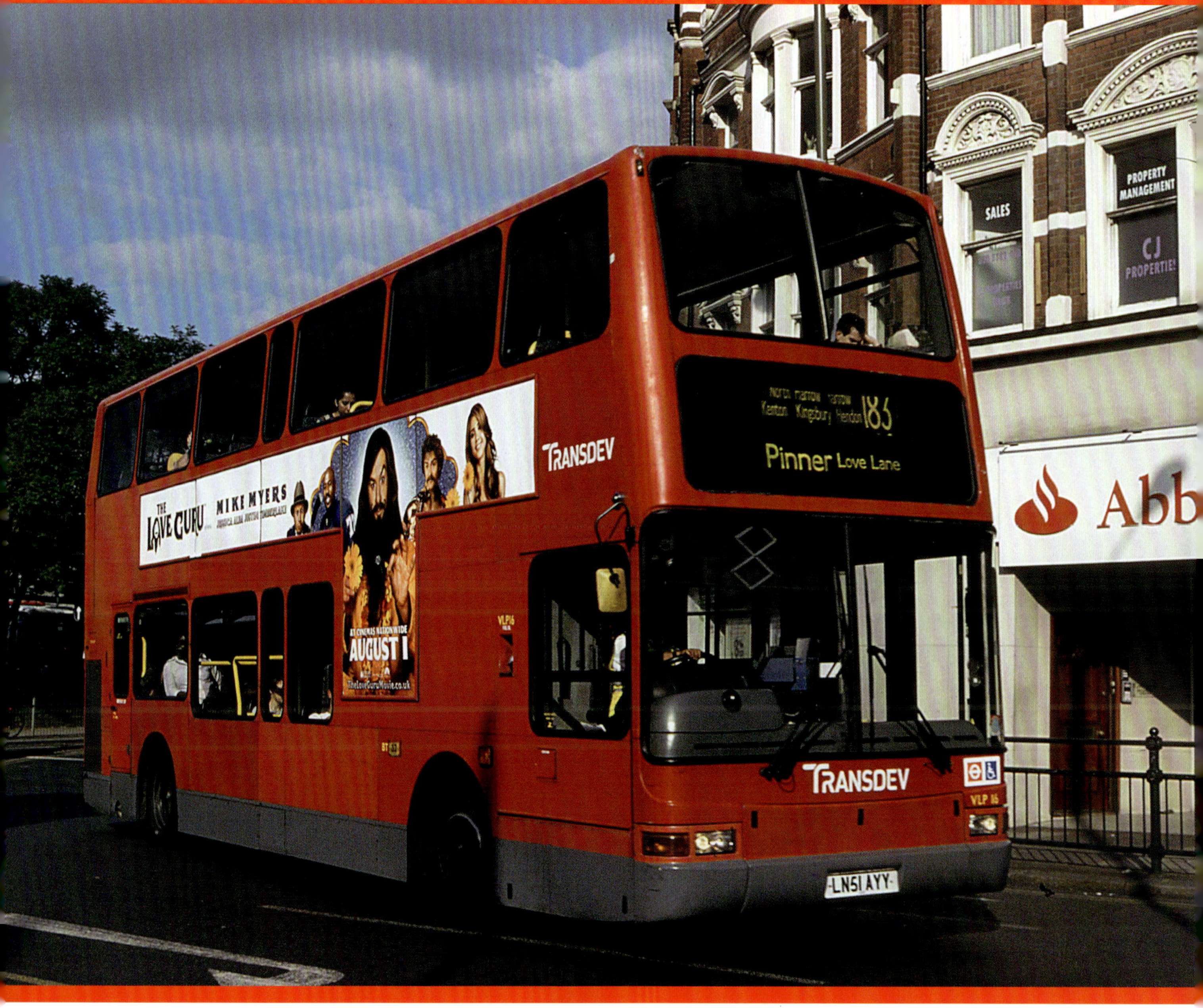

Matthew Wharmby

Cover: **Wrightbus' handsome Gemini body was developed specifically for the Volvo B7TL, helping the fortunes of both. Arriva London came late to the type, having been wedded to DAFs, but took nearly four hundred. This is VLW 22 (LJ51 DGY), seen in Wood Green on 18 April 2003.** *Author*

Back cover, top: **London General took 273 Wrightbus Gemini-bodied Volvo B7TLs as the WVL class, of which WVL 46 (LF52 ZRE) is seen at Hyde Park Corner on 4 July 2005, in front of Metroline's Plaxton President-bodied VPL 189 (Y189 NLK).** *Author*

Back cover, middle: **First alternated between Tridents and Volvo B7TLs for as long as each were available and amassed similar totals. VNL 32265 (LT52 WWL) was previously known as VFL 1265 and was taken for the 10's OPO conversion; on 21 October 2005 it is seen in Oxford Street on the 23.** *Author*

Back cover, bottom: **London United was an early Volvo B7TL customer, taking both ALX400s (VAs) and Plaxton Presidents (VPs). Flattered by the outstanding livery of the time, VP 124 (W472 BCW) is coming into Hounslow on 17 February 2007, at a time when operations were billed as Transdev.** *Author*

Title page: **Sovereign double-decked its 183 with 10.6m Plaxton President-bodied Volvo B7TLs. New as 2732, VLP 16 (LN51 AYY) is seen on 25 July 2008 leaving Golders Green.** *Author*

First published in Great Britain in 2021 by
Pen and Sword Transport,
An imprint of
Pen & Sword Books Ltd.
Yorkshire - Philadelphia

Copyright © Matthew Wharmby 2021

ISBN 978 1 52678 695 1

The right of Matthew Wharmby to be identified as author of this work has been asserted by him in accordance with the Copyright, Designs and Patents Act 1988.

A CIP catalogue record for this book is available from the British Library.

All rights reserved. No part of this book may be reproduced or transmitted in any form or by any means, electronic or mechanical including photocopying, recording or by any information storage and retrieval system, without permission from the Publisher in writing.

Designed by Matthew Wharmby

Printed and bound by Printworks Global Ltd, London/Hong Kong

Pen & Sword Books Ltd incorporates the Imprints of Pen & Sword Books Archaeology, Atlas, Aviation, Battleground, Discovery, Family History, History, Maritime, Military, Naval, Politics, Railways, Select, Transport, True Crime, Fiction, Frontline Books, Leo Cooper, Praetorian Press, Seaforth Publishing, Wharncliffe and White Owl.

For a complete list of Pen & Sword titles please contact

PEN & SWORD BOOKS LIMITED
47 Church Street, Barnsley, South Yorkshire, S70 2AS, England
E-mail: enquiries@pen-and-sword.co.uk
Website: www.pen-and-sword.co.uk

or

PEN AND SWORD BOOKS
1950 Lawrence Rd, Havertown, PA 19083, USA
E-mail: Uspen-and-sword@casematepublishers.com
Website: www.penandswordbooks.com

Contents

Foreword 5
Antecedents 6

London Bus Companies
Go-Ahead (London General, London Central and Metrobus) 8
London United 96
Metroline and Metroline London Northern 124
Arriva London North and Arriva London South 166
Arriva the Shires and Arriva Southend (Arriva Kent Thameside) 212
London Easylink 214
East Thames Buses 216
First London (First Capital and Centrewest) 224
Tower Transit 242
Sovereign 246
Travel London / Abellio 250
Sullivan Buses 262
Metrobus 264
TfL 265

Other London-area Volvo B7TL operators
Arriva Southern Counties; First Beeline and First Leicester; Ensignbus 266

London Tour Operators
London City Tour 270

Totals 272
Bibliography 272

Foreword

During the first half of the first decade of the 21st century, Volvo's B7TL and Dennis's Trident battled it out for supremacy in the capital, with DAF and Scania only minor competitors. When production of their respective first-generation low-floor double-deckers came to an end in 2006, order totals were almost exactly level, Volvo having achieved just over two thousand sales to London operators and Dennis a little more.

The Volvo B7TL had two solid predecessors in the underfloor-engined B10M (or Citybus) and the Leyland Olympian, which Volvo inherited from Leyland. From 2000 B7TL sales started and quickly drew pace with the competing Dennis Trident so that by the time production wound down after six busy years, London operators were operating much the same numbers of each. The myriad versions of the type in London remained reliable and lasted the decade and a bit expected of them, with the last regular examples drifting away in 2020.

My thanks to the regular band of intrepid photographers who filled in gaps where I wasn't able to go, and to the publishers for permitting this story to be told in the first place.

Matthew Wharmby
Walton-on-Thames, April 2021

Antecedents

Through the deregulation- and recession-caused destruction of the domestic British bus industry, Volvo had found itself the pre-eminent bus manufacturer in the country by the turn of the 1990s. Leyland had been taken over (with the unceremonious deletion of the majority of its product line all that was left to do on that front) and MCW had gone after a spirited decade and a half as Leyland's major competitor. Only Dennis remained as a rival, and they weren't up to much…

Until the Dart. After four or five years of rattly van-derived minibuses that really weren't built for the long term, Dennis produced the perfect bus for the straitened era it would be serving. As arm's-length municipals and former NBC companies were bought up at a song or simply driven ruthlessly out of business, the resulting big groups used Darts not only to replace the short-lived minibuses and then existing double-deckers as they aged, but to match the smaller number of passengers that would once have fitted into full-sized single-deckers.

Not that the double-decker was quite dead yet. The Olympian was the jewel in the old Leyland's crown, and the only model Volvo carried over, though it was now badged as a Volvo Olympian. Under this identity and with a degree of reworking to accommodate modern engines and interiors, Volvo sold twice as many Olympians as Leyland had before production ceased in 2000.

Right: **Tough as nails, almost absurdly light for its gargantuan carrying capacity and blessed with a truly frightening turn of speed, the Volvo B10M was described by various quarters as the perfect bus. In Citybus double-deck format it was just as accomplished, even if the East Lancs bodywork on the London & Country ones wasn't to everyone's taste aesthetically. It didn't matter, and in fact East Lancs survived the hard times to be able to participate in bodying the first-generation low-floor double-deckers like the Volvo B7TL and its Dennis Trident and DAF DB250RS(LF) rivals. On 2 March 1998 what was now Arriva London South VE 651 (H651 GPF) takes the comparatively short-lived Londonlinks livery into Euston on the 188.** *Author*

Left: **The Volvo Olympian was an improved and updated version of an already fine original, and sales supported that perception. Needing to replace ageing Metrobuses and Titans in the second half of the 1990s, the new operators of several former LBL subsidiaries took over 700 Volvo Olympians between them. One such repeat customer was Stagecoach, which specified models to its provincial long-wheelbase, low-height standard and 'Londonised' them only through fitment of an exit door and proper blinds. Here on 21 June 1999 at Oxford Circus is VA 50 (R150 VPU), delivered to Bow two years previously as a Titan replacement. The careers of these and other Volvo Olympians in London were to be cut short by what became TfL's imperative towards phasing in 100% low-floor operation long before it became legally mandatory, whatever the cost, and in this case Stagecoach could easily cascade buses out of London once replacing them with Tridents. Interestingly, the London operations of Stagecoach never ordered so much as a single Volvo B7TL.** *Author*

The simultaneous winding down of Volvo Citybus production on the underfloor B10M chassis made it imperative to design low-floor successors for both single- and double-deckers, and in 1999 Volvo thought it had the answer when it unveiled a vertical-engined B7L mockup and took it around the country, including to London. However, London operators declared they were not willing to depart from their trusted transverse-engine configuration and a hurried rethink had to be executed. This put Volvo a year behind DAF, who had set the ball rolling in 1998 with its own DB250RS(LF), and Dennis, whose UK-market Trident 2 made its debut in 1999, but by the turn of the century the new B7TL chassis was ready for bodying by Alexander, Plaxton and East Lancs.

Left: **Much interest surrounded Plaxton's construction of its first President body on a Volvo chassis, albeit a non-functioning mockup. It was put on display at various points (as here at Coach & Bus, held at the NEC on 10 October 1997) to whet appetites as the works geared up for mass production. However, the market at the time was firmly wedded to the transverse engine and expressed a strong preference for it in production models, thus setting back the timetable and enabling Dennis and, to a lesser extent, DAF, to get in on the ground floor with orders. Volvo's diligence was to pay off in the long run, however, as the reworked transverse-engined B7TL soon picked up enough orders to catch up to Dennis.** *Author*

Antecedents 7

Go-Ahead

AVL, PVL, EVL, WVL, VP, VWL and PVN classes

Even before Volvo had put what eventually resulted as the B7TL into production, London Central placed an order for forty-six in July 1998, against the tender awards for the 45 and 63, already operated by Titans from Camberwell and Peckham respectively.

Volvo's need to rework the prototype came about due to the preference of British operators for transverse engines, following the appearance in London of a non-functional demonstrator carrying a Plaxton President body. Go-Ahead's first order was firmed up by the beginning of 1999 as Alexander ALX400-bodied examples (the AVL class), but confidence in Plaxton was also expressed with a follow-on for 126 Presidents (PVLs) for the 89, 401 and 422 at Bexleyheath, the 37 and 77A at Stockwell and the 44, 77 and 270 at Merton.

The design rethink set Volvo back a year despite a solidly building order book, and Dennis's Trident scooped up some of the orders that might otherwise have accrued to Volvo; indeed, one potential big customer, Stagecoach, never took a single B7TL for London. Go-Ahead hedged its bets towards the end of 1999 by adding to its B7TL orders an order for 13 Plaxton President-bodied Dennis Tridents for the 88. By year's end the 89's need for new buses was factored in and seventeen more PVLs were ordered.

Right: **Elegant and symmetrical-looking with its blacked-out central staircase, the AVL class of ALX400-bodied Volvo B7TLs brought this combination to London for the first time. London Central, however, was to take no more after the first batch of forty-six, and they lasted only ten years in service. Seen at the south side of Blackfriars Bridge on 7 July 2000 is Camberwell's AVL 4 (V104 LGC).** Author

AVL 1, carrying a new livery of red with yellow-topped darker grey skirt and no cantrail band, was delivered on 5 December 1999, but further examples waited till January, when they were put to work training drivers pending service entry, which came on 28 January in the form of AVL 20 as PM126 on the 63. Camberwell followed on the 31st with its own route 45. This garage also introduced AVLs to the 12 on Sundays and N159 at night, while slipping them out on the 35, 40, 345 and 381. On Sundays the 36 was OPO with a Peckham allocation, which soon saw AVLs. All forty-six were in service by the end of February, but that was to be the one and only ALX400 order.

Above: **Peckham's AVL 26 (V126 LGC) is setting off from the old Crystal Palace Parade stand on 22 July 2000; it will make a U-turn at the roundabout a couple of hundred yards ahead and then return the way it came.** *Author*

Left: **The AVLs made it into the West End proper on Sundays with their use on the 12, which was OPO on that day. In Oxford Street on 2 April 2000 is Camberwell's AVL 12 (V112 LGC).** *Author*

Go-Ahead 9

Right: **More aerodynamic than the comparable ALX400, Plaxton's President body was an instant success and Go-Ahead London alone took 419 on Volvo B7TLs to produce the PVL class. On 2 June 2000 Bexleyheath's PVL 53 (W453 WGH) is at the first stop outbound on the 422.** *Author*

March saw the delivery and simultaneous entry into service of London Central's first PVLs, with PVL 6 on the 422 taking the honours on 9 March. The 422 took priority, this recently-gained route having been taken over with Titans, and after that was done the 229 and 401 could then be tackled, with predictable wanderings to the 51, 321 and 492. The 89's conversion was moved up so that PVLs 1-55 all went into Bexleyheath. Spanning the V to W half-year age letters, this they had done by the end of April, with the stragglers coming late from having trained Stockwell in advance of that garage's own batch, delivery of which followed immediately afterwards.

Right: **Although the modern fashion was for single-pane upper-deck front windows that didn't open, the unfortunate consequence was that vandals had a larger canvas on which to practise with their knives, as on Bexleyheath's PVL 5 (V305 LGC) coming into Lewisham on 5 May 2001. Etching was an absolute epidemic London-wise for several years in the first decade of the 21st century.** *Author*

Top left: **Plaxton thankfully built the President's upper-deck front handrails into the fascia rather than right across the sightline as on the ALX400. Go-Ahead's moquette of the time was distinctly discordant, but enabled similarly random pieces to be sewn in to replace ripped sections.** *Author*

Above left: **The rear aspect of the PVL was famously offset, as on Bexleyheath's PVL 49 (W449 WGH), seen on 2 June 2000 on the 229.** *Author*

Above: **The 401 descended from a London Country service and was one of the routes Bexleyheath converted from T to PVL in the spring of 2000; here is PVL 14 (V314 LGC) on 2 June.** *Author*

Left: **Not yet scheduled for vehicles newer than NVs was the 51, but on 14 April 2001 at Sidcup, Bexleyheath's PVL 30 (V330 LGC) has strayed.** *Author*

Right: **After nine years of Metrobuses, Stockwell was ready to upgrade when the awards of the 37, 77A and 88 proved successful. On 22 July 2000 PVL 77 (W477 WGH) is setting off from Wandsworth, the modern western terminus of a route 77A that had seen much curtailment from its peak.** Author

PVLs 56-96, with London General logos, began taking over Stockwell's 37, 77A and 88 (plus the 11 on Saturdays and Sundays and unscheduled visits to the 133, 196 and 295) from 7 June, after two had been used on this year's Chelsea Flower Show park and ride. Here it was Metrobuses that were replaced, though, as with Bexleyheath's Ts, two more years would elapse before all the old buses moved on.

As Stockwell's PVLs went into service, 52 more were ordered, which would take into account the requirements for routes 188 and 343, both won by London Central for takeover over the cusp of 2000/01, and the 280, retained by Merton and to add to its expected forty-seven PVLs, which began taking over the 44, 77 and 270 (plus the 22 on Sundays and school journeys on the 152 and 163 as well as visits to the 155, 164 and 219)

Right: **Forty-one PVLs came to Stockwell during the summer of 2000, but not quite enough had been ordered to fulfil the 88 at the increased PVR it would be adopting when reconfigured to absorb the 135 on 2 September 2000, so thirteen Tridents were added as well. At the Oxford Circus stand of the time is PVL 71 (W471 WGH), seen on 27 August 2000; a week later the 88 would be projected north to Camden Town.** Author

Left: **On 4 August 2000 the 37 is seen in the hands of PVL 65 (W465 WGH) at Peckham. This was the site of the former Peckham garage, now a bus station and car park for the large Tesco. In later years the replacement Peckham garage round the corner would come to operate the 37, but with AVLs rather than PVLs.** *Author*

Left: **Coming and going at Tooting Broadway on 9 September 2000 as Merton's conversion from M to PVL gets under way; on the left is M 947 (A947 SUL), passing PVL 109 (W509 WGH). The Metrobus would be sold during the following February.** *Author*

Left: **Facing in the other direction on 20 October 2001, both buses on the 270 and 280 are now PVLs, with PVL 117 (W517 WGH) in front of PVL 102 (W502 WGH). The 280 was taken over with its own batch, but mixing of batches was inevitable and indeed preferable.** *Author*

from 28 July. Ahead of schedule, the 280 also began to see PVLs from this batch. Stockwell's 88, already awaiting 13 Tridents (PDLs), was about to have the 135's northern end added as an extension, whch would require a few more buses still. Where Routemasters failed and required doored buses with conductors, Camberwell's AVLs stepped in on the 12 and Stockwell PVLs covered Waterloo workings on the 11.

DVLA-enforced holes in the availability of matching registrations for these buses were plugged ingeniously with marks where the third number matched the ten, viz PVLs 80 and 90 were W408 and W409 WGH. PVL 70 did not take a new registration at all, instead receiving 170 CLT from a sold Routemaster.

In September, another order was placed for 29 PVLs for the 118 and 172, the former being a capture from Arriva London South and the latter fielding London Central's last 100% allocation of Titans. October saw the PDLs arrive and join the PVL allocation at Stockwell, predominantly on their intended 88, while examples of the next PVL order began to arrive, going into service at Merton from the 25th. These differed by having forward staircases, increasing downstairs capacity by two seats. That was the 280 accounted for, followed in November by PVLs 156-160 for the 88's increase at Stockwell. It had now been decided to put the 188 into Stockwell as a London General contract, and on 2 December this commenced with PVLs 160-178.

2001 began with the introduction of a Putney allocation on the 37 on 6 January, using PVLs borrowed from Stockwell. The month was also characterised by the delivery of the PVLs intended for the 343 and 118.

Right: **One of the 280's designated batch when new was PVL 145 (X745 EGK), sporting a forward staircase, and on 21 March 2002 it is working a route 77 duty past the south side of Lambeth Bridge.** Author

Right: **After almost interminable wandering in the last decade, the 188 now settled at Stockwell and on 14 July 2001 PVL 156 (X556 EGK) is seen coming through Waterloo.** Author

Left: **The look of the PVL class was alarmingly different once you effectively removed the blinds, which is more or less what was done with the batch delivered for the 118 and 343. They haven't even been set correctly on New Cross' PVL 183 (X583 EGK), coming up to the Elephant on 19 May 2001, compounding the unattractiveness.** Author

A shock greeted them, however, as their blind boxes had been simplfied to virtual uselessness with just a number and a lower-case destination alongside. Protestations were made at the highest level, and on the next order for twenty-five PVLs, placed in February for the 171, compromised by reducing the via point blind to two lines so that a lower-case blind, by necessity taller, could be carried underneath. PVL 208 was held back to be included in this order.

The 343 duly bowed on 3 February, replacing the previous Stagecoach Selkent route P3 with new PVLs from New Cross. The 118 also passed from Arriva London South to London General, adding PVLs to Merton's

Left: **Merton's PVL 197 (X597 EGK) has somehow been fitted with an NN blind in all-capitals, which is more authoritative as a destination but next to useless without the accompanying via points. It is seen at Brixton on 14 April 2001.** Author

Right: **A rethink of blind policy produced this compromise on the PVLs ordered for the 171 and 172 in 2001, with one line off the via blinds to admit the taller letters of the destination. It looked reasonably modern and still helpful to the passenger. On 10 September 2001 New Cross's PVL 210 (Y801 TGH) is at Catford.** *Author*

already large fleet and mixing the batches throughout the five routes operated. One to fall out early was PVL 200, whose upper deck was destroyed by arson on 29 April; repairs to this and PVL 205, deroofed on 11 May, were effected by Caetano at Waterlooville.

Stockwell's PVL loans to Putney ended in March, even before the removal of the latter's route 37 allocation on 29 September. On 18 April the first of the PVL 208-249 batch began entering service at New Cross, displacing Ts from the 172 and NVs from the 171 by June and, as with the 343's batch, wanderings to the 21 and 321 were soon evident. At this point, New Cross's allocation on the 36 on Sundays found itself converted to PVL operation.

Right: **Turning off Waterloo Road on a one-day diversion being taken by all southbound buses on 23 June 2001 is New Cross's PVL 229 (Y729 TGH).** *Author*

Left: **The 321 had been carved out of the 21's outer end in 1997 with LDPs, these Dart SLFs being the only low-floor vehicles available at the time, but it was too busy for them and double-deckers substituted from time to time, first Ts and NVs and then PVLs when they arrived at New Cross. PVL 233 (Y733 TGH) works through Eltham on 7 July 2001.** Author

Warranty work carried out by Volvo on the oil seals forced the to-ing and fro-ing of PVLs during the spring and summer.

The rest of 2001 was quiet, but in September further Volvo B7TL orders were placed for retained tenders. As well as 19 PVLs for the 51, a new venture came in the order for 36 East Lancs Vyking-bodied B7TLs for Sutton's 93 and 154; all three routes were presently NV-operated and beginning new contracts on 1 December.

After Putney came off the 37 on 29 September, a new three-bus loan from Stockwell was instituted when three PVLs were outstationed at Waterloo for part of the 77A on Mondays to Fridays.

Left: **Straying from the 45 to the 35 and laying over at that route's Shoreditch terminus on 24 November 2001 is Camberwell's AVL 12 (V112 LGC).** Author

Go-Ahead – 17

Right: **Inevitably the 343's batch of single-line blinded PVLs at New Cross would appear on the 171 and 172 and vice versa; at Waterloo on 23 June 2001 is PVL 187 (X587 EGK).** *Author*

Below: **The first day of the 486 at Bexleyheath, 23 February 2002, saw Titans and PVLs join the established MD-class DAFs, and PVL 11 (V311 LGC) at the Bexleyheath terminus has had a makeshift blind made up for the route.** *Author*

Below right: **The first transfers of PVLs encompassed PVLs 50-55, which moved from Bexleyheath to New Cross. Here at Victoria on a Boxing Day OPO working of the 36 on 26 December 2002 is PVL 52 (W452 WGH).** *Author*

At the end of 2001 Go-Ahead continued to branch out from its established PVL; as well as four more to top up the 89 and sixteen more EVLs to take in the 213 at Sutton, there was an order for 27 with Wrightbus's new Gemini body already entering service with Arriva as VLWs. These, to be known as WVLs at London General, would furnish the 345, soon to be concentrated at Stockwell in its entirety. Finally, the 35 and 40's tender renewal would require replacement of their NVs, and forty more PVLs were ordered.

London Central operated several Christmas Day services at this time, and 2001's 712, 725 and 729 featured eleven AVLs.

The transfer from New Cross to Bexleyheath of the 486 to accompany its extension there on 23 February 2002 saw PVLs appear and they remained as regular visitors thereafter.

The EVLs began arriving in February 2002 and were put into service at Sutton beginning on 13 March. PVLs 250-272 were delivered at the same time but only the first four and the last six went to Bexleyheath, removing the garage's last Titans and cascading out some NVs to help do the same at Peckham; the rest were switched temporarily to Stockwell to double-deck the 345 prior to the WVLs' delivery, which ensued late in March.

Above: **The angular but broadly attractive East Lancs Vyking body made its debut on the EVL class of 52 vehicles, all allocated to Sutton for the 93, 151, 154 and 213. Seen departing Putney Bridge Station on 28 June 2003 is EVL 1 (PL51 LGA).** *Author*

Left: **New to Bexleyheath in March 2002, PVL 250 (PL51 LDJ) works a 422 through Woolwich on 20 April of that year.** *Author*

Go-Ahead – 19

Right: **In spite of its London Central fleetnames, PVL 254 (PL51 LDU) was one of a number put into Stockwell to help the first thirteen WVLs restore the upper deck to the extremely heavily pressed 345, and on 28 March 2002 it is seen coming onto the stand at Peckham.** Author

Right: **PVL 257 (PL51 LDY) was wrapped in gold for the Queen's Golden Jubilee during 2002, and on 7 October of that year is seen at Camberwell Green.** Author

Right: **The other low-floor double-decker liveried in gold for Londons General and Central was AVL 13 (V113 LGC), which on 7 October 2002 is seen on the 35 at Clapham Common.** Author

Left: **The handsomely curved Wrightbus Gemini body was an instant hit and propelled the bodybuilder to the forefront of the industry. The code specified by London General, WVL, gave rise to the 'Weevil' nickname hung on the Gemini ever after, and well it might, as the roofline was more than suggestive of a beetle's carapace. Here at the South Kensington stand of the 345 on 23 June 2002 is Stockwell's WVL 10 (LG02 KHH).** *Author*

An AVL and a PVL each helped celebrate the Queen's Golden Jubilee during 2002, with gold vinyls, paint over the tricky bits and a sponsor over the rear. Camberwell's AVL 13 was sponsored by Mars Celebrations chocolates and PVL 257, just into traffic at Stockwell, plugged Felix cat food. Both liveries lasted until January 2003.

On 27 April the 345 saw its first WVLs, but the tally there would only reach thirteen as the rest were diverted to Putney to assume the 85 on 29 June in lieu of the PDLs ordered for it; these Tridents joined forces with existing examples at Stockwell and a few more PVLs left for their proper home at Bexleyheath. The WVLs already at Stockwell started

Left: **The 85 had a second batch of PDLs pencilled in for its takeover by London General, but it was decided to concentrate Tridents at Stockwell instead and further WVLs took it over instead. Coming out of Putney Bridge Station on 1 July 2002 is Putney's WVL 24 (LG02 KHZ).** *Author*

Right: **The follow-on batch of EVLs were meant for the 213 at Sutton, but the first contingent had already made themselves familiar, so it wasn't unusual by any means for the rest to visit the 154, as EVL 48 (PJ02 PZF) is doing when seen at West Croydon on 19 June 2003.** *Author*

Below: **Having replaced Ts on the 35 and 40 in 1997, it was now time for the NVs to move on and in 2002 PVLs replaced them. On 15 March 2003 Camberwell's PVL 303 (PJ02 RFY) is seen at the Elephant & Castle.** *Author*

wandering to the 37, 77A, 88, 133 and 188, while those being readied for the 85 at Putney were broken in on the 170 in considerable numbers. Then came the 213's batch of EVLs and the PVLs for the 35 and 40. Three still at Stockwell were loaned to Commercial Services to perform the Wimbledon tennis service. Squadron entry of the new PVLs at Camberwell was from 8 July.

The 'Weevil' had taken; in July forty-four more WVLs were ordered to take over the 74 and its new offshoot 430. Putney's existing fleet had already started appearing on the 74 and the evening OPO arm of the 14 (and

Left: **Camberwell's brand new PVL 291 (PJ02 RDV) is shiny as it arrives at Notting Hill Gate during Carnival on 25 August 2002.** Author

consequent N14). Then came an even bigger glut of Volvo B7TL orders as expansion plans were drawn up for routes to be funded by the introduction of a Congestion Charge into central London; there would be forty-nine more WVLs for the 133 and its planned new offshoot 333 and forty-three PVLs for the 21 and 321, the latter being double-decked.

London Central's neighbour, London Easylink, collapsed in ignominious circumstances on the afternoon of 21 August and some of the PVLs rounding out Camberwell's latest fleet were requisitioned to help out on the 185, which had once been a Camberwell route anyway (and would be again, eventually!).

Left: **On 24 August 2002 at Lewisham, Camberwell's PVL 306 (PJ02 RGU) is assisting on the 185, which, following the collapse of London Easylink, would field an extraordinary variety of buses over the next year until a stable contractor was identified for it.** Author

October saw Putney's WVL contingent arrive, the first examples entering service on the 22nd and enough arriving in time for the 430 to commence on 23 November. The 170 was pushed out to Stockwell to make room and soon saw Stockwell's own WVLs. The 133/333 order was increased to fifty and commenced build, arriving in the mainland during December. This month also saw New Cross's next PVL batch commence delivery, the first going into service on the 21 and 321 on 21 December.

Nine PVLs moved from Stockwell to Camberwell on 23 November when the latter route was given a proportion of the 188. Camberwell's share was set to increase further from 10 February 2003, requiring the input of new PVLs otherwise intended for New Cross.

The expansion routes were introduced on 25 January 2003, the 333 out of Stockwell taking priority for as many WVLs as had been delivered by that date. On 2 February a Putney allocation of three WVLs was introduced to the Sunday 22, otherwise the province of Merton PVLs. Otherwise, the WVL allocations at Stockwell and PVLs at New Cross were completed over March and into April, all of these indirectly eliminating the last Metrobuses and Titans from Go-Ahead London. Stockwell was also receiving PDLs to bring Go-Ahead Trident numbers up to fifty and thereby displace PVLs from the 188's batch for NV replacement, mostly to New Cross, but PVL 176 went into Peckham, introducing the class there. Further PVLs from both the X-reg batch ex-Stockwell and new 52-reg examples were added to Peckham to

Above: **Putney quadrupled its WVL fleet at the close of 2002 when new examples arrived for the 74 and 430. Coming up to Roehampton, Earl Spencer on 23 November 2002, the first day of the 430, is WVL 33 (LF52 ZRP).** Author

Right: **WVLs and PVLs meet in Piccadilly on a Sunday OPO working of the 22, on which day Merton was still in the majority despite the introduction of a small Putney allocation which came off at lunchtime. This particular Sunday is 5 May 2003, when we see Putney's WVL 49 (LF52 ZRK) heading west and Merton's PVL 199 (X699 EGK) heading east.** Author

24 – Volvo B7TL

Left: **On 15 March 2003 at the Elephant, Stockwell's WVL 105 (LX03 EXV) sets off for Tooting Broadway on the 333, introduced several weeks earlier but otherwise a carbon copy of the old 95, withdrawn in 1991. There are some anomalies on this particular bus; its set of KM/NN blinds don't fit in the apertures and the transfers aren't Johnston, but it's new and has helped add capacity to the network as intended.** Author

start off new route 363, which commenced on 17 May with the commensurate withdrawal of the 63 back to Honor Oak. PVL 355 was late-arriving and was scooped up for 2003's Wimbledon tennis and Hampton Court Flower Show services out of the newish Plough Lane garage before heading to New Cross. Unfortunately it sustained an engine fire on 25 August and was removed for repair.

All the Ms and Ts having been disposed of, a batch of thirty WVLs was ordered in June to replace Stockwell's RMLs on the 11. A quiet summer was broken by the addition of eight WVLs to top up the 88 and thirty-four PVLs for the looming double-decking of the 155 plus general PVR upcounts for three retained tenders at Bexleyheath (routes 401 and 422) and Camberwell (the 45).

Left: **As the outer third of the 133 had been severed to create the 333, so did the 63 cede its roads south of Honor Oak to new route 363. It started with its own batch of PVLs, but PVL 176 (X576 EGK), seen at the Elephant on 20 October 2003, is an older one drafted into Peckham earlier.** Author

Right: **Now both operating PVLs were the 21 and its smaller sibling 321, also created by localising a section under its own number. Pointing south-east at Lewisham on 8 February 2003 are PVLs 316 (PJ52 LVT) and 246 (Y746 TGH), both of New Cross but the latter from the 171 and 172's batch new in 2001 .** *Author*

Right: **New into service at Stockwell in February 2003, PVL 333 (PJ52 LWN) was transferred to Peckham in time to take up on new route 363 on 17 May. On 19 May 2004 it is seen coming up to the bus station at Crystal Palace.** *Author*

Right: **Putney was apt to use its WVLs on the 170 and so did Stockwell when the route was transferred into that garage. The latter's WVL 115 (LX03 EEG) is seen at Clapham Junction on 6 August 2003.** *Author*

Left: **Not only have the unhelpful single-line blinds spread to WVL 151 (LX53 BJU), but the number font is in New Johnston, which is non-standard for blinds. The 11 was one-manned with WVLs like this on 1 November 2003 and the buses were branded shortly afterwards, as shown in this Liverpool Street shot of 13 May 2006.** *Author*

Mid-September saw the 11's intended WVLs start delivery, but none went into service as crew buses until the last night of the RMLs, 31 October, so that the RMLs could continue until the end of service. The new buses had white roofs to reflect sunlight. WVL 151 had a two-piece blind box, reflecting that the drift towards dumbing down information had not subsided. At least it was powered from the cab, removing the driver's need to get out and risk attack. Also coming in October were the latest Presidents, of which PVLs 356-361 went into Camberwell against the 45 and PVLs 371-389 for the 155 at Merton, both deployments occurring during November. Finishing the set were PVLs 362-371, not required until the 401 and 422 began their new contracts on 24 January 2004. Bexleyheath's existing PVLs began to go through refurbishment.

Left: **Twice converted to single-deck and twice suffering for it along the busy Clapham Road corridor, the 155 gained back a permanent double-deck allocation in November 2003 with the delivery of PVLs to Merton. On 15 July 2006 PVL 381 (PJ53 NKU) demonstrates at Clapham Common.** *Author*

Above: New for the 401 and 422 is Bexleyheath's PVL 367 (PJ53 SPX) at Woolwich on 22 May 2004. *Author*

Below: Caught at Hyde Park Corner on 5 July 2004 is Putney's WVL 46 (LF52 ZRE). *Author*

A concerted push against Olympians was now taking place; Bexleyheath's 03-reg PVL intake had threatened but not entirely ousted NVs, and the input into Stockwell of WVLs 152-159 in February 2004 saw five X-reg PVLs transferred into New Cross to do the same.

With Volvo B7TLs now firmly established on night routes, a move to renumber those matching their day counterparts was executed, with the N12 becoming 12 on 24 January and the N14, N37, N85, N88, N93 and N345 similarly losing their N-prefixes on 3 April.

All-over ads had crept back into fashion, helped by the success of the Golden Jubilee liveries, and in February 2004 WVLs 148-150 out of Stockwell were treated, with maximum customer impact envisaged on their captive route 11. WVLs 148 and 150 plugged musicals *The Lion King* and *Bombay Dreams* respectively, while WVL 149 donned shocking pink for designer Zandra Rhodes. The 11's other WVLs received blue side strips that served as discreet route branding, which didn't stop them from visiting other Stockwell routes if they had to.

The temporary withdrawal of artics from those routes operating them forced PVLs to visit New Cross's 436 for the first time at the end of March, and appearances continued even after the MALs were fitted with fire-suppression kits and restored to service.

In May WVL 149 lost its original ad for a new one in black touting the English National Opera (its performance-specific rear treatment being for *Carmen* and then for *The Pirates of Penzance*), and in June WVL 150 was given an ad for *Mamma Mia*.

Left: **Drumming up business for the musical version of** *The Lion King* **is Stockwell's WVL 148 (LX53 AYZ) at Victoria on 8 May 2004, six months after the conversion of the 11 to OPO.** *Author*

Left: **Wearing an all-over coat of shocking pink for Zandra Rhodes, WVL 149 (LX53 BJK) is working through Charing Cross on 28 February 2004.** *Author*

Left: **The Zandra Rhodes ad didn't last long on WVL 149 (LX53 BJK) and on 1 September it is seen carrying an ad for the English National Opera through Charing Cross.** *Author*

Above: Peckham's PVLs were liable to get out on the 381 before that route passed to Travel London; here at Waterloo on 25 February 2004 is PVL 333 (PJ52 LWN). *Author*

Above right: WVLs were odd on the 37 while the route was still based at Stockwell; on 29 May 2004 WVL 74 (LF52 ZPD), with larger numberplate transfers than was the official standard by that time, is in St John's Road, Clapham Junction. *Author*

After a very quiet summer, the latter end of 2004 saw action anew; when London Central's 381 was taken over by Travel London on 9 October (thus precluding any more AVL or PVL appearances), a gap at Peckham opened up which was filled by the transfer from Stockwell of the 37. Peckham took along five ex-Stockwell PVLs plus all nineteen of Camberwell's AVLs, introducing the latter to the 37 for the first time. Camberwell had ceded its route 188 allocation to Stockwell on 9 October but decided to send Peckham the AVLs, thus converting the 45 to PVL. Then the 12 was one-manned on 6 November with MAL artics; as part of this the Sunday AVLs and PVLs came off. London Central's next and final Routemaster route to be one-manned was the 36, and its replacement order, placed in September, constituted thirty new PVLs.

Right: The new face of the 37 from 9 October 2004 was AVLs from Peckham. With a blind with larger route number characters, AVL 46 (46 CLT, ex-V146 LGC) shows off the only ex-Routemaster registration on an AVL at Peckham on the first day. *Author*

Tendering had only begun to touch the original Volvo B7TL routes during 2004; the 89 and 280 were offered and retained and in November the 188 and 343 went out again, followed at the start of 2005 by the 118 and 172.

All four PVLs and the one AVL carrying ex-Routemaster marks lost them at the end of 2004; PVL 70 received previously unallocated W578 DGU. By the end of 2004 Bexleyheath's early PVLs had all been refurbished and the AVLs began to go away for treatment.

PVLs 390-419, stored since construction in November, now arrived and on 25 January 2005 were put into service at New Cross as crew buses for the last three days of such operation on the 36; full one-manning took place on the 29th. Those were the last of the PVLs, numbers topping out at 419 as what was now Alexander Dennis discontinued

Above: Crew-operated PVL 399 (LX54 GZL) works through Camberwell on the last day of Routemasters on the 36, Friday 28 January 2005. PVLs had replaced the route's RML minority at New Cross earlier in the last week and the RMs were set to go tonight. *Author*

Left: On 18 June 2005 at Victoria New Cross's PVL 393 (LX54 HAU) is now standard fare on the 36. This batch of PVLs was the last taken by Go-Ahead London. *Author*

Go-Ahead – 31

the President body and prepared to revamp the remaining ALX400 into the new integral Enviro400. Wrightbus thus had renewed opportunity to seize its business and did so, with a hefty order for fifty WVLs to secure the one-manning of the 14 and 22, London General's last two Routemaster routes.

The 89 started its new contract on 5 February and with it, lost the New Cross allocation. Bexleyheath thus received back five of its PVLs to reunite PVLs 1-55 once again.

Sutton had operated solely EVLs since 2002, but in February PVL 22 was loaned from Bexleyheath; similar PVL loans during the winter were to Merton and Peckham.

In February WVL 150's rear was amended to advertise a third opera, *The Barber of Seville*.

March saw the 188 and 343 awards announced, and both were lost to Travel London; this would precipitate major PVL transfers. With the 172's award still awaited, the 171 was tendered in April. June saw the 118 held on to, but the 37, 44, 77, 77A and 270 of the second large PVL batch were all offered.

May saw the delivery begin of the WVLs for Putney, now increased to fifty-two. Six were diverted to Stockwell to release PVLs to Bexleyheath to see off finally the NVs that had latterly been covering PVL refurbishment; lingering NVs at Merton were also polished off through transfers of PVLs there. After the Wimbledon championships, which used WVLs 164-166 guesting at Sutton, the takeover of the 14 and 22 could begin, the WVLs releasing Putney's RMLs one-by-one from late June until the routes' OPO conversion on 23 July, the same day as Merton's 280 began a new term with its existing PVLs. WVLs 192-211 featured an air-chilling system mounted above the staircase upstairs and unfortunately forcing the need to fit two smaller windows opposite, spoiling the elegant roof line. Ongoing modifications in the interest of noise reduction on all three B7TL classes obliged the hacking into engine covers of two more grille holes at either edge.

Sutton had only enough EVLs to furnish the PVRs for which they had been bought, so an increase to the 93 applying from 23 July had to be accomplished with PVLs 59 and 60, formalising the class there. PVL 98 soon joined it, itself replaced shortly after by PVL 80. The EVLs themselves continued to wander to LDP routes 80, 151 and 164.

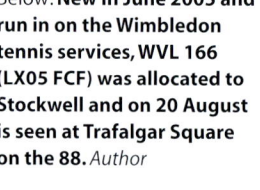

Below: **New in June 2005 and run in on the Wimbledon tennis services, WVL 166 (LX05 FCF) was allocated to Stockwell and on 20 August is seen at Trafalgar Square on the 88.** *Author*

Left: Two of the RML-replacement fleet of WVLs form up at the 14's Putney Heath stand on the last evening of crew operation, Friday 22 July 2005. They are Putney-allocated WVLs 184 (LX05 FAM) and 190 (LX05 EZV). *Author*

Below: With no more EVLs available to supply enhancements like the one needed on the 213, PVLs had to be seconded to Sutton and here at Kingston on 13 August 2005 is PVL 59 (W459 WGH), transferred from Stockwell. *Author*

Right: **Carnival services have always provided entertaining one-offs, and the 36X has been no exception down the years. Hitherto an RM route, from 2005 it was operated by the 36's new fleet of Volvo B7TLs, as PVL 408 (LX54 GYY) is doing when seen at Elgin Avenue on 28 August 2005.** Author

Now that the 36 had been one-manned, its Carnival offshoot 36X was operated by PVLs in 2005 and for some years thereafter. WVLs from Stockwell helped out on the 36 and this too would become a familiar feature of Carnival.

After an indifferent first half of 2005 for tendering, Go-Ahead received a whopping boost in August with the award of the 68, 468 and X68 from Arriva London South. The 171 was also retained with its existing PVLs and the 196 was won back from Travel London; although pencilled in for the group's first Enviro400 order, its likelihood of seeing Stockwell's PVLs and WVLs would be strong. Sixty-two more WVLs were ordered, which would take class strength to 273.

On 3 December 2005 the 188 passed to Travel London. Leaving Stockwell were WVLs 1-9, which struck up a new allocation at Camberwell, while W-reg PVLs into Merton and Bexleyheath finished off the last NVs

Right: **At the same spot but in a sunnier patch of the same day is Stockwell's WVL 153 (LX53 BGE), adding numbers to the normal 36 for Carnival.** Author

Left: **Mixed allocations between the four types of bodywork on Volvo B7TLs were inevitable as requirements were juggled between garages. Camberwell began operating WVLs alongside its PVLs on 3 December 2005, and on the 9th, when attention was otherwise focused on the 159's last Routemasters, WVL 5 (LG02 KGY) is heading south through Brixton.** *Author*

in the company, rendering the group 100% low-floor. As well as cascading NVs out of Merton, older PVLs from Stockwell released PVLs 195-205 to be hired to Metrobus to cover the 127, taken over on the 10th from the unfortunate Centra and operating for several months until the formalisation of its own contract with its own new buses.

The end of the year brought tendering victory for all the early PVL-operated routes at Stockwell and Merton; the 37, having since separated from this contingent, was to receive new Enviro400s.

On 14 December *Mamma Mia*-liveried advert bus WVL 150 was extensively damaged in an accident at Ealing while coming back off an N11 duty.

As part of the changes that saw Arriva London North's 29 become the last artic route on 14 January 2006, the 21 was extended from Moorgate to Newington Green to support it. On 4 February the 118 began a new contract,

Left: **Long ago the 21 had got as far north as Wood Green, but in modern times cross-town routes had gradually been pared back and back against the onslaught of traffic. However, the need to indirectly help out the 29 upon its conversion to bendy buses on 14 January 2006 prompted a revival of the 21 as far north as Newington Green. Setting off from Lewisham on its way there on 18 March is New Cross's PVL 320 (PJ52 LVX).** *Author*

Right: **Although the two-via-point blind on Stockwell's WVL149 (LX53 BJK) is an aesthetic downgrade, as is the going over of the faux radiator grille upon repaint to that section, the NSPCC advert offers some departure from the norm as it's carried towards Clapham Junction on 30 September 2006.** *Author*

despite its batch of PVLs having been transferred away to Metrobus, but the 343 and N343 passed to Travel London, releasing ten PVLs to store at Plough Lane in advance of their use at Sutton to double-deck the 151.

February saw a new TfL ad campaign mounted for the Oyster card, and Stockwell's WVL 135 joined Bexleyheath PVLs 270 and 271 in its signature blue. WVL 150 was repaired and lost its *Mamma Mia* ad for an orange one extolling the NSPCC, which was also applied to WVL 149. Sutton's EVL 21 became the first ad bus in its class in April, donning an Oyster scheme, and in May WVL 146 gained a black and white ad to celebrate the achievements of London schoolchildren.

On 18 March the 172 began a new contract with its existing New Cross PVLs, and on 1 April Camberwell took over the 68, 468 and X68 with WVLs 212-273, all now unfortunately with the coarsened blinds which were now standard. These were

Right: **The advert carried by WVL 146 (LX53 AYW) through Vauxhall on 23 October 2006 is as imaginative as could be without being immediately obvious as to who or what it was plugging; in fact it was commissioned to congratulate London's schoolchildren.** *Author*

36 — Volvo B7TL

the group's last B7TLs, as Volvo was now developing a new chassis which would hopefully cut down on some latterly discovered noise problems encountered with the vehicles' cooling fans. Appearances by PVLs on the 68 and 468 were matched by the new WVLs' wandering to the 35, 40 and 345. The 15th saw Metrobus take up the 127 in its own right and the hired PVLs move on, though they now passed to East Thames Buses under a third set of fleetnumbers. The 151 at Sutton received PVLs 179-188, 190, 191, 193 and 194 on the 22nd, followed on the 29th by the commencement of the 171's new contract, and Stockwell's takeover of the 196 on 6 May immediately introduced WVLs as guests of the scheduled new Es. When Merton took back the 200 from Centra on 20 May, a schoolday double-deck was included which became a PVL.

Above: **The final batch of WVLs in their B7TL form comprised sixty-two for Camberwell, whose takeover of the 68, 468 and X68 on 1 April 2006 represented a smashing victory over neighbouring Arriva London South. Only the simplified blinds let them down. Here on 17 September at Waterloo is WVL 268 (LX06 ECA).** Author

Left: **The southern half of the 68 and 468 pair was actually the better provisioned, despite its having cut Croydon off from town via the Camberwell direction when commissioned in 1994 as 68A. On 22 April 2006 WVL 246 (LX06 EAJ) is coming into Croydon town centre.** Author

Right: **Converted from M to LDP at the end of 1996, the 151 really needed double-deckers still and in 2006 it received some in the shape of PVLs from the single-line blinded batch that had spent their first five years at New Cross but had now lost their route 343. On 15 April 2007, with classic buses in the background on a highly-regarded local running day, Sutton's PVL 179 (X579 EGK) leaves Wallington.**
Author

Several changes surrounded the new London General PVL contracts applying from 3 June. The 77A lost its number outright, becoming 87, and the N77 was renumbered N87 to accompany it, in this way actually getting its old number back! Night bus N22 was withdrawn between Fulwell and Kingston so that the 281 could be given a night service.

On 7 June Peckham's 37 was converted to E operation, allowing its AVLs to return to Camberwell and oust the nine WVLs back to Stockwell. Three transfers of PVLs into Bexleyheath during July allowed three 51-reg examples to join the Commercial Services fleet. Eight from that batch were amassed, to oust NVs, and to that end they received gold fleetnames, gold fleetnumbers and two white

Right: **A fixture in inner Essex since time immemorial, the 87 had dwindled and dwindled in recent times until it was arbitrarily withdrawn so that its number could be re-used to replace the last suffixed route on the system, the 77A. This had similarly declined in importance until reaching parity with the similar 77 and under its new number would become a second-tier route at Stockwell. Setting off from Wandsworth on the 87's first day in this part of town, 3 June 2006, is WVL 115 (LX03 EEG).**
Author

relief bands. During August a quantity of the PVLs subbing at East Thames Buses moved on once again, this time to London United, where they stayed until November.

After repeated deferments, 11 November was the date that Merton's 44 was rerouted at Battersea via Chelsea Bridge to Victoria. The N44 followed suit, still reaching Aldwych but now via Victoria.

As 2006 wound down, the 22, 36 and school route 621 found themselves on tender, while refurbishments and/or repaints spanned PVLs from the W- to the Y-reg batches, with a small pool of early-numbered examples moving around the garages to cover. Whether refurbished or not, the tip-up seats downstairs were removed, the reduction of two or three seats on both AVLs and PVLs being worth the

Above: AVLs returned to Camberwell in June 2006; here at the Elephant on 4 February 2007 is AVL 16 (V116 LGC) with a modern blind. *Author*

Below: On 16 September 2007 Merton's PVL 125 (W425 WGH) has just performed a journey to Victoria on the rerouted 44. *Author*

Right: **It wasn't much consolation for a route that once got as far north as Wood Green only a generation previously, but the 14 found itself projected north the half-mile from Tottenham Court Road to Warren Street. In truth, its stand at the former had been obliterated by Crossrail construction and the route had to lay over somewhere. On 13 January 2007 Putney's WVL 54 (LF52 ZPP) is in Putney High Street; until recently an extra via point would have been added to new blinds to properly publicise the extension, but that wasn't allowed any more.** *Author*

risk of fending off the risk of lawsuits from people careless enough to get limbs caught in them. Otherwise, refurbishments involved the fitting of Rowan Telmac seating (as fitted to WVLs from new) to replace cracked or worn-out Fainsa Cosmic units. PVLs 82 and 131 became dual-purpose trainers through the addition of a removable instructor's seat.

On 13 January 2007 the 14 was extended from Tottenham Court Road to Warren Street; the 22 and 430 received similar PVR increases that saw the transfer from Stockwell to Putney of twelve 05-registered WVLs, which were replaced by the PVLs returning from London United. At Sutton the 93 was boosted again, taking PVL 266 from Commercial Services; the rest began to be fitted with coach seating.

In February EVL 21, PVLs 270 and 271 and WVL 135 all lost their Oyster livery. Tendering at the start of the year saw the 22 retained; the 621 had already been kept hold of but not the 625, which passed to Selkent on 3 January. Then in May the 36 was announced as retained with its existing PVLs.

Right: **WVL 158 (LX53 BDO) was transferred from Stockwell to Putney to increase the 14, 22 and 430 and fit in perfectly with its newer siblings already there. This shot was taken at Kingston on 15 September 2007.** *Author*

Left: **PVL incursions had broken the EVLs' majority at Sutton, and with the increase to the 213 more had to come in. Otherwise, EVL 42 (PJ02 PYZ) is going about its normal business in Eden Street, Kingston on 30 June 2007.** Author

On 24 February, the 200's school PVL was replaced by an E. Sutton needed further PVLs when the 213 was increased on 31 March, though four Es were ordered for this. The four PVLs in question were displaced from Stockwell by the last four to come back from loan at East Thames Buses.

In June, WVL 150 returned with a new body with single-line blinds like the 06-reg batch; it was put into service at Camberwell. Commercial Services PVL 251 received an advert for Madame Tussauds. On the 30th the 85 was boosted through the addition of four 53-reg WVLs transferred from Stockwell.

Summer 2007 proved quiet, but in August WVL 149 lost its NSPCC ad and PVL 412 gained one for Venezuela tourism.

On 1 September, after deferment enough for a whole school year to have elapsed, new route 639 was introduced at Putney to join the existing 670. Stockwell's N133 was withdrawn between Streatham and Tooting and rerouted to Mitcham. The 22's new contract began on 20 October.

Left: **Having already served at Sutton (see page 33), PVL 59 (W459 WGH) transferred to Camberwell in December 2005 and then to New Cross, under whose stewardship it is seen at Waterloo on 7 June 2008. As none of the PVLs already based had KM/NN blinds, a new set had to be commissioned, in which the route numbers were of rather larger dimensions.** Author

Above: **Taken for the 11 in the autumn of 2003, Stockwell's WVL 133 (LX53 AZF) finds itself instead on the 133 on 7 October 2006 at the Elephant & Castle. On 3 November 2007 the 133 was reallocated to Mandela Way, but this wasn't one of the buses that went with it.** Author

At the beginning of 2008, Sutton's EVL- and PVL-operated gamut of 93, 151 and 154 were tendered, plus the LDP routes they could also visit. Then came the 51 out of Bexleyheath. The 36 began its new contract on 9 February, the accompanying PVR boost awaiting five Es but being accomplished with PVLs. The N36 was withdrawn and replaced by new Selkent-operated N136. The 170 fell off the register for double-deckers from the 16th due to its extension to Victoria over the 239, along which there was a low bridge. On the same day as the 333's intermediate rerouteing via Stockwell, 8 March, its operating garage Mandela Way took over the afternoon duty on the 670, cross-linking from the 333.

WVL 101 lost its roof to fire set by arsonists on 18 January, and arson was also the finish for WVL 221 on 14 March, but this one was totally destroyed and became the first writeoff for the class.

April saw the Es for the 36's latest contract delivered and put into service. Tendering to Volvo B7TL-operated routes in the first half of 2018 put out the 35, 40 and 345 at Camberwell plus Sutton's 213. Sutton was boosted in May by the announcement that London General had made a clean sweep at Sutton, with new buses for everything, even if it did put a time limit on the EVLs on the 93, 151 and 154. The summer programme was then unveiled, involving the issue of tenders for the 21 and 321 and the 63 and 363. It had been a good spell for Go-Ahead, but now came some losses with the announcement in

A new garage bowed for WVLs when Mandela Way took on the 133 and N133 from Stockwell on 3 November so that the 24, won from Metroline, could be put into Stockwell a week later. Nothing but Es appeared on the 24, but when needs warranted, examples were taken from the 196 and WVLs or PVLs substituted; in fact a number of PVLs had to be drafted into Stockwell at the beginning to cover for the most late-arriving of the new Enviro400s.

Right: **For posterity, here is Camberwell's WVL 221 (LX06 DZD) at Waterloo on 8 April 2006, but it wouldn't live to see its second birthday, owing to being destroyed by fire outside its home garage.** Author

Left: **PVL 251 (PL51 LDK)** didn't last long as a service bus, being intended for greater purposes as a London General Commercial Services private-hire bus, but in Grosvenor Place on 30 September 2007 it is playing at being a Lincoln Town car limousine in this imaginative wrap for Madame Tussauds. *Author*

June that the 51 and school routes 602 and 603 had been lost to Selkent. On 7 June the N11 was revised at its western end to terminate at Ealing Broadway rather than Wembley.

2008 was the year of iBus, this innovative control and information technology being fitted to every London bus during the year. Many companies hired in vehicles to cover their own fleet going away for fitment, and in June Stockwell took on six Metroline TPLs, followed by six TNs from First London. Otherwise, a band of twelve PVLs roved from garage to garage as cover, completing London Central by August and then moving into Putney.

Advert buses came and went in 2008; in January WVL 148's *The Lion King* ad was freshened up, while PVL 412 resumed red in April and WVL 110 gained an ad for Visa in August. WVL 146 regained red in September.

As 2008 elapsed, the 14, 74, 85 and 430 went out for tender. A particularly bitter blow was the loss of the 35 and 40 to Travel London, though the 345 was retained.

Left: **The most visible effect of refurbishment on London Central's early PVLs was the replacement of their Fainsa Cosmic seating with Rowan Telmac Telford 20 units**, whose handles were yellow to match the handrails in general. Bexleyheath's PVL 27 (V327 LGC), serving Woolwich on 13 December 2008, has also had a new, post-1 September 2001 numberplate fitted, with the narrower characters. *Author*

Below: **The one-way system between the Elephant & Castle and St George's Circus was simplified to direct Waterloo and Blackfriars-bound buses along the same thoroughfare as those going south; on 25 May 2009 Camberwell's PVL 300 (PJ02 RFN) demonstrates.** *Author*

Below: **Despite its branding for the 11, Stockwell's WVL 138 (LX53 AZD) has been turned out on the 88 on 19 March 2009 and is seen in Trafalgar Square.** *Author*

The appearance of the iBus-cover PVLs at Mandela Way for the first time in September and October wasn't the class's first run-out on the 133 and 333. When the TNs went back to First, in came Tridents (TLs) from Blue Triangle to help out at Stockwell. Blue Triangle hadn't been a Volvo B7TL operator; indeed its debut order for the type was cancelled and replaced by the same TLs, but on 17 October Camberwell sent PVL 298 to Silvertown to man the 425; PVL 276 followed on the 22nd.

13 October saw Putney's 85 bolstered by three Enviro400-bodied Volvo B9TLs known as VEs.

On 6 December the 93, 151 and 154, awaiting new DOEs, started their new contracts at Sutton, while the 51 departed for Selkent. This loss freed enough PVLs from Bexleyheath to start getting rid of Stockwell's unloved PDL class of Dennis Tridents. As DOEs, which were still Tridents if you read the chassis plate, began taking over at Sutton from 8 December the first buses out were three PVLs, which boosted Silvertown's numbers to five; PDLs also headed there to ease out the original TLs. The year ended with the offering out of the 133 and 333 and the announcement that the 85 and 213 had been kept hold of.

In the Bexleyheath area on 24 January 2009, the 601 and 602 were taken over by Selkent and the 401 increased in frequency. March proved good for Go-Ahead; the 21, 63, 321 and 363 were all retained with new buses for the 21 and 63 and a night service for the 321. That month saw Stockwell's WVL 135 gain an all-over ad for *Monsters vs Aliens*. WVL 125 followed in May for *Terminator: Salvation*, this scheme lasting a month. Their route 11 was now up for tender.

So much for the EVLs; the new model of acquisition was leasing, so when contracts were up, vehicles were disposed of. Thus did the gathering of DOEs on the 93, 151 and 154 at the start of 2008 begin the process of cascading EVLs out of the company. Sutton's remaining PVLs also left, but remained in stock to be parcelled up between Stockwell and Silvertown. Eleven PVLs were converted to permanent trainers at this point, to replace NVs in the same role.

Left: After just the five years of their routes' contracts plus two for good performance, the EVLs came to the end of the road in 2009, with just three kept back to serve as iBus cover. On 2 August 2008 Sutton's EVL 25 (PN02 XCJ) is at North Cheam, setting off on a route 93 journey. *Author*

Not that the EVL was quite done; in the third week of March four gravitated to Putney to cover refurbishment of WVLs 14-27 and turned out on the 74, soon being joined by more. Putney's refurbished WVLs came back with their blind boxes converted to single-line spec and a hole cut into each bumper to carry an array of LED running lights. Seating was now to the darker and simplified blue and the noise problems that had bedevilled the type were just about ironed out through upgrading of the engines to Euro 5 standard.

May saw the announcement that the 14, 74 and 430 had all been retained with existing WVLs, which made up for the exit of the 35 and 40 on the 2nd. Forty 02-reg PVLs were made spare and were earmarked for refurbishment to provide the stock for the 213, 321 and 363, but AVLs 1-19 were also withdrawn and returned off lease.

The 345, its new contract having started on 2 May, was converted to E operation in the first half of June. That marked the end for Stockwell's PDLs, which last ran on 24 July.

Left: Refurbishment now came to Putney's first allocation of WVLs and incorporated some additional features over and above the usual reupholstering and deep cleaning. The blinds are now single-line efforts, there are two running light clusters in the bumper where foglights would have been in years of old, and the combined indicators and sidelight units have been replaced with up-to-date LED versions. WVL 15 (LG02 KHO) is rounding Hyde Park Corner on 25 May 2009. *Author*

Below: **LED spotlights and new blind boxes also came to the PVLs refurbished for the 213 and put into Sutton. PVL 289 (PJ02 RDO) looks appropriately smart as it comes into Kingston on 24 July 2011, its blinds already set for the return journey.** *Author*

On 4 July the 85 and 213 began their new contracts and the latter sprouted a night service. PVLs 282-297 began going through refurbishment for the 213, returning the class to Sutton and the treatment featuring the same single-line blind box conversion and addition of driving lights as on the 85's WVLs. The EVL class at Sutton held out until September, EVL 42 being the last operating there and leaving just half a dozen at Putney now that all the 85's WVLs had been refurbished.

Having already had dealings with East Thames Buses through the loan of PVLs in 2006, Go-Ahead now bought the company from TfL and assimilated it into London General on 3 October. East Thames Buses had inherited London Easylink's Volvo B7TLs and then bought its own, so coming into the fleet were Plaxton-bodied VPs 1-19 for the 185 and Wright-bodied VWLs 1-4 and 6-44 for the 1 and 180. Allocation between the second Mandela Way (wholly-VWL) and Belvedere (the other half of the VWLs and all of the VPs) was fairly fluid, with both types of Volvo able to visit the 42, 132, 661 and 669 and the portion of the 108 operating south of the river.

Right: **The Plaxton President-bodied Volvo B7TLs on the 185 since 2001 were still going seven years later under a third operator now that Go-Ahead had bought East Thames Buses. The acquisitions retained their fleetnumbers rather than becoming assimilated into the PVL class, as on VP 8 (X159 FBB), seen at Vauxhall on 7 February 2010 with a Go-Ahead fleetname.** *Author*

On 10 October the 21, 321 and N21 were renewed, the night route being diverted to Foots Cray so that a night service could be introduced on the 132, now a Go-Ahead route. In November the 21 was converted from PVL to WVL – not the time-honoured B7TL, but a continuation of the class code on what would become large numbers of B9TLs now that Go-Ahead had rediscovered its faith in Volvo buses. Then, on 14 November Peckham's 63 and 363 started new contracts and a week later the 14, 74 and 430 followed suit at Putney, their own 05-reg WVLs now passing through H&D Trim for refurbishment including the fitting of an air-cooling system upstairs. Unlike the previous Putney examples, the blind boxes and bumpers on these ones were left alone. PVLs 343-355 were refurbished for the 321, and to cover them at New Cross from 15 October came none other than EVLs 5 and 15 ex-Putney, which soon racked up appearances on the 21, 171, 172 and 321 but predominantly on the 172. EVL 17 was the last at Putney and continued on alone there well into 2010. The 63's new B9TL WVLs started service on 2 December, replacing the remaining AVLs.

The announcement of the future operator of the 133 and N133 in September proved a loss for London General, as it was awarded to Arriva London South. At the end of 2009 the 45, 88 and 155 were put out to tender again, followed in the first quarter of 2010 by Bexleyheath's 229, 401 and 422, Merton's 118 and New Cross's 172. The 11 was announced as retained.

Having already started reapportioning East Thames Buses' routes between existing garages, management loaned buses to them too; from 25 November PVL 170 served on the 185 from both Belvedere and Mandela Way West, slipping out on the latter's 42. Then two more PVLs were put into Belvedere. Now that the 132 was at Bexleyheath, it began to see PVLs, which also visited the 486 and B16 (though not beyond Eltham Green on the latter).

In November WVLs 146 and 147 received ads in alternating white and green for the M&G Recovery Fund.

Their work done at New Cross, EVLs 5 and 15 returned to Putney on 7 January 2010 to join EVL 17, this time to cover further WVL refurbishments now taking in the middle order of 02- and 52-registered examples. PVLs 313-325 and the first ex-East Thames VWLs were refurbished at the same time, the latter donning London General's grey skirt and yellow band.

AVL 8 was the last of its class in service on 8 January 2010, working on the 363, and all departed fleet strength without having managed a decade in action. The next B7TLs to leave didn't even achieve that, being taken from the 51-reg PVL batch new to Stockwell and now domiciled at Bexleyheath; their leased status made them fair game and they were replaced by X- and Y-reg PVLs.

Left: **Like the EVLs, the AVLs didn't manage ten years either when the Titans had served for twice as long and the Routemasters twice that again. Peckham's AVL 44 (V144 LGC) is coming round the Elephant & Castle on 23 October 2009. The last of the KM blinds, as fitted to Peckham buses by this point, boasted a substantially larger route number.** *Ian Jordan*

Right: **The former East Thames Buses VWLs looked splendid in their new London General livery (London General since the 1 was reallocated to Mandela Way) and with an accompanying new set of blue seats. VWL 28 (LF52 THX) is seen at Canada Water on 20 July 2010.** Author

Right: **Belvedere was kept open and remained the base for the 180; likewise the beneficiary of refurbishment, VWL 21 (LF52 TGY) is seen at Woolwich on 30 July 2011.** Author

Right: **On 7 February 2010 at Vauxhall Stockwell's PVL 15 (V315 LGC) is guesting on the 88, which, while pretty fluid in which of the several types operated appeared, tended not to use PVLs.** Author

Left: **WVLs came to Merton in 2011 to begin seeing off the garage's original batch of PVLs. Coming up to Clapham Junction on 8 October of that year is WVL 89 (LF52 ZNX).** Author

2010 otherwise kicked off with a loss, 23 January seeing the 133 depart for Arriva London South at Norwood together with the N133 at night; the 670's cross-working now came off the 14 at Putney. The 333 stayed put at Stockwell under a new contract. That made space at Mandela Way for the 1 to be put in from its formerly East Thames Buses neighbour, which took place on 6 February with its VWLs. This month saw Blue Triangle gain back a PVL when PVL 209 was sent to Rainham to form the one-bus 375's permanent allocation.

The early PVLs were definitely starting to shift now that the EVLs and AVLs had been eradicated; beginning on 3 March, 52-reg WVLs 72-104 made spare from the 133's loss began to take over at Merton, introducing the type to the 44, 77, 270, 280 and Sunday 22 with appearances (as had the PVLs) on the 155, 163, 164, 200, 219 and 355. A handful of PVLs drifted into Mandela Way and Putney at this point, the latter deployment constituting a permanent allocation that was still backed up by three EVLs, and further PVLs still, once away from Merton, were converted to

Left: **On 30 July 2011 PVL 321 (PJ52 LVY) heads through central Lewisham in one of those rare quiet periods before the town centre was pulled to pieces again and redesigned wholesale. The route was now shared equally between Bexleyheath and New Cross, and this PVL belonged to the latter.** Author

training buses or, in the case of Y-registered examples, seconded to Commercial Services.

In March WVL 138 received an ad for the film *How To Train Your Dragon*.

Mandela Way West was closed on 1 May and its routes were reallocated; the 185 went with VPs 1-14 and VWLs 1-4 and 6-10 to Camberwell and would continue to visit the 42, as that went there too. Bexleyheath gained school routes 661 and 669, taking with them VPs 16 and 17, and regained an allocation on the 321 (with PVLs 346-355 ex-New Cross), while Mandela Way proper took half the N1 from Belvedere. The 108's scheduled evening double-deckers on the southern half had come off Belvedere's 180 but now took their buses from the 321 at New Cross, thus converting from VWL to PVL operation. Camberwell and Mandela Way would loan back and forth much as the former Mandela Way West had to Belvedere.

In May the 45, 88, 118 and 155 were awarded to and retained by their incumbent Go-Ahead operators, all but the 118 with existing Volvo B7TLs. Similar good fortune accrued to Bexleyheath's 229, 401 and 422, all retained in June with new buses on the first and third. Meanwhile, 2010's spring and summer tranches put out the 68, 468 and X68 plus the 171 and school routes 639 and 670.

Mandela Way's PVLs proved temporary and all had gathered at Camberwell by May. July saw the loss on tender of the 172 to Abellio, the new identity since 2009 of Travel London. PVL 110, now with Commercial Services, received an all-over ad for Madame Tussauds (this time including the front), which it served on its dedicated new route 850 from 12 July-19 September. VWL 1 had a Bingo ad at this point but lost it in July.

The trio of EVLs finished their covering task at Putney and between 17-23 July moved to Stockwell for the same role, turning out on the 87, 88 and 333. Similar refurb cover to Belvedere's VWLs prompted PVL loans from Bexleyheath and Camberwell, while VP 17, sole member of its class left at Belvedere, visited Bexleyheath's 486. Having donned grey skirts over the year, Camberwell's VPs were now barely distinguishable from the garage's incumbent PVLs and were seen wandering off the 185 to the 42, 45, 468 and X68, with the latter's 06-reg WVLs on the 185 in return, plus one visiting Mandela Way's 1 later in the year.

September heralded the retention of the 68, 468 and X68 by Camberwell's 06-reg WVLs and the 171 was also kept hold of, though with new buses. The 639 was retained and intended to absorb the 670 with the next

Below: **On 18 October 2010 Bexleyheath's PVL 16 (V816 KGF) pulls into Lewisham at the end of another long journey on the 89, but its time was almost at an end and sale would follow in March 2011.** *Author*

Left: **2010 was also the last full year in service for PVL 104 (W504 WGH), which on 22 October at Waterloo finds itself working out of New Cross; the blinds are now the curtailed variety with two via points.** *Author*

school year. On 30 October the 11 and N11 commenced their new contracts at Stockwell and Camberwell's 45 followed suit on 13 November, with the expectation that its PVLs would be refurbished. The winter tranches were then published, offering out the 89 among others.

Advert WVLs 138, 146 and 147 lost their pieces in September but WVL 135 gained one the same month for *Despicable Me*. During the month five discarded PVLs were taken back on lease to furnish an 851 operated by Blue Triangle into the Olympic Park then under construction west of Stratford. Blue Triangle had also picked up school contracts 673 and 674 plus a diagram on the 150, which commenced on 16 October with PVLs 66-68, refurbished for the purpose and divided between Silvertown and Rainham. When not needed at Silvertown, PVLs 66 and 67 were turned out on the 474. PVL 110 finished its summer work and lost its ad to join them.

On 11 December the 88 and 155 began a new contract each, the former undergoing a partial conversion to E operation between 27 November and mid-December and thus dislodging five early PVLs to New Cross as WVLs 1-13 went through refurbishment. The 670 survived and was reinstated in the spring term of 2011. On 30 December the conversion of the 118 from PVL to E began and Bexleyheath's 229 and 422 began to receive their new B9TL WVLs on 6 January. Putney's stand-in PVLs departed to help Stockwell cover its WVL refurbishments, while 53-reg examples (minus six departed off lease) were held back for treatment for the 401 when Bexleyheath's ten-year-old PVLs otherwise departed. Some were added to the fleet of Blue Triangle at Rainham, which otherwise stored withdrawn examples prior to their disposal. All the first batch of PVLs had been withdrawn by February, when Bexleyheath's treatment to B9TL WVLs was completed.

Refurbishments in the first half of 2011 worked methodically through the 11's batch of WVLs and the 02-reg PVLs still at Camberwell for the 45, followed by the successive 53-reg PVL batches for Bexleyheath's 401 and Merton's 155. In February WVL 147 gained an ad for G-Star Raw but WVL 135 regained fleet livery upon its own refurbishment in March. At the same time, whether refurbished or not, the 11's WVLs lost their route branding and in fact a TfL edict went out that Go-Ahead, like other contractors, had to abandon their livery from now on and repaint everything red.

Contract awards in February kept the 89 (with new buses) and took school routes 624, 625 and 658 from Stagecoach Selkent while keeping the 655.

On 19 March 2011 the 172 departed for Abellio, standing down a dozen Y-reg PVLs, but 2 April saw the 68, 468 and X68 renewed under Camberwell's existing 06-reg WVLs. On 30 April the 171 was renewed but since the beginning of the month its own PVLs were already giving way to new B9TL WVLs. The same fate followed for the PVLs based at Docklands Buses' Silvertown on the 474.

Right: **The 337 was taken back by London General with a more-or-less route-bound batch of twelve Es, but flexibility meant the appearance of whatever else Stockwell could put out, and just such an occasion on 10 July 2011 has produced WVL 107 (LX03 EXZ), coming into Richmond.** Author

A new pitch for WVLs wasn't scheduled but inevitable when Stockwell took back the 337 on 28 May under a new London General contract otherwise meant for twelve new Es. Similarly, New Cross's takeover of Abellio's 129 on 4 June introduced rogue PVLs alongside the scheduled EDs.

Three ad B7TLs in May were WVL 130 and Commercial Services PVLs 248 and 249 for Malaysia tourism, the latter pair only for this year's Chelsea Flower Show. PVLs 221 and 222 from the same outfit had already been converted to single-door and PVL 224 became an open-topper, gaining the splendid London General livery. The first all-red Go-Ahead London buses had to appear sooner or later, and they were WVLs 147 and 148, their ads removed upon refurbishment. Capital One sponsored WVLs 14 and 131 between June and October, advertising its Click card.

Right: **PVLs from PVL 208 had side blind boxes that took the same route panels as on the front, but that too was dumbed down to just one arbitrary via point, as on Camberwell's PVL 307 (PJ02 RGV) passing through Brixton on 30 July 2011.** Author

Left: **The reallocation of the 42 to Camberwell on 10 May 2010 permitted the appearance of WVLs alongside its usual Scania OmniTowns, and in Bishopsgate on 11 June 2011 we see WVL 256 (LX06 EBJ).** Author

Leasing terms cost Go-Ahead its first two WVLs in June, at the same time as Y-reg PVLs lost from the 171 and 172 continued to leave the fleet. Refurbishment now got started on the 06-reg batch of WVLs now that their routes were secure for five more years.

2011's summer tenders offered out the 22, 280 and 621; the 22 and 280 were announced in August as retained with new buses and the 621 was lost to Stagecoach Selkent.

In August WVL 130 lost its ad but recently-repainted WVL 147 gained another one, this time for Google Maps. G-Star Raw returned in September, sponsoring WVL 105 with a picture of Gemma Arterton. Both lasted until the following February.

An emergency deployment for sixteen recently-refurbished PVLs was due to the failure of all the new Enviro400s for the 453 to be delivered on time to take over from artics

Left: **The purge of artics during 2011 led to the double-decking of the two new routes that had been introduced with them, but the 453's intended contingent of Es were not all in place in time for the changeover on 24 September 2011, so PVLs stepped in. Here in the Old Kent Road on that first day is PVL 303 (PJ02 RFY), loaned by Camberwell to Mandela Way.** Author

Go-Ahead 53

Right: **Peeping through the metal fencing at Putney Bridge station's northbound District Line platform gives a little-seen view of the roofs of vehicles on stand round the corner from the outbound stops. As can be seen, the standard is now white roofs, though this innovation has singularly failed to accomplish what front upper-deck opening windows did for many generations and clear heat through rapid air circulation. This is Merton's PVL 372 (PJ53 NKM) on 13 April 2011.** *Author*

Right: **After its time spent carrying various ad liveries along the 11, Stockwell's WVL 150 (LX53 BJO) suffered accident damage so severe that it had to be rebodied, and the replacement had single-line blinds. It is seen at Vauxhall on 19 November 2011.** *Author*

Right: **Refurbishment-installed spotlights blazing, PVL 335 (PJ52 LWP) at Clapham Junction on 8 October 2011 brings the type back to the 37 for a day when Peckham couldn't manage to field one of the usual AVLs.** *Author*

Left: **The EVL class may have barely registered in London bus histories (this account likely to be their only valediction!), but three lingered after withdrawal to serve as iBus fitment cover for three more garages, and on the last of those deployments, EVL 17 (PN02 XCD) is seen at Waterloo on 24 September 2011 when on attachment to Camberwell.** Author

on 24 September; Mandela Way, reprieved from plans to close, was their host for a month; their place on the 45 at Camberwell was taken by WVLs (B9TLs) arriving for the similar double-decking of the 12.

The three EVLs that had stayed behind long after their siblings had departed transferred from Stockwell to Camberwell in the middle of September and turned out on the 68, 468 and X68 as WVL-refurbishment cover; VWL 10 loaned from Mandela Way also visited the X68. A particularly weird working was of Rainham's PVL 159 on East London Transit routes EL1 and EL2.

The 12 was double-decked on 5 November with the B9TL variant of WVLs, but the B7TL versions still at Camberwell soon turned out in support, as did PVLs shortly after.

After a brave extended innings, EVLs 5, 15 and 17 finally bowed out on 30 December and left Camberwell for sale.

At the end of 2011 the 36 found itself offered out, while the 624 and 625 continued from Mandela Way and Bexleyheath respectively;

Left: **VP 2 (X151 FBB) is the complete Go-Ahead London bus in this Lewisham view of 25 March 2012, East Thames Buses and London Easylink long forgotten, but there wasn't much time left for the class and sale ensued in December 2013.** Author

Go-Ahead — 55

Right: **You can tell that PVL 348 (PF52 WPY) is a Bexleyheath motor in this Lewisham shot of 4 August 2012, due to the characteristic front windscreen-carried Times New Roman running number cards that only that garage favoured. The 321 juggled its resources back and forth in the PVL era, and six weeks after this shot was taken, Bexleyheath would withdraw again.** *Author*

the 658 was assumed with new buses. When the 22's award was made (back to London General), its by-no-means exhausted WVLs were planned to be re-used on the 257, won by Blue Triangle at the same time.

On 28 January the 89 was renewed and its earliest PVLs replaced by new Es, leaving just PVLs 346-355 and 362-370 for the 321 and 401. All had been refurbished, and like the 06-reg WVLs still being done, were outshopped still with grey skirts and black between the window frames.

Needing money desperately, FirstGroup began selling off chunks of its London operation and on 31 March Northumberland Park became a London General garage, bringing across all its vehicles. Among these were seventeen Plaxton President-bodied 10.6m Volvo B7TLs, which were rechristened from VNL to PVN class and continued on the 67 with visits to the 259, 357 and 476. The 67 was up for tender so the longevity of the PVNs, now entering their second decade, was far from assured. This point in time saw the

Right: **Another set of Volvo B7TL acquisitions prompted a new code as Go-Ahead picked up what First London could no longer handle. Again, rather than incorporate the 67's seventeen buses at Northumberland Park into the PVL class, London General named them PVNs rather than continuing their cumbersome First codes. This bus, seen at Wood Green on 11 August 2012, started as VTL 1307, then became VNL 32307 but settled as PVN 2 (LK03 NHG).** *Author*

Left: **On 7 April 2012 Merton's PVL 145 (X745 EGK) serves Tooting Broadway on the 77. It had eighteen months left in service.** Author

36 announced as retained with a proportion of new buses, while the 44, 77, 87 and 270 now found themselves out again. The 425, still capable of fielding B7TLs at Silvertown, was also tendered.

31 March was also the date the 19 and 249 were taken over by London General. Merton was in charge of the latter and immediately put out PVLs alongside its brand new B9TLs.

March 2012 saw Commercial Services' PVL 71 given an all-over ad for the Warner Brothers Studios Tour and set going on this year's route 850 there on 12 March. PVLs 219 and 223 were two more single-door conversions for the unit, and LED blind boxes were fitted to the others. A handful of PVL repaints in the spring were to all-red but with a white tape band.

Go-Ahead's participation in Olympics support didn't include any B7TLs other than WVLs 272 and 273 seconded from Bexleyheath to Silvertown and the regular Commercial Services PVLs worked to their full capacity, but some local routes were augmented for the duration of the Games; between 16 July and 13 September Silvertown's D8 was double-decked and long-discarded PVLs were hired back to add a supplementary service

Left: **The PVLs' generation of double-deckers had omitted the white tape band inherited from LBL, but London General Commercial Services restored it as part of their own livery and a handful of 2012 repaints gained it on its own, without the skirt. Silvertown's PVL 72 (W472 WGH), put into Docklands Buses' fleet, is seen at Stratford on 4 August 2012, during the period that the D8 was double-decked for the Olympics. Passenger numbers later justified its permanent conversion to double-deck.** Author

Right: **Another new territory for PVLs by 2012 was the 425, normally the province of Scanias. Here at Stratford on 4 August 2012 is PVL 66 (W466 WGH).** *Author*

Right: **Double-deck extras on the 108 during the Olympics were by necessity restricted south of the river; a lucky chance at Lewisham on 4 August 2012 catches New Cross's PVL 323 (PJ52 LWA) arriving and PVL 211 (Y811 TGH) leaving, each with different blind displays.** *Author*

Right: **Then there was the 129, just a stub of a route since plans to extend it to Peckham were cancelled, but it was right in the middle of an Olympics staging area and thus needed double-deckers like PVL 91 (W491 WGH), coming up to North Greenwich on 4 August 2012. Like the D8, the 129 was later double-decked permanently.** *Author*

Left: **Visa is sponsoring Putney's WVL 14 (LG02 KHM) in this Kingston shot of 11 July 2012 .** *Author*

to the 425, operated by Northumberland Park between 27 July and 12 August. Out of the Olympic area, Camberwell operated a supplementary service on the 74 with PVLs. Overall, the corporate sponsors of the Games were obliged to plug as much product as possible, to which end WVLs 14, 16, 212, 216, 231, 248 and 271 were given all-over ads for Visa and WVLs 215, 219 and 241 ones for Samsung.

So recently acquired, the 67 was announced in July as lost to Arriva London North. On 21 July the 280 began its new contract, waiting for new Es to oust its PVLs and WVLs. The month also saw the clean sweep of Merton's 44, 77 and 270 and Stockwell's 87, all of whose WVLs would be joined by a proportion of new buses and Es cascaded from the 24. In mid-September, PVLs 390-404 were transferred from New Cross to Merton

Left: **On 4 August 2012 WVL 271 (LX06 ECE) has gravitated to Bexleyheath and is also in a wrap for Visa. The 132 was yet another route that benefited so much from the restoration of its upper deck during the Olympics that double-deck buses were later instituted permanently.** *Author*

Right: **The appearance of new Es on the 36 prompted the transfer of the displaced PVLs to Merton to upgrade the age profile there. Setting off from Putney Bridge Station on 28 July 2013 is PVL 390 (LX54 HAA).** Author

as the proportion of new Es for the 36 came off temporary Olympics duty to release them. Refurbishment was on the cards for these buses too, and in any case their first task was to displace fifteen W-reg PVLs for withdrawal. Shortly afterwards an order was placed for Es to complete the route and free up the rest of the 54-reg PVLs.

On 29 September Bexleyheath withdrew from the 321, giving New Cross back PVLs 346-355 and simultaneously dropping the cross-links to the 661 and 669, which now operated independently. The 22 and N22 started their new contracts on 20 October, awaiting new B9TL WVLs and WHVs.

Following the successful conclusion of the Olympics and Paralympics, the Visa-sponsored WVLs 216, 248 and 271 regained red between September and November and the Samsungs came off in November. With

Right: **Repainted WVLs looked surprisingly uncomfortable with all the black bits painted over. WVL 189 (LX05 FBC) was meant for transfer to Northmberland Park to take over the 257, but until that happened, worked a little longer at its original Putney and on 11 August 2012 is seen in Putney High Street.** Author

Left: **On its intended 257 on 7 September 2013, Northumberland Park's WVL 202 (LX05 EZU) hasn't been treated quite as well as the flowerbed it is passing outside Leytonstone station.** *Author*

the simultaneous standing down of the D8's PVL enhancement, normal business could be got back to. 13 October was the date set for the takeover of the 257 from Stagecoach East London; since the acquisition of Northumberland Park, plans were revised to put it in there, but not enough of the 22's new buses had been delivered in time to displace the higher-numbered 05-reg WVLs needed, so on the 13th a handful of PVLs were reactivated and put into Putney for a last hurrah of the class. The 257 immediately saw PVN visitors. As it happened, the 22 was done out of its new buses, which were switched to the 74 on the grounds that Putney High Street, most of which was served by the latter, had pollution issues which would best be alleviated by keeping the WVLs on the 22.

13 October also saw the 42's propensity to attract B7TLs continue upon its transfer from Camberwell to Mandela Way; these were now VWLs, which were also known on the 453 as well as continuing to be loaned to Camberwell. That garage's own PVLs, meanwhile, took in the 436 for the first time.

When the 24 was lost to Metroline on 10 November half its E complement was put into Merton pending the order of eighteen new EHs for the 87. The equivalent number of X-reg PVLs made spare weren't out of work for long; the need to double-deck the 132 during the Olympics was felt successful enough to implement permanently and at the tail end of November fourteen of the PVLs were transferred from Merton to Bexleyheath for an official 1 December start date. Neighbouring Belvedere and Bexleyheath traded their VPs VWLs with aplomb despite being allocated to separate companies within Go-Ahead (London General and London Central respectively) and one result of this saw a VWL on the 401, a new route to rack up. At London General's core, Putney's tenure with the PVL class came to an end on 13 November when PVL 170 was withdrawn.

Below: **In a shade of pink that became notorious the longer it went on, PVL 113 (W513 WGH) is seen at Hyde Park Corner on 11 August 2012, working out of Putney while the garage's normal WVLs were helping out Northumberland Park.** *Author*

Right: **On 21 August 2014 PVL 163 (X563 EGK) is seen at Eltham on the 132, now restored to double-deck operation but fairly soon to upgrade to Es.** *Author*

Below: **This is the last summer for PVL 118 (W518 WGH) as it rounds Hyde Park Corner on attachment to Putney on 27 May 2012; it was sold in October.** *Author*

Putney also engineered swaps that soon rotated refurbished WVLs 189-205 into their rightful position at Northumberland Park. WVLs 206-210 then made their way to Merton.

Mass ad blitzes had proven a successful strategy during the Olympics, and at the end of 2012 Apple picked up the baton, splurging heavily on vinyl wraps to plug its iPod. Just nine of eighty buses to don basic white with a choice of subsidiary colours (just like the product in question) were WVLs 16-18, 37, 118, 133, 139, 233 and 251. This was only a short-term contract, three lasting until December and the rest regaining red in January.

The rest of the 36's Es arrived in time to meet the route's new contract applying from 9 February 2013, and the residual PVLs left for Merton. The resulting cascade of movements out of Merton (even as a surplus was used to add capacity to the 219 while six of its LDPs were sent elsewhere) put B7TL-based WVLs into two new bases; Putney and Bexleyheath, the former to cover refurbishment of the last of its own examples. In April the four Putney WVLs moved on to Mandela Way while Stockwell and Camberwell got one each; PVL 79 was otherwise Camberwell's last. A further Gemini, WVLs 93, was converted to open-top over the summer and repainted into General livery for Commercial Services.

Left: **Even though Bexleyheath and Belvedere fell under different arms of the Go-Ahead London organisation, the natural neighbours swapped buses on a regular basis, which saw PVLs pop up on the 180, otherwise the province of VWLs. Coming though Lewisham on its way north-east is PVL 369 (PJ53 SRO) on 4 August 2012.** *Author*

Left: **Apple's iPod bus campaign of late 2012 positively deluged the streets with buses; one of them was Camberwell's WVL 233 (LX06 DZR), seen crossing Waterloo Bridge on 25 November 2012.** *Author*

Left: **Stockwell's WVL 139 (LX53 AYM) rounds Trafalgar Square on 25 November 2012; this was the green and yellow version of the four available.** *Author*

Right: **On 1 April 2013 Stockwell's PVL 203 (X503 EGK) climbs out of Clapham Junction on the 87. It lasted four more years.** Author

On 13 April Merton's 200 gained two double-deck school journeys; it was also up for tender and was retained. 27 April saw the 67 pass to Arriva London North, but six of the seventeen PVNs were retained to replace the similarly-inherited PDN-class Tridents; the rest went into reserve, with Blue Triangle's school routes eyed as a future pitch.

New contracts commenced on routes 44, 77, 87, 270 and N87 on 1 June, with all the buses needed in place including the E40Hs (EH class) for Stockwell's 87, which came in May. The same frustrating last-minute switch that TfL had applied to the 22 in violation of its contract terms was repeated on emissions grounds and the EHs went onto the 88 instead, indirectly replacing the Y-reg PVLs from Stockwell. Finally, four new Es completed Merton's new-bus component and displaced WVLs to add to Bexleyheath.

The four refurb-cover WVLs of 52-reg age moved from Mandela Way to Camberwell in

Right: **Merton's WVL 86 (LF52 ZNU) heads north from Tooting Broadway on 16 June 2013.** Author

64 – Volvo B7TL

Left: **The X68 was a unique partial express route that alone was allowed to depart from the strictest letter of its routeing in that once it got past its stopping points, it didn't really matter which way it went to get to its first set down at West Norwood; hence WVL 234 (LX06 DZS) at Waterloo on 15 March 2013 is opting to take the 59 road via Brixton rather than follow its stopping partners via Camberwell.** Author

May and more joined them in June to cover the fitting of Eminox SCRT emissions regulators to B7TLs' exhausts. The caravan proceeded on to Peckham in July, introducing the type there for the first time. A more ambitious initiative was the fitting of Camberwell's WVL 243 with a Williams Gyrodrive electric flywheel which would mimic the stop-start nature of hybrids, reducing fuel consumption in a similar manner but saving weight by comparison.

Merton lost the chance to field PVLs on the 249 with its reallocation to Stockwell on 1 June, but the 257's B7TL-type WVLs gained a new opportunity when the 20 was reallocated from Rainham to Northumberland Park on the 22nd. By compensation Blue Triangle gained eight WVLs and PVNs 7-17, all for school routes 608, 652, 656, 667, 679 and 686. Silvertown still had PVLs, but their chance to use them on the 425 was lost on 6 July when Tower Transit took over this route.

Left: **Looking tired but still serviceable on 14 April 2013 is Merton-operated PVL 112 (W512 WGH) at Streatham. The characteristic asymmetrical rear of the President body on Volvo B7TLs has been added to during the bus's lifespan with two extra ventilation grilles chopped into each wing in a desperate attempt to baffle the noise problems the B7TL was subject to as it aged.** Author

Above: The VPs inherited from East Thames Buses came to the end of the road in 2013 as WVLs made spare from the 11's conversion to Borismaster were transferred to Camberwell to replace them. The blinds on WVL 132 (LX53 AZD), while still minimal, are now white on black, justified as still being a contrasting colour and designed to make up for the dayglo yellow on previous blinds fading quickly. This shot was taken at Vauxhall on 24 February 2014. *Author*

The B16 had fielded VPs and PVLs for some time, but with its withdrawal from the demolished Ferrier Estate on 27 July Bexleyheath could now push them all the way up the main road to Kidbrooke Station.

For the 2013 summer season, Commercial Services' PVL 217 was given an ad for 'Middle School' by James Patterson and turned out on the 850. One fixture to have moved on was the 36X, New Cross's perennial Carnival one-off; this year it operated Es instead of PVLs.

It was now the time of the Borismaster, and London General's first route to receive the LT class was the 11 from 20 September; the surviving 53-reg WVLs found themselves transferred to Camberwell to see off the VPs from the 185 by 4 November. The VWLs also at Camberwell increased numbers at Belvedere, whose loans to Bexleyheath now added the 89, 229, 422 and 486 to the class's tally, with 53-reg PVLs on the 180 in response. The Eminox-cover WVLs introduced Silvertown to the

Right: The treatment of PVL 224 (Y824 TGH) to General livery for Commercial Services was truly splendid. It is seen outside Merton garage on the occasion of its open day on 17 November 2013. *Author*

Left: **Merton's WVL 79 (LF52 ZPK), leaving Tooting Broadway on 16 June 2013, looks strangely naked without its signature London General grey skirt; in fact, with its black window edging retained, it could pass for an Abellio 'V' if it got as far as the Elephant.** Author

type, while the 132 at Bexleyheath received a proportion of Es ex-Stockwell to partially upgrade it from PVL. Sales of ordinary WVLs now commenced, as opposed to ones going back off lease. WVL 79 was repainted all-red, producing an unfamiliar aspect, and finally for the autumn, three WVLs were put into Sutton on 1 November, introducing the B7TL variant there for the first time; effectively for a boost to the 93, they soon visited the 151, 154 and 213.

WVL 243 re-entered service on 26 November, its flywheel producing the expected 20-30% fuel savings. WVL 83 was sent away to become the second Commercial Services convertible open-topper, and 2013 ended with Bexleyheath's 661 and 669 out to tender, subsequently successful. VPs 15-17 were stood down there in December and were the last of the type in service; as they left the fleet, the first VWLs started to accompany them.

Left: **One of three WVLs transferred to Sutton to boost the 93 on 1 November 2013 was WVL 76 (LF52 ZPG). It is seen coming north through Wimbledon on 12 January 2014.** Author

Substantial inroads had now been made into the PVL class, and the beginning of 2014 saw three Commercial Services examples replaced by three Scanias coming from Metrobus.

Repaints to Merton-based 54-reg PVLs from the start of 2014 introduced all-red to the class, however belatedly. In January three WVLs joined Northumberland Park as refurbishment cover for the 231's ENs; their newer siblings had already strayed to this route from the 257, and from about now the 357 became fair game for them.

Following Go-Ahead's decision to bring Metrobus into the London operations' fold in the same manner as had Blue Triangle and Docklands Buses, replacements for ageing Volvo B7TLs started to be pulled from this source; after the 54 and 75 were lost back to Stagecoach Selkent a raft of Optare-bodied Scanias were brought to Rainham in May to eject the PVNs from its school routes, save PVN 17 which escaped to Silvertown until the end of July. The pool WVLs spent time at Rainham but moved on to New Cross in June; once there they turned out in strength on the 129, double-decked on the 7th mostly with rather newer Es. Further movements during the summer allowed Silvertown to dispose of its last PVLs.

For the duration of the closure of Putney bridge to all but foot traffic during the

Above: **On 5 April 2014 at Waterloo WVL 271 (LX06 ECE) adds variety to the 1, otherwise still the province of Mandela Way's VWLs.** *Author*

Right: **PVLs had now become the latest generation of Go-Ahead London trainers. On 3 December 2014 a number of them were seen ambling uncertainly around Woolwich, and this is PVL 64 (W464 WGH).** *Author*

Left: **The closure of Putney Bridge during the summer of 2014 left not a lot of room for affected routes to turn around, so rather than just subjecting them to awkward U-turns at each head of the bridge, some sections were combined. Refurbished and repainted Merton PVL 395 (LX54 HBB), with a set of its own LED lights fitted above the headlights rather than in the bumper, is coming out of Lower Richmond Road on 28 August, having stood at the Putney Common stand otherwise occupied by the 22 since time immemorial.** Author

summer of 2014, local routes were curtailed or cleverly combined; where WVLs were concerned, the 430 was split across the bridge but the 270 coming from the south was diverted to Putney Common to cover the 22.

It had been a strikingly quiet year for Go-Ahead, with many contracts extended by two years, but in the autumn programme the 151 and 155 were two PVL-operated London General routes to find themselves out to tender. The 661 and 669 began their new terms on 4 October, but there was another 669, a Surrey school route operated by two Commercial Services PVLs which soon gave way to Scanias.

After a couple of years with no adverts on WVLs, a new one bowed in September with the treatment of WVL 34 to one for Rimmel, lasting three months. WVL 177 followed in October for Penny for London.

Left: **On 20 November 2014 at Tooting Broadway, Merton's PVL 377 (PJ53 NKO) was entering its twelfth year as a stalwart of the 155, but the route was up for tender and would be receiving new vehicles whoever won the contract.** Author

Go-Ahead – 69

Right: **The big 06-reg batch of WVLs began to shift in 2014 as the 68's complement was replaced by Es themselves displaced by Borismasters. WVL 240 (LX06 DZZ) was one parcelled out to New Cross to put an upper deck on the 129, and on 26 March 2015 it is seen drawing up to North Greenwich.** *Author*

Borismasters continued to pour into the capital; in the few weeks from 18 October a further complement was deployed to Mandela Way to take over the 453 and thereby displace its Es to Camberwell for the 68 and 468. 06-reg WVLs thus to move out were apportioned between a wide variety of garages, numbering four to Merton for the 44, three to New Cross for the 129, three to Silvertown for the D7, four to Stockwell to cover refurbishments to the first five EHs and finally twenty-one to Metrobus at Orpington to replace Scanias on the 161 beginning on 7 November, with visits to the 320 and 353 by the end of 2014 and the 126 during 2015.

London General Commercial Services was thrust into the forefront on 12 January 2015 when troubles at London Bridge compelled three extra services to be put on temporarily; the PVLs' participation was on the 21. PVL 224 with this unit gained a blue livery for the London By Night Sightseeing Tour.

Right: **Silvertown was also a beneficiary of ex-Camberwell WVLs, putting them on the D7 but also letting them wander to the 474, which had its own (albeit of the later B9TL variant). On 17 March 2015 WVL 250 (LX06 EAP), leaving the new bus station at East Beckton, shows off the wealth of vent holes hacked into the engine cover and rear sidewalls.** *Author*

Left: **It's not by night and it's not London as such, as PVL 224 (Y824 TGH) swings into the London Bus Museum at Brooklands on 19 April 2015. This was the livery of the popular after-hours tour of London that was entrusted to Commercial Services.** *Author*

Left: **Metrobus had now been folded entirely into London General, but Metrobus fleetnames kept this august identity alive even as its historically Scania-based vehicle preference gave way to cascaded Volvo B7TLs like WVL 230 (LX06 DZN), coming into Woolwich on 18 October 2015 after the conversion of the 161. Frustratingly, the buses never did lose their previous Camberwell codes for all the years they were based at Orpington.** *Author*

Left: **The other main Metrobus route to see former Camberwell WVLs was the 320, which had more recently been extended up from Bromley North. Here at Catford, Rushey Green on a sunny 27 February 2015 is WVL 224 (LX06 DZG).** *Author*

Right: **A big push by the Philippines tourist authority saw several London buses treated to ads extolling various parts of the island archipelago; this one, on Putney's WVL 164 (LX05 FCD) was for Siargao, an island off the north-east coast of Mindanao. The shot was taken in Eden Street, Kingston, on 23 January 2015.** *Author*

In January 2015 five Putney WVLs were liveried to plug tourism to the Philippines; these were WVLs 160, 162-164 and 181 and their contracts lasted for a year. February saw WVL 177's ad changed to one for Peru.

The Borismaster invasion had now proceeded to the 12, and aside from transfers of B9TL WVLs, two of Camberwell's remaining 06-reg contingent passed to Mandela Way to join PVL 233, hitherto working alone alongside the 1's VWLs.

The 42 had transferred to Camberwell the previous 13 October so was not subject to B7TL incursions any more unless Camberwell chose to put out one of the 185' WVLs.

In May 2015 awards kept the 155 with London General but with new WHVs ordered to replace its 53-reg PVLs; the 129, 639 and 670 were also out, followed in the summer by the 85, 213 and four south-east London routes still fielding Volvo B7TLs, the 1, 132, 180 and 185. In June Sutton held onto its double-deck

Right: **Neither PVL 229 (Y729 TGH) nor VWL 18 (LF52 TGU), the latter a loan from Belvedere to Bexleyheath, had that much time ahead of them when captured together on 11 May 2015 on the 401's stand at Bexleyheath. The VWL was sold in 2016 and the PVL became a trainer.** *Author*

Left: Converted from MAL artic to WHV and WVL (B9TL), the 12 very occasionally saw an appearance by a 'proper' Weevil, as in this Elephant & Castle appearance by Camberwell's WVL 78 (LF52 ZPJ) on 18 January 2015.
Author

complement, though the WVLs supporting the 93 and the PVLs on the 151 were due to be replaced. The same fate was likely for the older buses on the 129, announced as retained in August. The summer tenders were announced at that point and threatened PVLs on the 321 and 363 and WVLs on the 14 and 430, whoever won them. Even before the 14's award, forty-two WHVs were ordered in the interest of continuing to fight pollution in Putney High Street, blamed on buses.

A staff shuttle between Vauxhall and the Battersea Power Station construction site was mounted on 1 June with three Commercial Services PVLs based at Waterloo. WVL 177 lost its ad in June but WVL 166 gained one for Sunglass Hut for two months.

LTs now reached Stockwell's 88 from 22 August; its EHs could now take over the 87 and displace Es to see off Euro 2-spec PVLs still working; PVL 203 was the only one left at Stockwell and was withdrawn first, followed

Left: In its later years, PVL 232 (Y732 TGH) roved around London Central and London General, filling in on its own for a short while and then moving on again. In this Kingston shot of 6 October 2015 it is working out of Sutton, having come from Peckham the previous month, but would soon head on again, to Camberwell.
Author

Go-Ahead 73

Right: **Converted to open-top and repainted into London General colours complete with gold leaf fleetnames and fleetnumbers, WVL 93 (LF52 ZNE) looks absolutely outstanding on the occasion of its display on 5 September 2015 at Camberwell garage open day.** *Author*

Below: **Most unusual on the 171 out of New Cross on 10 October 2015 at Waterloo is WVL 97 (LF52 ZNK), transferred in during June 2014 and ending up spending two and a half years there.** *Author*

by the 132's contingent at Bexleyheath. Those PVLs thus leaving the fleet in September were the first B7TL sales in a year, but four WVLs ex-Stockwell were transferred in shortly after to keep the B7TL type alive, with four more bolstering numbers at Northumberland Park.

Putney's WVLs were reprieved when the new WHVs arriving in August were switched to Metrobus to start edging out Scania Omnidekkas. On 2 October the school served by the 639 and 670 was relocated from Putney to Battersea and the routes amended to match.

The 85's award was announced in October as a loss to London United, but the 213 would be staying put at Sutton. The winter tranches were announced, setting the clock ticking on WVL-operated 333 at Stockwell, though the 401's PVLs were assured two more years.

On 5 December the 93 and 151 started new London General contracts at the latter and the 155's new term commenced a week later. Its new WHVs began to displace Merton's 53-reg PVLs; while handfuls topped up Stockwell and Camberwell and a few into Commercial Services, PVL 375 was the first into Metrobus Croydon for an allocation aimed at taking Scanias off the 64 for its last months before transfer to Arriva London South.

Following the withdrawal of Silvertown's last two PVLs in October, eight remaining Euro 2 PVLs lasted to the end of 2015 and into 2016, three at New Cross, two at Camberwell and one each at Bexleyheath, Merton and Mandela Way. The last mentioned's PVL 233 came off after 25 January.

In February the 321 and 363 awards were made back to their incumbents, though the 52- and 03-reg PVLs on each would depart in favour of cascaded and new buses respectively.

From 6 February 2016 the 68 began converting to LT operation; there were still a handful of 06-reg WVLs at Camberwell following the takeover by Es, but this batch continued to spread, members now heading to Croydon where they replaced Scanias on the 127. Due to the need for B7TL WVLs to

Left: **Another early Weevil oddment is WVL 85 (LF52 ZNT), seen at Peckham on the 63 on 16 December 2015.** *Author*

be sent to Rainham for an increase to the East London Transit routes, the 249, tendered in February, was converted to PVL with the balance of the 53-reg examples ex-Merton. Euro 2 buses were no longer permitted after 1 April, making Camberwell's PVL 169 the last such on the day before. Most of the rest of the WVLs were now put on notice when Go-Ahead swept the 14, 185, 430, 639 and 670 in the same tranche that kept the 1 and 180 and thus threatened all the VWLs. A combination of E40H MMCs (EHs), MCV-bodied Volvo B5LHs (MHVs) would put an end to them by the beginning of 2017. Then, in May, the 333 was awarded to Arriva London South.

On 30 April the 35 and 40 came back to Camberwell on new London Central contracts after five years at Abellio, with the 345 going the other way; PVLs could now appear once again and did so on the 40 at least. When the 85 was taken over by London United on 2 July, a chain of reallocations

Left: **Metrobus had been cascaded WVLs and now it was time to give it some PVLs as Scanias fell well and truly out of favour. Still carrying the Merton codes from its original (and hitherto only) garage, now Croydon-allocated PVL 375 (PJ53 NKM) is coming around the bus station at Addington Village on 25 March 2016.** *Author*

Go-Ahead – 75

Right: **Always second-tier even despite its conversion to double-deck under Arriva London South, the 249 was designated to sacrifice its newish B9TL-WVLs to bolster East London Transit and receive ageing PVLs in exchange. Perhaps this contributed to its loss on tender, straight back to Arriva London South, but on 4 May 2016 Stockwell's PVL 388 (PJ53 NLE) is seen setting off from Clapham Common.** *Author*

to fill the space left at Putney saw the 77 reallocated from Merton to Stockwell, taking PVLs 405-419 with it. Of WVLs 14-27 stood down, three went to Camberwell and two each to Stockwell and New Cross with two reactivated at Putney, but Stockwell passed its examples to Camberwell and Sutton took one before sales of that batch commenced. Putney's own WVL 57 gained an ad for T Systems in June, carrying it till August.

With the 45, 257 and 280 out for tender, August saw the 249 awarded to Arriva London South and on the 27th the 64 left Metrobus for the same company, with PVLs 371-377 divided between Belvedere and Stockwell.

Orders ensued against the contracts for the 14, 185, 363 and 430 and the first of the resulting MHVs arrived in September to convert Camberwell's 185 in the two weeks

Right: **The loss of the 85 by London General to London United on 2 July 2016 didn't mean the immediate withdrawal of its 02-reg WVLs despite their age; they had been refurbished, after all, and in ones and twos dotted around the fleet were still considered useful. WVL 25 (LG02 KJA) was transferred to Camberwell and is seen on 11 August at the Elephant & Castle.** *Author*

Left: There are roadworks going on at Eltham Church on 19 July 2016 as Bexleyheath's PVL 365 (PJ53 SPU) makes the right turn to head north. This day saw examples of six types on the 132, of which this PVL was the only representative. *Author*

Left: WVL 118 (LX03 EEM) was transferred from Stockwell to Bexleyheath in October 2015 and on 18 February 2016 is seen in Bexleyheath town centre on a route 401 duty. *Author*

Left: Bexleyheath's WVL 120 (LX03 ECW) was another transfer from Stockwell, this time in March 2016, and is seen on a scorching-hot 19 July setting off west from Bexleyheath as BX101 on the 486. This bus would move about over the next couple of years, coming back to Bexleyheath twice again and then heading to Merton to form the WVLs' rearguard there. *Author*

Go-Ahead

Right: **Stockwell took over the 432 with the B9TL versions of WVLs, but very occasionally it would stick out something older, as on 15 June 2016 when PVL 388 (PJ53 NLC) is seen at Brixton, coming off a duty which would later pick up again and continue all day.** *Author*

Right: **There was older and then there was positively ancient, which is what the original batch of WVLs were in modern terms by 30 August 2016, when Stockwell saw fit to put out WVL 3 (LG02 KGV) on the 249 at Tooting Bec.** *Author*

Right: **WVL 121 (LX03 ECY) was transferred from Stockwell to Bexleyheath in October 2015 and spent over two years there; on 26 November 2016 it is seen at Woolwich on the 422.** *Author*

Left: **Still looking spry in the morning sunshine of 2 April 2016, VWL 33 (BX04 AZV) crosses Waterloo Bridge. It was sold in February 2017.** *Author*

following 27 September and spanning its contract renewal on 1 October. The recently-opened River Road garage allocated to Blue Triangle took the 474 from Silvertown on this day and added its seven WVLs, stopping them from appearing on the D7. The 1, 132 and 180 also started new contracts on 1 October and Mandela Way's allocation of WHVs started taking over the 1 on the 17th, with VWL 17 the last to go after 5 December.

On 8 October the 321 was renewed, awaiting a chain of transfers before its PVLs could go. The 21st saw the debut of the MHV class at Peckham, which in concert with new EHs replaced the 363's PVLs, which had continued to see service on the 63 as well. PVL 335 was Peckham's last on 11 November as the 363's contract spooled out. Peckham also transferred B7TL WVLs out to Belvedere to start the conversion of the 180 from VWL.

Left: **On 26 October 2016 Peckham's PVL 341 (PJ52 LWW) has reached the Elephant after a trip on the 363 and is about to lay over, but its career was almost over and it would be sold the following January.** *Author*

Go-Ahead – 79

Right: **Putney's long association with the WVL ebbed away after 2016; here at Putney Bridge on 11 March of that year is WVL 179 (LX05 FBV), but by this time next year it would have gone.** Author

Putney's large new fleet of WHVs commenced operation on 31 October, in time for the contract renewals on the 14 and 430 on 19 November. The long-established WVLs on these routes and continuing to figure on the 22 and 74 began to stand down, the pace accelerating in December as the accompanying allocation of EHs arrived, late due to a last-minute change to specify E40Hs instead of Volvo B5LHs.

On 3 December 2016 the 118 found itself reallocated from Merton to Metrobus Croydon, taking its Es with it and precluding WVLs or PVL appearances. However, this was a short-term measure and on 28 January 2017 it moved again to Stockwell, which could now impose its own B7TLs; it was also doing so on the 249 and 432 at this point. Stockwell had space made by the 333's departure for Arriva London South on 21 January.

Right: **Under tendering, the 333 had been lost to Arriva London South and thus time is running out for WVL 8 (LG02 KHE) as it passes through Brixton on 25 September 2016.** Author

Left: **The VWL class bowed out early in 2017, consigning remaining memories of East Thames Buses to the history books (i.e. this one!). Without the usual extension of the yellow banding round the pointy Gemini bumpers is VWL 26 (LF52 THU) at Greenwich on 4 October 2016.** *Author*

The conversion of the 21 from B9TL WVL to LT operation had started on 5 December but proved very slow, as was the resulting displacement of those WVLs to the 321. Those conversions and that of the VWL-operated 180 were completed in January; Camberwell's VWL 10 was the last of all, coming off on the 24th following the completion of the 185's upgrading using the EHs ordered against the 42 but in reality mixed with the 185's own MHVs. Bexleyheath could still field B7TL WVLs as spare buses even after the 89's renewal on 28 January, while the PVL-operated 401 was now out on tender again since the end of 2016. As for the more recent WVL operations, Metrobus's 161 was also offered out and Northumberland Park's 257 was announced as lost to Stagecoach.

Despite heavy sales at the beginning of 2017 that saw over fifty B7TLs, including 39

Below: **With the loss of the 257 to Stagecoach, this route would now have circulated round all four local operators. When captured at Stratford on 31 October 2016, Northumberland Park's WVL 111 (LX03 EDV) was carrrying a side blind in the front box.** *Author*

Right: **You can barely see the join on WVL 83 (LF52 ZNR) as it reposes outside the Old Vic on 16 January 2017 with its roof on. This was the second WVL to be converted to open-top and repainted into London General livery.** *Author*

WVLs, leave the fleet in February alone, VWL 10 found itself reactivated by Camberwell on 9 February and served on the 185 till the 27th, but that was truly the end for that class, while New Cross's PVLs 343 and 352 lasted until 10 March and PVL 320 saw the class out there after service on the 18th. Despite being only fifteen years of age, WVL 1 was sold to the London Bus Museum at Brooklands, becoming its most modern exhibit.

In March the 45, still mostly PVL at Camberwell with a handful of WVLs in support, was awarded to Abellio. The PVL class found itself on the ropes at this point, however, the 401's examples at Bexleyheath coming off in the last week of March and 1 April seeing Merton's contingent (mostly on the 44, 270 and 280 with schoolday visits to the 163, 200 and 655) decimated by an influx of WHVs made spare from the takeover of

Right: **One of the survivors of the 2002 PVL batches whose other members had otherwise been returned prematurely off lease or converted to Commercial Services vehicles, PVL 272 (PN02 XBW) is seen at the Elephant on 16 March 2017 as a Camberwell bus. The 45 wouldn't be its major pitch for much longer, however, and it was sold after the route passed to Abellio.** *Author*

the 19 by Arriva London North. On the same day the 249 departed for Arriva London South and its 53-reg PVLs were stood down at Stockwell. This garage, however, was part of an experiment that saw WVLs 94 and 95 converted to VantagePower hybrid configuration, not that the vehicles were terribly successful; neither lasted beyond the end of 2017. Stockwell's 77 was now the only wholly-PVL route left there and this was out for tender by mid-2017. PVL 288 took itself out of consideration with a well-documented crash into a building at Lavender Hill on 10 August.

WVL withdrawals at Camberwell and Putney during April reduced numbers to just four at the latter, and the last there was WVL 165 operating an N22 duty in the early hours of 23 May. Even the 06-reg WVLs found themselves having to look over their shoulder into their second decade, and more so when the 161 was awarded and concurrently lost to Stagecoach Selkent. Then came the loss of the 468, Camberwell's remaining repository of the 06-reg WVLs, awarded to Arriva London South in July, and in August the 196, still a strong possibility for Stockwell WVL holdouts, was awarded to Abellio.

In June Metrobus Croydon's WVL contingent was increased by three 06-reg examples, nominally as cover for fellows going away for conversion to single-door format for the X26; there were now six based and used on the 119 and 127.

Late in the day for the WVL class, WVL 269 received an ad for the London Metropolitan University in July 2017, losing it upon withdrawal in March 2018.

In September the 77 was announced as retained by London General and new EHs were put on order for it. Merton's PVLs continued to decline as WVNs were put in during the month, but the opportunity was taken to use PVLs 390-396 to join earlier

Above: **The last WVL to receive an all-over ad was Camberwell's WVL 269 (LX06 ECC), still going on the 468 after eleven years. It is seen at the Elephant & Castle on 11 November 2017.** *Author*

Left: **WVL 239 (LX06 DZY) was transferred from New Cross to Metrobus Croydon in February 2016 and on 17 August 2017 is seen leaving Tooting Broadway as another unusual deployment to the 127, B5LH WHV 62 (BF65 WJE) from the 119 and 202, arrives.** *Author*

models at Commercial Services. On 14 October Northumberland Park's 257 was taken over by Stagecoach East London, but eight of its 05-reg WVLs proceeded to Bexleyheath as refurbishment cover. Then went the 45, passing from Camberwell to Abellio on 11 November, and that was the end of PVLs there.

A new site at Morden Wharf had replaced Belvedere and Mandela Way, but no B7TL WVLs worked from there until WVL 120 spent three days on loan in December 2017, working the 180.

2018 began with the 401 and 422 removed from Bexleyheath on 20 January with their move to Arriva at Dartford; although its five PVLs and fourteen WVLs were withdrawn (three PVLs and four WVLs to live on by transferring to Morden Wharf), three WVLs were reactivated in March and lasted all the way through 2018 and into 2019.

Sutton's PVL fleet started to drift away in January, its last on the 213 being PVL 289 on 13 March; Morden Wharf lost its three PVLs after 6 February and the six WVLs in March, while PVL 377, a lone example left at Croydon, finished on 23 February.

On 17 March the 161 departed for Stagecoach Selkent, Orpington passing three WVLs each to Croydon and Stockwell but losing thirteen on aggregate, and on the 31st the 468 was taken over by Camberwell. That finished off WVLs 18, 22, 25 and 27 from those that had been ejected from Putney a year earlier, plus much-wandered WVL 90 and finally WVLs 252-270.

Things were really winding down now for the Volvo B7TL at Go-Ahead London. River Road lost WVLs 113-117 in May, while at Stockwell, the 196 passed to Abellio on 5 May and the 77 started a new contract on 2 June, with new EHs taking over in the following

Right: **Both before and after the 257's departure from Northumberland Park, its refurbished 05-reg WVLs would turn out on the 357, as WVL 204 (LX05 EZA) is doing when sighted at Walthamstow Central on 4 January 2018.** Author

Right: **PVL operation at Sutton came to an end early in 2018; prior to that, Sutton's PVL 292 (PJ02 RDX) is seen in Kingston on the morning of 25 May 2017.** Author

month and easing out PVLs 405-419. The last in service at Stockwell was PVL 417, taken off an N87 duty at 1.05 am on 23 June. WSD-class Streetdecks simultaneously replaced six 05-reg and three 06-reg WVLs hanging on at Merton on the 44, but PVLs 282, 284 and 296 dodged the axe. But even the trainers were starting to leave, VP 19 departing in May and VP 18 in August; PVLs 399-404 were designated to replace them.

Orpington operated its last WVL on 9 July and Stockwell's WVL 96 was the last there, working on the 87 on 1 August, and then New Cross's last example left after 22 October. But the endgame wouldn't quite come; PVL 282's withdrawal from Merton in September left just two of the class in service, and of those, PVL 284 made its way to Bexleyheath on 15 November to strike up an allocation there once again!

Above: **Already reallocated to Stockwell, the 77 operated PVLs until June 2018. On 26 October 2017 one of them, PVL 411 (LX54 GZC), works through Tooting.** Author

Left: **Seen at Sutton station on 18 June 2017, Merton's WVL 206 (LX05 EZC) was sold in June 2018. Older WVLs still, however, continued on into 2019.** Author

Right: **WVL 96 (LF52 ZNJ) returned to Stockwell in March 2016 after five months at Camberwell, and on 6 January 2018 is seen at Charing Cross on the 87, which tended to get the oldest buses still available at Stockwell. Withdrawal and sale came in September.** *Author*

The position as 2019 bowed was the following, with just seventeen Volvo B7TLs operated by all five of the constituent companies of Go-Ahead, though since 2017 all were now under London General's unified and increased O-Licence. Merton had hold of WVLs 119-121 and PVL 296, using them predominantly on the 280 with appearances on the 270 and 655; Bexleyheath's WVLs 196-198 liked to stick to the 89, while PVL 284 was less discriminating, having been recorded on the 132, 486 and 625 as well. At Croydon, WVLs 238-240 were three of five remaining of the old 68/468/X68 batch and worked the 127 alone, and Northumberland Park had WVLs 111, 189, 204 and 205, spread among the 20, 191, 357, 476 and 616. Finally, WVLs 249 and 250 were at River Road, having come

Right: **WVL 235 (LX06 DZT) came to New Cross in January 2015 after the 68 was converted to E operation and spent three and a half years there; on 22 April 2018 it is seen at Marble Arch on the 36, otherwise long since converted to E operation and about to move on to the next generation of EHs.** *Author*

Left: **When this photograph of WVL 197 (LX05 EZO) was taken at Lewisham on 14 December 2018 Bexleyheath could still put three WVLs into the field. They lasted until the following March.** *Author*

there in October 2016 for school routes only and therefore stuck to the 679 (WVL 249) and 649 and 652 (WVL 250).

On 23 March 2019 the 20 departed for CT Plus, taking it out of contention for Northumberland Park's four B7TL WVLs. The transfer of its B9TL WVLs to Bexleyheath enabled WVLs 196-198 to stand down after the 28th, leaving just PVL 284. This enjoyed a private hire on 4 May, on which it explored a range of historical Bexleyheath routes, and, with four weeks still on its ticket, continued on in service. Even after that it was relicensed for another year, though its fellows at Merton started to fall out finally, WVLs 120 and 121 and PVL 296 coming off after service on 3 June. A new set of blinds into PVL 284 included the 291, otherwise the province of

Below: **Since coming to Bexleyheath, PVL 284 (PJ02 RCU) had divided its time equally between the 89, 132 and 486, and on 21 April it was encountered as BX7 on the 89 at the very end of that Easter Sunday's daylight, crossing Blackheath.** *Author*

Above: **Merton garage of London General took three WVLs and one PVL into 2019, much as the previous Metrobuses had held out for years after their own official replacement. On 10 May south of Tooting we see WVL 121 (LX03 ECY), its second repaint finally looking tired.** *Author*

Morden Wharf but which on 3 June gained a couple of workings put into Bexleyheath to work off school route 658 in the afternoon; its first day on the 291 was 17 June. Five days later the 51 was transferred from Metrobus Orpington to Bexleyheath, and on the 25th PVL 284 turned out on that too. It wouldn't be the last time either.

WVL 119 was now on its own at Merton, and after service on the 270 on 1 August its tenure came to an end. When the school year came to an end, River Road's WVLs 249 and 250 took August off but on 4 September the kids came back and so did the two WVLs.

The valiant holding out of Bexleyheath's PVL 284 came to an end after ten months of

Below: **PVL 296 (PJ02 RFE), Merton's sole PVL, tended to make its home on the 270 at the end of its life; the route was generally a mix of anything Merton could throw at it from its stocks. On 10 May 2019 it crosses Tooting Broadway.** *Author*

turning out daily on anything and everything, and Monday 9 September was designated its last day. It was a busy one as well, bookending both morning and afternoon 661 rosters with work on the 132, before returning to that route as BX88 until finishing at North Greenwich at 20:29. That was the end at Bexleyheath, at London Central and of the PVL class in general. But there were still surprises in store; on 17 September WVL 204, otherwise withdrawn from Northumberland Park after 23 August, was reactivated at Metrobus Croydon to serve as refurbishment cover, taking its complement to four – or at least until WVL 240 was taken out of service after 27 September.

The 357's London General contract was renewed on 29 February 2020, but only enough new BYDs for the 212 had appeared, so WVLs 111, 189 and 205 soldiered on. But then came coronavirus, or COVID-19. The resulting sudden convolution of society forced London's bus passengers inside under lockdown from 23 March, and from the 30th bus timetables were put on a Sunday footing, with surplus vehicles mothballed. River

Above: **Metrobus's late-transferred trio of 06-reg Weevils continued into 2019 on the 127. Though Metrobus's practice is to carry its running numbers on vertical pieces of paper mounted in the windscreen, Croydon's WVL 238 (LX06 DZW), captured at Tooting Mitre on 10 May 2019, is still carrying New Cross's code from the London Central garage it had come from.** *Author*

Left: **Amid the spectacle of the withdrawal of Merton's Volvo B7TLs, a handful of WVLs continued on at Northumberland Park, held against the requirement for school route 616 but capable of turning out on the 191 and 357 every day. On 12 August 2019, weary-looking WVL 111 (LX03 EDV), with a side blind in the front box and a Stockwell garage code, is doing so on the latter. The removal of the ungainly not-quite-roundabout at Walthamstow Central has made photography opportunities easier, but the price has been the pulling of the 97 and 357 out of the bus station altogether.** *Author*

Right: **As Metrobus never used the KM/NN blind box specification or its DDA-tolerated successor, WVL 204 (LX05 EZA), transferred from Northumberland Park to Croydon, had to accept a side blind. After a while it had its own unique set made up and is carrying it with pride in this Tooting Broadway view of 30 July 2020, by which time this bus and WVL 239 had defied the apparent end of the WVL class and of Volvo B7TL operation as a whole.** *Author*

Right: **Schools routes, while more recently separated out into their own distinct timetables, haven't had the same obligation to provide the newest buses, not least due to vandalism concerns. Thus the long-term retention of two ageing Weevils at River Road, where they lived a peaceful semi-retirement during term times only. The imposition of the coronavirus lockdown looked to have doomed them, but both were resuscitated in September 2020 with extra attention paid to their schools status, as in this 15 September shot of WVL 249 (LX06 EAO) at Gants Hill. Although it couldn't muster a blind for the 679 by then, it was carrying the specified windscreen card. Six long years after having left Camberwell, that garage's code has remained obstinately in place!** *Author*

Road's WVLs 249 and 250 had already come out of service after the spring term, and for the rest it appeared to be the death blow. As their replacement by new electric double-deckers progressed, Northumberland Park's last Volvo B7TLs operated on 2 April (WVL 111), 6 April (WVL 189) and 7 April (WVL 205, on the 476). Croydon's then followed, WVL 204 coming off the 127 at 23.30 on 18 April, and the simultaneous removal of Arriva London North's two VLAs after the 24th seemed to mark the end for the B7TL after twenty years of service in London. Even so, the eight surviving London General WVLs remained licensed and on 18 July WVL 238 was sighted back on Croydon's 127. WVL 239 followed suit on the 21st and WVL 204 returned on the 24th. The loss of the 405 to Arriva on 29 August was projected to release vehicles to replace them finally, but the need identified for extra buses as children were compelled to return to school obliged WVLs 204, 238 and 239 to keep going. That saw Northumberland Park's WVL 205 reactivated on 5 September and the River Road pair later that week.

Only 58% of pre-lockdown passenger numbers would return to London's buses, and the sharply reduced income now put TfL's very survival in question without a bailout. The extra schools services were given until the autumn half-term unless funds were released by central Government, but even after that threat was warded off, Go-Ahead made a final push against its six surviving Volvo B7TLs. Croydon thus withdrew WVL 238 after 10 October and WVL 239 after

the 15th, with Northumberland Park's WVL 205 finishing at four o'clock on the 20th after one last go on the 616. Meanwhile, River Road's WVL 249 had managed just four days (8, 15-17 September) since its resuscitation, but WVL 250 had worked the 679 in both peaks since 9 September. At 16:10 on 23 October it came off service, but WVL 204 dodged the axe yet again. It moved from Croydon to Merton on 2 October and took up a dedicated posting on school route 655, prolonging it into 2021. A third lockdown stopped it in its tracks after Friday 8 January, but it was resuscitated, yet again, on 10 March and remains available for the 655; perhaps another volume will be needed to cover its eventual end!

Above: **The third London General garage to revive its Weevils after the lockdown ebbed was Northumberland Park, although WVL 205 (LX05 EZB), the lone example to be relicensed there, was now no longer able to turn out on the 191 (which had passed to Arriva London North) or the 357 and 657 (converted to Ee), so was used when necessary on the 616 and 675 during school times, with forays to the 476 mounted only when absolutely nothing else could be scraped up. On 15 October 2020 it is seen setting off from Edmonton Green on the second working of three scheduled on a Thursday, but it was to last just five more days, spending 19 October on the 476 and then completing one more 616 diagram, morning and afternoon, on the 20th.** *Author*

Above left: **Not even an increasingly worsening pandemic could stop WVL 204 (LX05 EZA); revived again and again, it solidified its claim to being the last Volvo B7TL in London service with a transfer from Metrobus Croydon back to Merton, where it dug its heels in on schoolday route 655. As twilight closes in on 2 December, it is at South Wimbledon, almost at the end of the single eastbound afternoon peak journey. WVL 204 completed the autumn term and, after taking Christmas off, returned to traffic on 5 January 2021, but lockdown throttled its career again. Until 10 March, that is, when it sneaked back onto the 655 and stayed put.** *Author*

Registrations

AVL 1-46	V101-110, 211, 112-120, 221, 122, 223, 124-146 LGC
PVL 1-143	V301-308, 209, 310-315 LGC, V816 KGF, V317, 218, 319, 220 LGC, V921 KGF, V322 LGC, V923 KGF, V324, 325, 226, 327, 228, 329-332, 233, 334-338 LGC, W439, 840, 441-443, 544, 445-449, 499, 451-454, 998, 456-459, 996, 461-469 WGH, 170 CLT, W471-479, 408, 481-489, 409, 491-498, 399, 997, 501-504, 905, 506-509, 401, 511-514, 415, 516-519, 402, 521-524, 425, 526, 527, 428, 529, 403, 531-534, 435, 536-539, 404, 541-543 WGH
PVL 144-207	X544, 745, 546-549, 599, 551-554, 615, 556-559, 616, 561-564, 656, 566-569, 707, 571-579, 508, 581-589, 509, 591-598, 699, 502, 501, 702, 503, 504, 705, 506, 507 EGK
PVL 208-249	Y808, 809, 801, 811-819, 802, 821-828, 729, 703, 731-739, 704, 741-749 TGH
PVL 250-312	PL51 LDK/N/O/U/V/X-Z, LEF, PN02 XBH/J-M/O/P/R-W, PJ02 RAU/X, RBO/U/V/X-Z, RCF/O/U/V-Z, RDO/U/V/X-Z, REU, RFE/F/K/L/N/O/X-Z, RGO/U/V, TVN-P/T/U
PVL 313-355	PJ52 LVP/R-Z, LWA/C-H/K-P/R-X, PF52 WPT-Z, WRA/C-E/G, PL03 AGZ
PVL 356-389	PJ53 NJZ, NKA/C-F, SOF/H/U, SPU/V/X/Z, SRO/U, NKG/H/K-P/R-T/W/X/Z, NLA/C-F
PVL 390-419	LX54 HAA/E/O/U, HBA/B, GZG/H/K-P/R/T, GYV/W/Y/Z, GZB-F, GZU-W/Y/Z
EVL 1-52	PL51 LGA/C-G/J/K/N/O/U, PN02 XCA, PL51 LGW/X, PN02 XCB-E, PL51 LFE, PN02 XCF, PL51 LFG, PN02 XCG, PL51 LFJ, PN02 XCH/J-M/O/P/R-T, XBX-Z, PJ02 PYU-Z, PZA-H/K/L

Registrations

WVL 1-27	LG02 KGP/U/V/X-Z, KHA/E/F/H/J-M/O/P/R/T-Z, KJA/E/F
WVL 28-121	LF52 ZSO/P/R/T, ZRO/P/R/T-V/X-Z, ZSD, ZPZ, ZRA/C-E/G/J-L/N, ZPN-P/R/S/U-Y, ZTG/H/J-P/R, ZPB-E/G/H/J-M, ZNP/R-Z/D/E/G/H/J-O, ZLZ, ZMO/U, LX03 EXV/W/Z/U, EDR/U/V, EEA/B/F-H/J/M, ECV/W/Y
WVL 122-159	LX53 AZP/R/T-W/Z/A-D/F/G/J/L/N/O, AYM-P/T-W/Y/Z, BJK/O/U, BEY, BGE, BFK, BDY, BBZ, BAA, BDO, BAO
WVL 160-211	LX05 FBY/Z, FCA/C-F, FBD/E/F/J-L/N/O/U, EJZ, EYM/O, FBV, FAA/F/J/K/M/O/U, FBA-C, EZV/W/Z/K-P/R-U, EYZ, EZA-H
WVL 212-273	LX06 DXS-W/Y, DZA-H/J-P/R-W/Y/Z, EAA/C/F/G/J-M/O/P/W/Y, EBA/C-E/G/J-P/U/W/Z, ECA/C-F/J

Date	Deliveries	Licensed for Service
12.99	AVL 1	
01.00	AVL 2-25, 27-29, 32, 33	AVL 2-16 (**Q**), AVL 20-24 (**PM**)
02.00	AVL 26, 30, 31, 34-46	AVL 17-19 (**Q**), AVL 25-45 (**PM**)
03.00	PVL 2-11, 13-17, 19, 21-33, 37, 39, 41-43, 46	AVL 46 (**PM**) PVL 2-4, 6, 8-11, 13-17, 22, 24, 25, 27, 28, 30, 32, 33, 37, 39 (**BX**)
04.00	PVL 1, 12, 20, 30, 34-36, 38, 40, 44, 45, 47-49, 51-55	PVL 1, 5, 7, 19-21, 23, 26, 29, 31, 34-36, 38, 40-43, 46-49, 51-55 (**BX**)
05.00	PVL 18, 50, 56-65, 67-69, 71	PVL 12, 18, 42-46, 50 (**BX**) PVL 56, 58-60 (**SW**)
06.00	PVL 66, 70, 72-80, 84-90, 92, 93, 97, 100, 101, 105, 106	PVL 57, 61-72 (**SW**), PVL 97, 100, 101 (**AL**)
07.00	PVL 81-83, 91, 94-96, 99, 102-104, 107, 109-117, 120-122, 124	PVL 73, 74, 76-83, 85-93, 95 (**SW**), PVL 75, 84, 94, 96, 99, 102-107, 109-117, 120-122, 124 (**AL**)
08.00	PVL 108, 118, 119, 123, 125-143	PVL 98, 108, 118, 119, 123, 125-143 (**AL**)
09.00	PVL 98	
10.00	PVL 144, 145, 147-155	
11.00	PVL 146, 156-178	PVL 146, 148, 150, 153-155 (**AL**) PVL 156-174, 176, 177 (**SW**)
12.00		PVL 175, 178 (**SW**)
01.01	PVL 179-190, 193-199, 201-203	PVL 179-190, 193, 194 (**NX**), PVL 195-199, 201-203 (**AL**)
02.01	PVL 191, 192, 200, 204-207	PVL 191, 192 (**NX**), PVL 200, 204-207 (**AL**)
04.01	PVL 208-228, 230, 231, 234	PVL 208-228, 230, 231, 234 (**NX**)
05.01	PVL 229, 232, 233, 235-249	PVL 229, 232, 233, 235-249 (**NX**)
02.02	EVL 1-11, 13, 14, 19, 21, 23	
03.02	EVL 12, 15-18, 20, 22, 24-33, 35 PVL 250-272 WVL 1-3	EVL 1-26, 28, 29, 31, 32 (**A**) PVL 250-253 (**BX**), PVL 254-266 (**SW**)
04.02	EVL 34, 36 WVL 4-9	EVL 27, 30, 33-36 (**A**), PVL 267-272 (**BX**) WVL 1-9 (**SW**)
05.02	WVL 10-21	WVL 10-13 (**SW**)
06.02	WVL 22-26 EVL 37, 39, 42-45, 48 PVL 273-289	WVL 14-26 (**AF**) EVL 39, 44 (**A**) PVL 26
07.02	EVL 40 PVL 290-301, 305 WVL 27	EVL 37, 40, 42, 43, 45, 48 (**A**) PVL 273-301, 305 (**Q**) WVL 27 (**AF**)
08.02	EVL 38, 41, 46, 47, 49-52 PVL 302-312	EVL 46, 49, 50, 52 (**A**) PVL 302-312 (**Q**)
09.02		EVL 38, 41, 47, 51 (**A**)
10.02	WVL 28-31	WVL 28-31 (**AF**)
11.02	WVL 32-53	WVL 32-53 (**AF**)
12.02	WVL 54-81, PVL 313-342	WVL 54 (**AF**), PVL 313, 317, 318, 320 (**NX**)

Date	Deliveries	Licensed for Service
01.03	WVL 82-90	WVL 58, 61, 62, 64, 66-68 (**AF**), PVL 314-316, 319, 321-325 (**NX**), PVL 326-331 (**Q**), PVL 332-342 (**SW**)
02.03	WVL 91-108	WVL 91-108 (**SW**)
03.03	WVL 109-121, PVL 343-348, 350-354	WVL 110-112, 116 (**SW**) PVL 343-348, 350-354 (**NX**)
04.03	PVL 349	PVL 349 (**NX**), WVL 109, 113-115, 117-121 (**SW**)
06.03	PVL 355	PVL 355 (**PL**)
10.03	WVL 122-151, PVL 356-382	PVL 356, 358 (**Q**)
11.03	PVL 383-389	PVL 357, 359-361 (**Q**), PVL 371-389 (**AL**) WVL 122-151 (**SW**)
01.04	PVL 362-370, WVL 152-159	PVL 362-370 (**BX**)
02.04		WVL 152-159 (**SW**)
01.05	PVL 390-419	PVL 390-419 (**NX**)
05.05	WVL 160, 161	WVL 160, 161 (**SW**)
06.05	WVL 162-177, 179	WVL 163, 167, 169 (**SW**), WVL 164-166 (**A**), WVL 168, 170-177, 179 (**AF**)
07.05	WVL 178, 180-211	WVL 178, 180-211 (**AF**)
03.06	WVL 212-273	
04.06		WVL 212-273 (**Q**)

Re-registrations
11.00 PVL 125 from W425 WGH to WLT 625
02.01 PVL 32 from V332 LGC to WLT 532
04.01 AVL 46 from V146 LGC to 46 CLT
02.03 PVL 257 from PL51 LDY to 257 CLT
09.03 WVL 60 from LF52 ZPX to VLT 60
10.04 WVL 94 from LF52 ZNG to WLT 694
11.04 PVL 32 from WLT 532 to V332 LGC
11.04 PVL 70 from 170 CLT to W578 DGU
11.04 PVL 125 from WLT 625 to W425 WGH
11.04 PVL 257 from 257 CLT to PL51 LDY
01.05 WVL 94 from WLT 694 to LF52 ZNG
01.05 AVL 46 from 46 CLT to V146 LGC
02.06 WVL 60 from VLT 60 to LF52 ZPX

Acquired with East Thames Buses, 03.10.09
VP 1-19   (X149, 151-154, 157-159, 161-169, 171, 172 FBB)
VWL 1-4, 6-44   (LB02 YWX-Z, YXA/D-H/J-N, LF52 TGN/O/U/V/X-Z, THG/K/N/U/V/X/Z, TJO/U, BX04 AZW/V/U/Z, BAA/U/V, BBE/F/J, BKL/K/J)

Acquired with Northumberland Park garage ex-First London, 31.03.12
PVN 1-17   (LK03 NHF/G/P/T/V/X-Z, NJE/F/J/N/V/X-Z, NKA)

Disposals
02.09 EVL 7-11, 13, 18, 28-30, 34
03.09 EVL 1, 2, 14, 16, 19, 22, 25, 26, 32, 33
       WVL 221
05.09 EVL 12, 31, 35, 36
       AVL 1-19
06.09 EVL 20, 27
07.09 EVL 43-52
08.09 EVL 3, 4, 6, 21, 23
10.09 EVL 37-42

Disposals

01.10	AVL 20-46
03.10	PVL 257, 258, 261, 262, 271, 279, 280
05.10	PVL 259
06.10	PVL 40-43, 47, 51, 52, 54, 74, 77, 78, 81, 250, 266
07.10	PVL 39, 44-46, 48-50, 53, 55, 260, 267
09.10	*Re-acquired on lease:* PVL 250, 258-260, 266
12.10	PVL 277
01.11	PVL 255, 256, 268, 269, 356-361
03.11	PVL 10, 11, 13-16, 18, 20-29, 31-36, 98, 99, 172-174, 177
04.11	PVL 100-105, 107, 108
05.11	PVL 1-9, 12, 17, 19, 30, 37, 38, 109, 111, 156-158, 197, 208, 212, 213, 227, 228
06.11	PVL 179-187, 239-243, 246, 247, 249, 251-254
	WVL 127, 128
08.11	PVL 188-194
11.11	PVL 243
12.11	PVL 250, 258-260, 268
01.12	EVL 5, 15, 17
03.12	PVL 58, 91, 210, 211, 270, 273-275, 278
06.12	*Re-acquired on hire:* PVL 58, 91, 210, 211
10.12	PVL 56-58, 84, 87-91, 106, 116-119, 125-128
11.12	PVL 189, 190, 276
01.13	PVL 65, 71-73, 93, 114, 121, 122, 124, 144, 168, 171, 175, 176, 178, 201, 202, 210, 211
02.13	PVL 63, 83, 146
07.13	WVL 124-126
10.13	PVL 61, 79, 85, 94, 145, 204, 205, 214, 216, 234-238
	WVL 80, 88, 89, 99
12.13	PVL 147, 149, 150, 153, 155, 156, 206, 207, 226, 230, 231
	WVL 78
	VP 1, 2, 4, 9-17
	VWL 1, 2, 4, 7, 8
01.14	PVL 209, 217, 225
02.14	*Re-acquired:* WVL 78
06.14	PVN 7-16, VP 5-8
07.14	WVL 91
	PVL 110, 112, 113
08.14	PVN 17
09.14	PVL 67, 68, 70, 95-97
09.15	PVL 162-167
12.15	PVL 115
01.16	PVN 4, 6
02.16	PVL 151, 215, 220
	PVN 3
04.16	PVL 152, 154, 169, 170, 203, 232, 233
	PVN 1, 2, 5
	WVL 72-74, 76-78, 86
07.16	PVL 159, WVL 101
08.16	WVL 14-17, 20, 21, 23
09.16	PVL 293
10.16	VWL 28, 30, 36-38, 41
	WVL 129, 130, 134, 142, 149
11.16	PVL 329-333, 337, 339, 342
	VWL 11, 15, 23, 32, 34, 42, 43
	WVL 19, 28, 35, 36, 40, 44, 51, 59, 69, 71, 123, 158, 175, 176, 184, 185, 242-245
12.16	VWL 6, 14, 17, 18, 21, 26, 27, 40, 44
	WVL 33, 56, 65, 85, 97, 100, 122, 150, 162, 181, 183
01.17	PVL 324, 325, 341, 344, 346, 350
	VWL 9, 12, 16, 19, 20, 24
	WVL 37, 42, 43, 45, 50, 53, 57, 60, 68

Disposals

02.17	PVL 319, 322, 334, 347, 349, 351, 354
	VWL 3, 13, 29, 33, 35, 39
	WVL 1, 5, 6, 9, 12, 13, 31, 34, 38, 41, 46-48, 52, 58, 61-63, 66, 67, 70, 81, 87, 139, 141, 146, 147, 155-157, 166-168, 171, 173, 179, 186-188
03.17	WVL 4, 10, 54, 145, 160
04.17	PVL 372
	VWL 22
05.17	PVL 343
	VWL 10, 31
	WVL 3, 49, 164, 172, 178, 180
06.17	PVL 321, 323, 343, 345, 352, 378, 379
	WVL 2, 8, 29, 30, 32, 55, 64, 92, 98, 106, 132, 135, 148, 161, 163, 169, 174
07.17	PVL 64, 69, 82, 131, 380
	WVL 7, 39, 105, 140, 161, 163, 236
08.17	PVL 62, 129, 130, 384
	WVL 11, 26, 109, 110, 131, 133, 136, 138, 151, 182, 273
09.17	PVL 371, 373, 376, 382, 386
	WVL 165, 271
10.17	PVL 86, 92, 387-389
	WVL 107, 170, 177
11.17	PVL 123, 132, 133, 160, 244, 272, 288, 298-312, 314-318, 326-328, 367, 368, 375, 381, 383, 385
	WVL 154
12.17	PVL 60, 66, 76, 161, 313, 369
	WVL 82, 104, 112, 143, 144, 152, 153, 159, 251
02.18	PVL 245, 281, 283, 286, 287, 292, 294
	WVL 84, 103, 191-194, 199
03.18	PVL 120, 285, 289, 377
	WVL 24, 108
05.18	VP 19
	PVL 75
	WVL 113, 116, 137, 190, 195, 200-203, 214, 215, 218, 220, 223, 227, 229, 252-270
06.18	PVL 405-419
	WVL 117, 206, 207, 209-213, 216, 217, 219, 222, 224-226, 228, 230, 246-248
07.18	WVL 118, 232, 233, 237, 241
08.18	VP 18, PVL 295, WVL 75
09.18	PVL 80, 135, 140, 265, 282
	WVL 96
10.18	PVL 362-366, 370
	WVL 22, 27, 90, 115, 208, 231
12.18	PVL 134, 136, 137
01.19	PVL 248
	WVL 18, 25, 114
03.19	WVL 102
06.19	WVL 120, 121
	PVL 296
07.19	WVL 119
09.19	PVL 284
01.20	WVL 240
02.20	WVL 94, 95
06.20	PVL 219, 222, 223
07.20	PVL 392, 394-396
	WVL 272
10.20	WVL 111, 189
	PVL 391
11.20	WVL 250
12.20	WVL 238, 239, 249
03.21	PVL 221, 390
04.21	PVL 138, 139, 141, 142, 224, 229, 397, 399-401
05.21	PVL 402, 403

London United

VA, VP, VR, VE, VLE and VLP classes

After three batches of Alexander-bodied Volvo Olympians, London United stuck with Volvo when what became the B7TL was announced, placing an order for 45 as early as August 1998, even though delivery was unlikely before the turn of the century. These were against retained contracts for the 71, 111 and 220 and would be carrying Alexander ALX400 bodywork. Further tendering success at that time meant that the 337 and H32 would be needing new buses as well, and in March 1999 26 more Volvo B7TLs were ordered, but this time with Plaxton President bodywork.

Production was in full swing by the second half of 1999, with over 500 vehicles on Volvo's order books as Olympian production ceased at the same time. Bodying then commenced, and at the beginning of February 2000 London United took delivery of its first ALX400s. This time a block of registrations had been booked (by the dealer, meaning Birmingham marks) with no care for whether the fleetnumbers would match, and after V176 OOE was seen carrying VA 70 it was decided to resume the Volvo Olympians' class code but jump to 60, thus rendering the batch for the 220 and 111 VA 60-104. The 120 replaced the 71 in the

Below: **The ALX400 body at its debut was a handsome creation that didn't depart too drastically from established London standards; the London United VAs delivered in 2000 had proper blinds with detailed information and their central staircases neatly divided each half of the saloon. Arriving at Wandsworth on 22 July 2000 after a journey on the 220 is Shepherd's Bush's VA 67 (V183 OOE).** Author

Left: **The route branding applied to Shepherd's Bush's VAs was generic in nature, choosing to play up the accessible nature of the buses rather than the route they served. Just as well, because on Sundays their remit expanded from the 220 to take in the 94 as well, which was OPO on that day of the week. On 2 April 2000 VA 81 (V204 OOE) is in Oxford Street.** *Author*

queue for new buses and the latter would have to wait another two years to replace its trusty but elderly Metrobuses.

The bodying of London United's first 45 ALX400s was split between Falkirk (VA 60-78 and 99-104) and Belfast (VA 79-98). Service entry onto the 220 at Shepherd's Bush was on 21 February with VAs 60 and 61, and by the end of the month the new buses had appeared on the Sunday OPO 94, night routes N9 and N11 and wandered to the 49. Hounslow put VA 74 out on the 120 on 16 March and converted the full route from LLW on the 18th; visits to other Hounslow routes took

Below: **Hounslow's brand new VA 77 (V193 OOE) is seen setting off from the garage's accompanying bus station on 20 May 2000, shortly after B7TLs had ousted LLWs from the 120. VPs were now arriving to join them.** *Author*

London United – 97

Right: **Fifteen of the new VAs into Hounslow were route-branded for the 111, featuring a Boeing 747 nose to play up the route's role as a local link to Heathrow Airport. Seen at Hounslow on 21 April 2000 is VA 91 (W124 EON).** *Author*

in the 111 and H32, which were planned for their own VPs shortly, plus the Sunday OPO 9 and night routes N94 and N97. The 111 was intended to have a dedicated VA batch with route branding, with the graphic of a Boeing 747 and the legend 'One Eleven' - the fifteen buses treated were VAs 63, 74, 76, 78, 88-93, 95 and 100-103, though naturally they didn't stick wholeheartedly to the 111 when flexibility was at a premium.

The VPs followed, the class's service debut at Hounslow being on the 120 on 13 April, and once the 337 and H32 were converted there was full intermixing with VAs on the 111 and the predictable visits to the 81, 116, H22 and H98 plus the 222 when it came to London United and just once on temporary route 509 commissioned to link the stricken Hammersmith Bridge with the Underground hub.

Right: **The VP class of Plaxton President-bodied Volvo B7TLs looked dynamite in their new livery of London United red and two greys, though everything did that was treated to this scheme. As with the VAs, similar resignation to the DVLA's foibles produced another batch of mismatched registrations that were simply thrown at the order, mandated gaps and all, and thus do we see Hounslow-based VP 121 (W468 BCW) at Wandsworth on 22 July 2000, having converted the 337 from M operation in the spring.** *Author*

When a Routemaster wasn't available at Shepherd's Bush, a VA could be put out with a conductor, and even more rarely, the 72 saw VA workings but only as far south as the top end of Hammersmith Bridge. Hounslow's participation in the regular splitting of the 281 on Twickenham rugby match days saw VP participation for the first time.

London United paused after this outlay, ordering just three Tridents as the 81's double-deck component that could helpfully be evaluated against the VAs and VPs. It seemed that the Trident prevailed, as the 131 and 267 had TAs ordered for them at the end of 2001 followed by a larger contingent still for the 65 and 71.

Above: **Other than the route-branded contingent for the 111, Hounslow's VAs and VPs were intended to be mixed in operation, and accordingly at Richmond on 19 November 2000 VP 123 (W471 BCW) has pulled up alongside VA 98 (W133 EON).** Author

Left: **On Sundays Hounslow operated the 9, despite being a long, long way from that route's western extremity at Hammersmith, but neither Shepherd's Bush, operator of its RMLs on weekdays, nor Stamford Brook could spare enough OPO buses. Working through a quiet Charing Cross on 27 August 2000 is VA 87 (W117 EON).** Author

Right: **Though the Volvo B7TL had a lump offset to the nearside which concealed various mechanical items, the ALX400 body specified a reasonably-sized rear window that stretched at least most of the way across the saloon; Plaxton's solution was asymmetrical and rather more awkward. On 11 March 2000 Shepherd's Bush's VA 69 (V185 OOE) has found itself turned short at Putney Bridge Station.** Author

On 24 September 2000 VA 75 was deroofed under Isleworth station bridge on its way back to Hounslow after a duty on the 337; it was rebuilt at Caetano in Waterlooville and prompted the fitting of a radio-linked audio alarm that alerted drivers if they were about to approach a low bridge. Shepherd's Bush's VA 69 was damaged by fire caused by electrical problems, but this one was repaired by Yeates of Loughborough.

The assumption of historically Country Area and LCBS route 406 on 31 January 2001 was accomplished with Hounslow buses, and before long VAs and VPs began to appear alongside the scheduled Ms. Its transfer to Kingston on 30 June put paid to that, however.

Despite London United having leaned towards Tridents, the company ordered three Volvo B7TLs in June, this time with

Right: **This shot of Hounslow's VP 114 (W461 BCW) was taken in mid-afternoon on 11 August 2001 at the garage entrance, but at least shows what the blinds for the N9 looked like, albeit with one via point scrubbed out to reflect the route's diversion via Putney instead of Barnes the previous autumn.** Author

Left: **The Wrightbus Gemini body and Volvo B7TL combination produced the VR class at London United, and they looked splendid, but only three were ever operated. Here at North Weald bus rally on 25 June 2003 is VR 228 (BD51 YCT), dressed for its usual route 267 operated by Fulwell.** *Author*

Wrightbus's new Gemini bodywork. They arrived in January 2002 as VR 226-228 and a late change in their deployment put them into Fulwell rather than the intended Hounslow. They entered service on the 267 from 28 February, quickly visiting the 65, 71, 85, 131, 281 and 290.

In association with the Queen's Golden Jubilee in 2002 fifty TfL buses were liveried in gold vinyl and one of them was Hounslow's VP 130 between March and December. Its sponsor was Felix cat food.

One of the expansion routes commissioned to tie in with the forthcoming introduction of the Congestion Charge in London was the 148 (including night bus N148) linking Shepherd's Bush and Camberwell. Awarded to London United, nineteen ALX400-bodied Volvo B7TLs were ordered for it, reviving the VA class after two years of Trident orders.

Left: **London United's contribution to the Queen's Golden Jubilee where Volvo B7TLs were concerned was VP 130 (W478 BCW), based at Hounslow. Seen at Kingston during May 2002, its sponsor was Felix cat food.** *Haydn Davies*

Above: **There was a new Transdev-oriented London United logo and a rebalancing of the ALX400 design by the time the VAs for new route 148 came along in the autumn of 2002. The staircase aperture on VA 310 (SK52 USJ), seen at Victoria on 22 January 2003, is so enormous that it blots out most of the lower deck. The 148, however, proved a roaring success and quickly moved to the forefront when prioritising vehicle renewal.** Author

However, its start date was moved up to 5 October 2002 so the TAs ordered for the 57 would have to deputise until the Volvos were delivered. The 220's VAs would also turn out occasionally, but in November the expected B7TLs started delivery and by January VA 293-311 were all in service on the 148.

During the summer of 2002 Shepherd's Bush's VAs had wheelchair ramps fitted to make them fully DDA compliant, and were followed in this process by the VP class.

On 3 November London Sovereign was bought by Transdev; at this time the 183 operated 2717-2733, seventeen Plaxton

Right: **London Sovereign came into the Transdev fold on 3 November 2002 and gained common purpose with London United. Occupying a middle ground between the old red and black livery and new London United fleetnumbers at Golders Green on 28 June 2003 is what was now VP 2732 (LN51 AYY).** Author

President-bodied 10.6m Volvo B7TLs. They hadn't actually carried their fleetnumbers but in March 2003 had them applied in London United's small yellow style. Later in the spring VP class codes were added.

Repaints to the 220's VAs began in March 2003 and on 30 August VR 226-228 joined them at Shepherd's Bush when the 220 received a PVR increase. They soon appeared on the 94 and 148, and later on the 72's northern section.

An order for ten more 10.6m Volvo B7TLs was placed in August to cover the retention of the 292 at Sovereign; its characteristic blue and cream Olympians had already given way to spare VAs (the Olympian variety). Mechanical problems at Edgware were pressing enough to require the hire of four NVs from London Central.

Originally pencilled in as VP 379-388, the 292's B7TLs, when they arrived, were formally reclassified VLP 18-27, allowing VP 2717-2733 to become VLP 1-17. The new examples entered service on 25 November, in advance of the 292's 6 December contract renewal date. By the end of 2003 existing Volvo B7TL routes 183 and 337 were all out to tender and the H32 had been retained and renewed. The 337 was awarded to Arriva, representing the VA/VP classes' first loss. 24 January 2004 saw the N94 and N148 lose their suffixes.

Above: **The three VRs were transferred from Fulwell to Shepherd's Bush on 30 August 2003 and joined forces with the VAs on the 220. Pictured coming up to Shepherd's Bush Green on 5 January 2004 is VR 226 (BD51 YCR).** *Author*

Left: **Ten new 10.6m Volvo B7TLs with Plaxton President bodywork took over the 292 at the end of November 2003, and they could also be seen on the 13, as VLP 23 (PJ53 OUW) is doing in Oxford Street on 21 October 2005, this being the last day of crew operation on the 13.** *Author*

London United • 103

Right: **Following the conversion of the 94 to OPO on 24 January 2004, the 9 remained RML-operated for another seven and a half months. Inevitably, the route's new Volvo B7TL complement arrived and eased off most of the Routemasters before the axe fell. On 1 September 2004, three days before that event, VR 228 (BD51 YCT) is in support at Charing Cross, with a conductor aboard.** *Author*

The conversion of the last Routemaster routes to OPO was the catalyst for large double-deck orders between 2003 and 2005; where London United was concerned, the 94 had already been done with TLA-class Tridents, but the 9's one-manning, set for 4 September 2004, would be done with a fleet of Volvo B7TLs, this time with East Lancs bodywork. Thirty-six 10.6m examples of a new VLE class were ordered, alongside ten 9.9m VEs which would assist in the restoration of the upper deck to the 49 to accompany its own retained contract. The VLE order was then increased to 45 so that the DAFs inherited from Arriva London South (and new to Capital Logistics) could be replaced from the 114.

During 2004 the 183's batch of VLPs received assault screens. 29 May saw the 337 depart for Arriva at Wandsworth and eleven

Right: **The 49 was about the last route that was appropriate for single-deck operation, but after five years of DP-class Dennis Dart SLFs it was now time to give it back its upper deck, and this was in the form of ten new VEs, helped by VAs leaving the 337 upon its loss to Arriva. Already based at Shepherd's Bush, VA 72 (V188 OOE), now carrying a post-2001 numberplate, is pictured south of South Kensington on 18 June 2005.** *Author*

Left: **The VEs for the 49 arrived in advance of the 9's VLEs, but were put to work straight away on the 9 to let the bulk of its Routemasters stand down. On 4 September 2004, the first day of the 9's new life as an OPO route, VE 1 (PG04 WGN) is coming down Piccadilly towards Hyde Park Corner. Company livery by now on new deliveries was basic red with just a grey skirt.** *Author*

VAs were transferred to Stamford Brook to start the 49 off. Before they entered service, however, three were put into Edgware temporarily, taking their route 111 branding to the 114 and 183 (and once to the 13). Then came the VE class of ten shorter buses, which trained drivers and then, from 4 August, went into service on the 9, displacing its Routemasters. As well as visiting the 148 and 220, a number ran the 94 augmentations for Notting Hill Carnival, but the 9's one-manning on 4 September saw it reallocated from Shepherd's Bush to Stamford Brook with the VLEs (that had commenced on the 49 on 20 August) and the 49 came the other way, consolidating with VAs and VEs. At night the N9 at Hounslow was renewed but the N10 passed to First London; accordingly most of the N97 was transferred from Shepherd's Bush to Hounslow to fill the gap.

Left: **The longer length of the 10.6m VLE is evident in this Park Lane view of VLE 22 (PA04 CYE) on 5 September 2004. The 9 was reallocated to Stamford Brook upon its OPO conversion.** *Author*

The unfortunate imperative towards all-red began to affect London United, which had perhaps the best post-privatisation livery of all ex-LBL companies; continued repaints to the 220's batch of VAs by June saw four repainted into red with just a grey skirt and white tape divider, and the new VEs and VLEs were red with grey skirt only.

VLEs 27-39 were next, the first entering service on Edgware's 114 on 9 September with the full set in position within four days (including the associated wanderings to the 13, 183 and 292). They debuted a new London Sovereign fleetname with Transdev logo to its right, and VLE 32 onwards had white roofs. Stamford Brook's new VLEs, meanwhile, added the 391 to their quiver; this was normally a Dart route but had, much earlier, replaced a double-deck service in the area (the 27). Finally, VLE 40-45 were delivered in October for a boost to the 148 applying from 6 November. But London United had once again been tempted away from the Volvo B7TL, this time by Scania's latest offering, and the first of the resulting SLE class was ordered in sufficient numbers to complete the 114. No further B7TLs were ordered, and London United also ignored Volvo's subsequent B9TL until its B5LH hybrid variant was developed.

Of the existing complement, those on the 120, 220 and N97 were assured another five years at least when London United were awarded their contracts once again. As red repaints progressed, the earliest VLPs lost their black skirts in favour of grey ones. On 22 October 2005 a night element was introduced to the 220.

Right: **The DAF DB250RS(LFs) brought over from the 60 to Sovereign were non-standard there and were disposed of in favour of a new batch of VLEs for the 114. VLE 35 (PO54 ACU) demonstrates at South Harrow on 29 May 2005.** Author

Right: **This lucky capture of VA 88 (W118 EON) at Richmond on 5 November 2005 illustrates the second of just two days it was able to work the 391 as a loan from Shepherd's Bush to Stamford Brook. The route was perfectly capable of fielding double-deckers and did so regularly ever after. Repaints were now into this simplified livery with just a grey skirt and white line above it.** Author

Above: **The 148 had grown sufficient to need substantial augmentation, and six VLEs were added to its VA complement on 6 November 2004. VLE 45 (PO54 OOG) was the highest-numbered of them and is seen on 13 May 2005 coming round what was previously a roundabout at County Hall, but which had recently had its York Road end pedestrianised.** Author

On 4 and 5 November 2005 Shepherd's Bush loaned VA 88 to Stamford Brook, which put it out on the 391; otherwise two-thirds of the route was transferred to Fulwell on the 12th. The takeover of the 27 by London United on that day was accomplished with new SLEs from Stamford Brook, but the odd VLE was apt to appear. VP 105 was transferred to Edgware and subsequent VA loans from Shepherd's Bush to Stamford Brook in 2006 saw the type turn out on the 9; in the reverse, loaned VEs visited the 391.

On 4 April 2006 Transdev announced a new corporate identity by which the corporate title would supersede local identities; thus vanished the London United and London Sovereign fleetnames, though their legal identities remained unchanged. VLP 3 was the last Sovereign B7TL with a black skirt, losing it in August.

Left: **VP 105 (W448 BCW), another recipient of a simplified repaint and without even the white band to cheer it up, served a very long spell at Sovereign, and on 8 May 2007 is seen at Edgware carrying the new all-encompassing Transdev logos phased in during 2006.** Author

Right: **Sovereign's VLPs lost their black skirts for grey ones without the benefit of a full repaint. On 17 February 2007 VLP 24 (PJ53 OUX) calls at Pinner.** Author

Right: **One of Shepherd's Bush's correct complement for the 49 is seen on 30 September 2006 at Clapham Junction in the form of VE 3 (PG04 WGU).** Author

Right: **One repaint along and also fitted with post-2001 numberplates with thinner characters is Hounslow's VA 74 (V190 OOE); it is pictured almost at the end of a route 120 journey on 17 February 2007.** Author

Polish-built Scania Omnicities were now Transdev's preferred double-deck type, but the debut order for the 148 was late coming so buses had to be hired in order that school routes 697 and 698, two tendering victories over First, could commence on 2 September 2006. These were six PVLs from London General, similar to company VPs and on their third spell of loan after periods at Metrobus (route 127) and East Thames Buses (mostly the 132). For the duration of their stay they were known by the VP fleetnumbers given to them when at East Thames Buses. The delivery of the SPs and their entry into service in October freed VAs 75-79 to pass to Hounslow and assume the 697 and 698 alongside the garage's other double-deck routes. Another school route was commissioned in the form of the 696 and allotted to London United for introduction on 22 January 2007.

Hefty increases to PVRs were now the norm; on 11 November a big boost to the 27 prompted the transfer to Stamford Brook of seven VLEs and VR 228, displaced from Shepherd's Bush by further incoming SPs.

Regular closures to the Central Line cast the 94 as the most important route needing augmentation, and on 6-7 January 2007 loaned Edgware VPs and VLPs aided Stamford Brook VLEs alongside the usual Shepherd's Bush runout. 7 April saw six Hounslow VPs visiting.

The entry into service of SO-class Scanias on the 148 in August 2007 displaced seven VAs from Shepherd's Bush to Hounslow, displacing TAs to Fulwell. At the same time, VR 227 joined VR 228 at Stamford Brook. Simultaneous iBus fitment to London United vehicles led to the loan to Shepherd's Bush of Tridents both indigenous and borrowed, in the latter case TNs from First. VEs 1-4 also spent a period on loan to Stamford Brook. After serving at Fulwell and then Tolworth, the First TNs moved to Hounslow in December to let that garage's VP and VA fleet go away for iBus fitment and thus complete London United. Sovereign followed in January 2008, that company's standardisation on Volvo B7TL chassis maintained by the loan of six VPs from Hounslow.

Below: **London General's PVLs were similar enough to London United VPs that the latter referred to them by the VP codes the six loaned examples received when at East Thames Buses. During October 2006 VP 29 (X502 EGK), normally known as PVL 200, is seen almost at the end of a route H32 journey based out of Hounslow.** *Haydn Davies*

Right: **On 6 April 2007 Shepherd's Bush's VA 303 (SK52 URZ) is seen on the 220 at Shepherd's Bush Green, having been edged off the more important 148 by new Scanias. This allowed earlier VAs to move to Hounslow.** *Author*

On 2 February 2008 a big boost to the 148 came about as the result of a longer-term Central Line closure, and in addition to Shepherd's Bush's usual miscellany, Tridents (TAs and then TPLs) came from Metroline to assist. An accompanying White City shuttle was served by three Hounslow TAs loaned to Shepherd's Bush.

A quiet 2008 thus ended with the tender and retention of the 49, 114, 183 and H32 (the latter two with new buses), plus arson damage and repair to VLP 18 and the fitting of VA 69 with plug doors. As 2009 progressed, the refurbishment of Sovereign vehicles necessitated the loan of VEs from Shepherd's Bush and VPs from Hounslow, but as further

Right: **Old and new London United liveries meet in Wood Street, Kingston on 20 September 2008 as VP 129 (W477 BCW) passes fellow Hounslow VP 125 (W473 BCW) on the 111.** *Author*

Above: **The 27 under London United was SLE-operated, but from time to time its Scanias were assisted by VLEs wandering from the 9. Calling at Notting Hill Gate on 19 June 2009 is VLE 14 (PG04 WHT) .** *Author*

Scanias (SPs) arrived to take over the H32, the Volvo B7TL fell out of favour and by May three examples each of the VA and VP classes had been put in store at Hounslow Heath and advertised for sale in the trade press.

Tendering proved stable for the Volvo B7TL-operated routes; the 111 was announced as retained in August 2009 on the basis of new buses and the 49, 114 and 183 began new terms on 5 September. On 10 October the 81 was converted to full double-deck and the 222 partially so, reactivating the VAs and VPs that had otherwise been stood down. VPs were also transferred to Sovereign to bulk out the 183 until its own new SPs arrived. When that took place from the end of September, VLPs 1-17 were withdrawn. Without even having reached a decade in stock, three VAs were sold in November. Their low longevity wasn't a record by any means, however; seven-year-old TAs were going off lease and finally London United declared themselves sick of trying to make the nine overweight and unreliable SO-class Scanias work and got rid of them. The 148 was thus now all-SP but continued to field VPs and VEs as fit.

As 2010 opened, VLPs 18-27 were put through refurbishment so as to stay on the 292. A partial repaint to VR 228 cost this bus its grey skirt and VR 226 donned red later in the year, just before all three VRs were reunited at Shepherd's Bush. It was extraordinarily rare for anything other than a contracted SP to work on the 10 following its assumption by London United out of Stamford Brook on 30 January, but on 18 August VLE 43 managed it.

May 2010 saw the 111's new contract activated and its VAs and VPs replaced by new SPs, but three of the 52-reg variety departed and several more went into store, leaving the 81, 120, 222, 696 and 697 with a VP or VA complement at Hounslow. On the ground, VAs tended to be preferred over VPs.

Refurbishments to Edgware VLEs during the summer and autumn of 2010 necessitated VPs coming to Sovereign again, though the class was otherwise being hollowed out by the return of eighteen of them off lease. The ten-strong VE class was also refurbished so as to remain on the 49 under the terms of its contract.

Above: **VA 97 (W132 EON)** out of Hounslow has managed to last until 24 May 2011 without a repaint, and was looking suitably tired when seen setting off from Hounslow. It is hard to see what sort of use its blinds are with just two via points and all that wasted black space. *Author*

Between 4-20 November 2010 the 94 received enough ADH-class Enviro400 hybrids to convert two-thirds of the route from TLA; the Tridents displaced stayed at Shepherd's Bush to replace the 220's VAs. At the close of 2010 the 9, tendered during the year, was announced as retained with the incumbent VLEs, and the 697 and 698 stayed put too.

Corporate wrangling within Transdev during 2010 had repercussions on London United and Sovereign; on 4 May Transdev agreed to merge with Veolia and the RATP withdrew its 25% stake in the form of London

Right: The 52-reg VAs gravitated to Hounslow after their early career on the 220 and spent the rest of their lives adding the upper deck back to routes 81 and 222. Coming through Hounslow town centre on 12 May 2012 is VA 304 (SK52 USB). *Author*

This was the death knell for the VA class; Tolworth's transfer of TAs 281-283 to Park Royal to release ADHs 1-3 to Hounslow doomed VAs 62, 74 and 91, all of which last operated on 4 October on the 111, H32 and 120 respectively. Tolworth's VA 80 ran last on 28 October and 19 November saw Shepherd's Bush's VA 64 and 90 run for the last time on the 49. VPs 105-111 at Hounslow were now all that remained of London United's original Volvo B7TL intake.

Between September and November 2013 VLE 3 carried an ad for the Burj Khalifa in Dubai. October saw the 49's result announced, but London United lost it to Abellio and would thus be standing down the VEs in 2014.

On 2 December Hounslow's VPs ran for the last time, replaced by TAs ex-Tolworth, but on the 4th VPs 105, 107 and 108 were loaned to Hounslow Heath and did a diagram on the H91 as rail extras; that was their last hurrah. After several months in store, first at the defunct Twickenham garage of the former NSL Services (aka NCP Challenger) and then Hounslow Heath, the first two were revived as private-hire buses.

2014 brought the return of the prodigal son when RATP purchased London Sovereign from Transdev with effect from 20 March and formalised on 28 April. Thus, back came the VLEs still operating on the 114 and the newer ten VLPs on the 292, with appearances by each on the 183. London United immediately despatched loans to its restored partner,

sending VEs 2, 9 and 10 for a couple of months.

The reallocation of route 131 from Fulwell to Tolworth with its TAs on 31 May 2014 permitted visits by the 57's VLEs, which would soon have a greater impact on the route than first realised. This was due to complaints arising from the quieter parts of the 57 against the loud noise of the VLEs' cooling fans, a longstanding problem with the Volvo B7TL which had ultimately cost Volvo orders for its B9TL successor. Thus were TAs restored to the 57 and the VLEs swapped to the 131.

Above: **When Borismasters took over the 9, its VLEs were redeployed to Tolworth to take over the 57 from TAs, though there weren't quite enough for that task and some Tridents had to remain. On 22 June 2014 VLE 11 (PG04 WHP) is in Eden Street, Kingston.** *Author*

Left: **In three years with the rump of Transdev, Sovereign had not added to or subtracted from the VLE or VLP classes based at Edgware on the 114 and 292 respectively. On the afternoon of 9 September 2014 VLE 28 (PA04 CYL) is seen at Harrow, now without fleetnames until something to the RATP style was run up for Sovereign.** *Author*

Right: **Following their making spare from the 49, six of the VEs replaced a like number of SLEs from Sovereign's 114 and were then joined by the rest, more or less. On 10 April 2016 VE 8 (PG04 WGZ) comes through Harrow's fussy one-way system towards the bus station. They would leave in turn even before the 114 passed to Metroline West.** *Author*

After the loss of the 49 to Abellio on 6 September, VEs 1-6 were sent to Sovereign at Edgware on a permanent basis to replace SLE 1-6. As 2014 rolled into 2015, VE 10 went to Edgware and VE 7 was loaned to Hounslow Heath at the beginning of February, turning out on the 116 and 285 once each. That month saw VP 110 converted to single-door and given a new livery for the private hire department, which was soon rechristened United Motorcoaches; its front was grey in a swoop extending to mid-body and then along the upper deck. VP 106 followed suit in May.

A quantity of SPs moved into Tolworth during the summer, but they neither threatened the VLEs nor managed to clean out the TAs still based there. The 131's

Right: **Noise problems persisted on the B7TL to the end, and it put the wind up some residents of the leafier parts of Kingston, who complained about the racket made by the VLEs sent to replace the 57's TAs. With a couple of years still on its contract, an expedient was fashioned by which they were swapped to the 131, and on 21 July 2015 at Tooting we see Tolworth's VLE 6 (PG04 WHJ).** *Author*

Above: **Most post-LBL companies created a private-hire arm, but London United took longer to do so than most. When it did, however, the result was the stylish United Motorcoaches livery of grey and red. Carrying it at Hemel Hempstead on 3 April 2015 is VP 110 (W454 BCW).**
Russell Young

contract was extended for two years as it was, ensuring that the VLEs would stay put until 2017 irrespective of the 57's result, which was up in the air by that point. October 2015 saw that particular announcement in the form of another negative for London United; it would be returning to London General after nineteen years. The VLE class was, however, threatened at another point when the 114 was awarded to Metroline West in December after a period out to tender. Almost all of the VEs had now gathered at Edgware by the end of 2015, so their tenure was not what could be secure either.

A renumbering scheme was in the offing for 2016, and its main effect was to lump buses into blocks of thousands. For Volvo B7TL purposes, VLEs 1-39 became VLEs 40501-40539 and VEs 1-10 became VE 40601-40610, with the surviving VA trainers numbered between VA 40360 and VA 40398, VPs 105-111 to VPs 40705-40711 and VLPs 18-20, 22-27 to VLPs 40718-40720 and 40722-40727. VLP 21, also known as trainer TV 1, became VLP 40331. It wasn't worth physically renumbering the B7TLs at this stage and only United Motorcoaches VA 81, numbered VA 40381, carried its new number when it was deroofed under a hotel canopy in August.

VLE 13 of Tolworth found itself a guest on Fulwell's 281 on 27 May, but these buses could no longer work on the 57 after 2 June when it passed to London General at Merton. It was TAs that managed to survive, however, regaining the 131, and the VLEs were withdrawn, plus VE 9 that had tagged along at Tolworth.

Someone at London United had rather jumped the gun when it came to ordering new buses for the 72; assuming that Hammersmith Bridge would have been rebuilt sufficient to take double-deckers once again, the company took many more VH-class Volvo B5LHs than would subsequently be needed. Since Hammersmith Bridge had barely been touched since its initial damage in 1984, the VH deployment was changed and plans were made to send them to Edgware to see off the last VEs and VLEs. This they did by taking over the 13 during July so that its original-spec VHs could cascade to the 114 and 183. After the VEs had been seen off, a handful of ex-Tolworth VLEs displaced leased classmates from the VLE 27-39 batch and were then withdrawn themselves when the 114 passed to Metroline West on 2 September, leaving just VLEs 18, 20, 22 and 23 for school routes 605, 618 and 619. VLEs 6

Right: **Symbolically seeing off the VLE class from stage service is this rear shot of Tolworth's VLE 22 (PA04 CYE) in Kingston on 28 May 2016. Enough survived on the 131 to take the type into 2017.** *Author*

Below: **The 114's dedicated VLE batch also managed to make it into 2017. Coming off the stand at Ruislip station on 13 May 2016 is Edgware's VLE 30 (PA04 CYS).** *Author*

and 15 clung on at Tolworth and VLEs 14 and 16 pitched up at United Motorcoaches. Here they were renumbered VLEs 40514 and 40516 and were repainted into the grey livery worn by buses allocated to the Kingston University contracts, themselves about to take delivery of plush new VHs.

Three of Edgware's five VLE survivors gravitated back to Tolworth in January 2017 and boosted numbers there to six, though VLE 23 returned to Edgware and held out there until 10 February. United Motorcoaches could now field four VLEs. Of the ten VLPs still going on the 292, VLPs 23 and 24 were detached for conversion to VantagePower hybrid propulsion.

Tolworth's brief renaissance ended on 21 March when VLE 6 ran on the 131, and then it came time to sweep away the 292's VLPs, the last of which ran on 25 May in the form of VLP 25, first on the 605 and then the 292. And that was it for the service career of the Volvo B7TL at London United and Sovereign, but for the two VantagePower motors; that is, if they ever managed to make it into service. They were reclassified VH 45223 and 45224, swiftly amended to VLP 45253 and 45254 to denote their newly hybrid configuration and returned to traffic in June and September 2017 respectively. It was not the happiest of systems, however, and appearances in service proved comparatively rare. In the end VLP 45254 last operated on 17 May 2018 and VLP 45253 on 9 July, both on the 292.

Above: **The last Volvo B7TLs in normal service at London United or Sovereign were the VLPs on the 292. On 10 April 2016 VLP 26 (PJ53 OVA) is seen at Edgware, with a month left to go for the class, although two were revived as VantagePower hybrids for a spell.** *Author*

Left: **Relegated to backup duties for Kingston University, what was now VLE 40516 (PG04 WHV) makes the best it can out of an otherwise unadorned overall grey livery when seen at Kingston on 26 October 2016. Almost forgotten thereafter, this and VLE 40514 saw an unexpected renaissance from 6 October 2020 when pressed into use as auxiliary school buses on the 406 and 418, which had been transferred to Tolworth that year and now needed post-pandemic support.** *Author*

Right: **Two of the 292's VLPs were fitted with VantagePower equipment that effectively turned them into hybrids, but the system wasn't the magic bullet that would turn ageing diesel buses into low-emission motors and, like the two WVLs similarly fitted at London General's Stockwell, lasted only a short time. For posterity, performing a schoolday 605 through Burnt Oak on a splendidly-clouded 7 July 2017 is VLP 45253 (PJ53 OUW), not quite convinced yet of its ultimate numerical identity but standing out through its attractive black window surrounds on each deck.**
Tommy Cooling

London United reallocated the United Motorcoaches operation from Twickenham to Hounslow Heath on 16 October 2017. The takeover of the Kingston University routes by new VHs obliged the two VLE spares, 40514 and 40516, to lose their branding and become just grey.

2018 saw the last VLEs cleared out other than the two grey examples, leaving just nine VAs that soldiered on as trainers divided between various London United garages. Finally, its remit made unviable by a combination of factors, United Motorcoaches was disbanded on 21 December.

Registrations

VA 60-104	V176-194, 202-208 OOE, W116-119, 122, 124, 126, 127-129, 131-134, 136, 137-139, 141 EON
VP 105-130	W448, 449, 451-454, 457-459, 461-469, 471-478 BCW
VR 226-228	BD51 YCR-T
VA 293-311	SK52 MKV, MSO, MPU/V/X/Y, URV-Z, USB-D/F-H/J/L
VE 1-10	PG04 WGN/P/U-Z, WHA/B
VLE 1-45	PG04 WHC-F/H/J-N/P/R-Y, WJA, PA04 CYC/E-H/J-L/P/S, PO54 ABZ, ACF/J/U/V/X-Z, ADU/V, OOD-G
VLP 18-27	PJ53 OUN/P/U-Y, OVA/B

Date	Deliveries	Licensed for Service
02.00	VA 60-70, 79, 80	VA 60-62, 65-70, 79, 80 (**S**)
03.00	VA 71-78, 81-91, 93, 94, 96-100, 103	VA 71-73, 81-86 (**S**), VA 63, 64, 74-78, 87-91, 93, 94, 96-100, 103 (**AV**)
04.00	VA 92, 95, 100, 101, 104	VA 92, 95, 100, 101, 104 (**AV**)
	VP 109, 110, 112-115, 117-119, 121, 123, 125-127, 130	VP 109, 110, 112-115, 117-119, 121, 123, 125-127, 130 (**AV**)
05.00	VP 105, 107, 108, 111, 116, 124, 128, 129	VP 105, 107, 108, 111, 116, 124, 128, 129 (**AV**)
06.00	VP 106, 120, 122	VP 106, 120, 122 (**AV**)
01.02	VR 226-228	
02.02		VR 226-228 (**FW**)
11.02	VA 293-295	VA 293-295 (**S**)
12.02	VA 296-306	VA 296-302 (**S**)
01.03	VA 307-311	VA 303-311 (**S**)
11.03	VLP 18-27	VLP 18-27 (**BT**)
07.04	VE 1-10, VLE 1-14	
08.04	VLE 15-26	VE 1-10 (**S**), VLE 1-11, 13, 14, 16 (**V**)
09.04	VLE 27-39	VLE 12, 15, 17-26 (**V**) VLE 27-39 (**BT**)
10.04	VLE 40-45	VLE 40-45 (**S**)

Acquired with London Sovereign, 03.11.02
2733 (LN51 AZA-G/J/L/P/R/T-Z)

Renumbered
2717-2733 to VP 2717-2733, 06.03 and then to VLP 1-17, 11.03
VLP 23, 24 to VH 45223, 45224, 06.17 and then to VLP 45253, 45224, 09.17

Loaned from London General, 24.08.06-02.11.06
VP 21, 22, 27-30 (X699, 504, 597, 596, 501, 501 EGK)

Passed to Transdev with the split of London United and Sovereign, 03.03.2011
VLP 18-27, VLE 27-39

Acquired from Transdev with London Sovereign, 20.03.2014
VLP 18-27, VLE 27-39

Disposals
11.09	VA 67, 69, 70
01.10	VLP 1-17
03.10	VA 297-299
06.10	VP 128-130
08.10	VP 113-127
05.11	VA 66, 68, 100
06.11	VA 73
08.11	VP 112
10.12	VR 226-228
	VA 293-296, 300-311
02.13	VA 95
04.13	VLE 25, 40-45
12.13	VA 79
01.14	VA 63, 75, 77, 82, 88, 94, 97, 99, 101-104
02.14	VA 74, 80, 90, 91
03.14	VA 85
05.14	VA 62, 64, 65, 71, 86, 92
10.14	VA 72
12.14	VA 76, 93, 96
09.16	VE 1-10
10.16	VLE 1-5, 7-9, 11, 12, 27-39
02.17	VLE 17, 19, 20
03.17	VLE 18
04.17	VA 81, 87
06.17	VLP 18-20, 22, 25-27,
	VLE 15
07.17	VLE 24
10.17	VLE 6
02.18	VP 105, 107-109, 111
06.18	VLE 21
07.18	VLE 13
08.18	VLE 10, 22, 23, 26
01.19	VP 106, 110
08.19	VLP 21
10.19	VLP 45253, 45254
02.20	VA 40360, 40361
01.21	VA 40378
05.21	VLE 40514, 40516

Metroline

VP, VPL and VW classes

Already used to the Dennis Trident, Metroline, in the person of its smaller constituent Metroline London Northern, envisaged something different against the retained contracts for the 271 and W7 in the middle of 2000. Mindful of the Volvo B7TL's alleged greater hill-climbing capabilities and needing that skill on both services, an order was placed for 27 Plaxton President-bodied examples on the longer chassis option. Shortly after, requirements for the 52 as well as a planned increase to the 134 prompted the order to be increased to sixty.

The resulting VPLs 135-161 began delivery to Holloway from Volvo's Brimsdown premises (Duffield's) during December 2000, and at that point their deployment was changed; instead of the 271 and W7 they would be entering service on the 43, with TPs displaced to the intended routes. This began in earnest on 17 January 2001, and sure enough, the new VPLs began wandering to the 17 and 134 plus the 10 on Sundays. With the V-class Volvo Olympians staying put, it was Ms that the brunt of withdrawals hit at this time.

Below: **On 19 May 2001 in Upper Street Holloway's VPL 144 (X644 LLX) is leading VPL 137 (X637 LLX); the headway has gone a bit awry somewhere! Differences from the previous Plaxton bodies on TPs are the forward staircases and gasket windows, two choices that would be persisted with.** *Author*

Left: **A further change was implemented upon the introduction of the second batch of Metroline VPLs; this was blind boxes reconfigured to be of the same depth and thus capable of carrying the necessarily taller destinations with mixed upper- and lower-case wording. Seen setting off from North Finchley on 2 March 2002 is VPL 163 (Y163 NLK), with two replacement wings still in factory grey.** *Author*

Forty-two more VPLs were then ordered to furnish the 82 and 113. The original 27 completed delivery in January and the next sixty followed during March. Of these, VPLs 162-167 went to Holloway and VPLs 168-194 commenced the conversion of the 52 and N52 at Willesden from 21 March. These had DDA-compliant blinds with two lines of via points, but also very small fleetnumbers, which made one-look identification even less straightforward after the mismatch of available registrations that were booked for them. Willesden's VPL intake were also tasked with covering the 6 and 98 on Sundays

Below: **The 10.6m President body's extra length by comparison with previous generations of buses made for an elegantly-proportioned vehicle, even if capacity still wasn't anywhere close to that of the Metrobuses, Titans or Olympians. Willesden's VPL 196 (Y146 NLK), calling at Hyde Park Corner on 5 April 2003, didn't have to have a mismatched registration, but Y196 NLK had already gone onto stablemate VPL 170.** *Author*

Metroline — 125

Right: **Since coming back to Willesden from Armchair, the 260 had replaced its Ms with AVs, but by the summer of 2001 the 52 was fielding VPLs and could now let them wander. On 28 July VPL 186 (Y186 NLK) rounds the war memorial at Golders Green.** Author

when they were OPO, though the 98 saw them less than did the 6. The 260 was a new venture for the type, however.

July 2001 saw the delivery of the next 42 VPLs commence and Potters Bar's 82 saw its first example on the 24th. However, gearbox problems with a dodgy ZF batch saw the five that had entered service by the 29th pulled off service and sent back to Duffield's at Brimsdown for attention under warranty. This being addressed, a full complement arrived in August and completed the 82, with visits to the now extra-London 84 and 242, and a little later, the 231 and 310A.

Right: **On Sundays the 6 and 98 were OPO, but since the demotion to single-deck of the 302 and 297, could not spare enough double-deckers for each. The 6 tended to be favoured for the VPLs when they came, and on Bank Holiday 5 May 2003 at Charing Cross we see VPL 195 (Y144 NLK).** Author

Those VPLs intended for Edgware's 113 spanned the registration system changeover applying on 1 September and lost their booked Y-registrations for new 51-marks. Service entry at Edgware was on 17 September, with wanderings from the first day to the 107 and 240. The conversion was completed by October, but the next major order favoured Tridents and it would be another year before Volvo B7TLs were ordered again.

VPL rarities at this time were the 4 and W7 from Holloway and the 297 out of Willesden. On Christmas Day the latter put its Volvos into action on special routes 714 and 716.

Above: **Potters Bar's 82 converted from M to VPL in August; VPL 201 (Y201 NLK) is at Golders Green on 28 July.** Author

Far left: **With the modern DDA-compliant blind apertures the same height, sometimes the blinds were put in the wrong way round, as on Potters Bar's VPL 202 (Y202 NLK) at Victoria on 26 August 2001.** Author

Left: **Edgware's 113 was next in line for M to VPL conversion; on 7 June 2002 VPL 233 (Y233 NLK) waits time at Oxford Circus.** Author

Right: **Metroline began dual-sourcing between Dennis Tridents and Volvo B7TLs, taking each in both lengths and from two bodybuilders. Thus did established allocations begin to shift; it was decided to convert Potters Bar to Trident and the VPLs came to Holloway to upgrade the 134 from TP. At North Finchley on 1 June 2002 VPL 157 (X657 LLX) gets ready to head south.** Author

In the first half of 2002 began the first of what would become numerous type shuffles within the two Metroline companies. When new TPLs arrived in February, fifteen replaced Potters Bar's only recently-introduced VPLs, which headed to Holloway to take over the 134 and thus cascade TPs to double-deck the C2. Before they went, Potters Bar's VPLs visited the 317 and finally the 263, put into that garage on 1 February.

Three VPLs were liveried in gold for the Queen's Golden Jubilee, whose celebrations spanned the spring, summer and autumn of 2002; VPLs 163, 188 and 219 from Holloway, Willesden and Edgware respectively.

3 May saw the completion of the 82's conversion from VPL to TPL, although three VPLs came back to assist in the aftermath of the Potters Bar rail crash. And then it came time to release VPLs from Holloway itself;

Right: **Three Metroline VPLs constituted the company's contribution to the Queen's Golden Jubilee celebrations, with one from each garage operating them. Calling at Muswell Hill on 6 May 2002 is VPL 163 (Y163 NLK).** Author

Left: **VPL 210 (Y143 NLK)**, still carrying its original Potters Bar codes, is seen at Burnt Oak on 18 August 2002, not long after the 204's conversion to VPL and two weeks before its transfer from North Wembley to Edgware. *Author*

further TPLs into the garage during May allowed the Volvos to head to Edgware for the 204, operated by its North Wembley outstation. The 240 was on the books for conversion from M to VPL at this time but was taken out of consideration due to the need to supply vehicles to increase PVRs across the board.

After fourteen years with Grey-Green and its Arriva successor, the flagship 24 was awarded to Metroline London Northern in March and the company swung back to Volvo for this order, specifying 31 Plaxton President-bodied 9.9m chassis to start a VP class. Dual-sourcing was more or less the case now, as the order straight after that comprised 81 TPs.

On 31 August the 204 was reallocated from North Wembley to Edgware, though its VPLs made the move two days earlier.

Left: **On 1 April 2002 VPL 214 (LK51 XGH)** is seen at Edgware bus station near its home garage, still plated for the N98 duty it had come off the previous night but evidently without something else to go on to by the next afternoon. *Author*

Right: The 24 was taken up by Metroline London Northern on 9 November 2002 and restocked with 31 new VPs, the shorter chassis being chosen due to a tight turn at the Pimlico end of the route. VPLs and TPLs very rarely appeared on the 24 for the same reason. Seen at Camden on 7 April 2003 is Holloway's VP 330 (LR52 BNE).

Below: **On 22 February 2003 VP 325 (LR52 BMY) from the 24's batch is seen at the Nag's Head on its way through a visit to the 271.** *Author*

The 24's takeover date was 9 November, but the delivery of VPs 317-347 cut it fine, with the first examples arriving only on 30 October, so the route (and its night counterpart N24) had to be assumed with eight of the outgoing Arriva Volvo Citybuses taken on hire. These lasted until 16 November, and even after that TPs and VPLs turned out on the 24 as fit.

VPLs 163 and 188 lost their gold livery in December, leaving VPL 219 to carry it all the way to April 2003. Between November 2002 and March 2003 five VPLs were loaned between Willesden and Edgware.

2003 began with another VP order, this time for 29 to furnish the 260 and its planned new offshoot 460, both awarded to Metroline

Left: **Prior to receiving new VPs, the 260 was curtailed at Golders Green, forming a larger overlap with the new 460 than was usually the case when routes were split. Setting off from the route's new terminus on 21 September is Willesden's VP 470 (LK03 GKC).** *Author*

in December 2002. But prior to that, more TPs arrived, and one of their duties was to displace ten Holloway VPLs to Edgware during April so that the 240, by now the last route with an official allocation of Metrobuses, could lose them at last. The next TPs also started off the new 460 on 28 June until VPs 466-494 arrived, which took place in July; Willesden's 260, which had been bulked out with spare but extremely elderly Ms, took priority for conversion, which commenced on the 11th. Then followed the 460, whose operating garage was Park Royal, otherwise known as Harlesden but renamed to attract staff perhaps put off by the low reputation of the location. VP 468 had been in service less than a month when it was taken under Old Oak Common Lane railway bridge on its way back to Willesden early on 21 August and deroofed.

Left: **Willesden garage forecourt provided a handy turning point for the new 460, even if the route was operated by Park Royal. On 26 March 2004 VP 484 (LK03 GKF) has arrived and will turn around shortly.** *Author*

Metroline – 131

Right: **Holloway juggled its Volvo B7TLs and Dennis Tridents for as long as it had them; early in 2004 it was decided to make Perivale a Trident shed and put its intended new VPs into Holloway instead. Here in the Holloway Road on 12 February 2005 is VP 498 (LK53 LXP).**
Author

The endgame in the act of replacing the capital's Routemasters was now approaching, and it was decided to treat the 6 and 98, which constituted Metroline proper's entire allocation, in one fell swoop. In August seventy VPs were ordered, for delivery in time for the proposed OPO conversion on 27 March 2004. Right on the heels of that came a stroke of luck for Volvo, as an existing order for 17 TPs for the 297 at the recently-opened Perivale was changed to one for sixteen VPs. However, that deployment changed on the fly as well; as their delivery approached, Metroline decided to put them into Holloway and displace 03-reg TPs to Perivale instead. This took place from 18 December.

VPs 512-580 (this order having ceded one bus to the previous) were built over the turn of

Right: **The 6 and 98's venerable RMLs were replaced up to and including 27 March 2004 by 69 new VPs. It wasn't quite the same, even if the vehicles were as generally attractive and personable as Willesden's VP 549 (LK04 CVL), shortworking to Oxford Circus with a stablemate on 9 April.**
Author

2003/2004 and stored prior to being brought to the capital beginning in February. Even before they commenced easing Willesden's RMLs off the 6 and 98 from 10 March, they contributed indirectly to the withdrawal of the company's remaining Metrobuses that month, leaving a hard core at Potters Bar that lasted six months longer.

Just as VP 468 had its repairs completed, VPL 142 was another deroofing casualty, this time under Finsbury Park station bridge on 2 March while coming off a W7 journey.

The 6 and 98 were gradually turned over to crew VPs and one-manned on 27 March, following which they visited the 52, 260 and 302. On another sector, the Routemasters' unpopular putative replacements, the articulated Mercedes-Benz Citaro G buses, were suffering from fire issues that prompted TfL to take them off the road temporarily. To this end, Metroline loaned six VPLs and drivers to First to assist on the 18 on 25 March, and on the 26th the aid came in the form of six VPs not yet needed at Willesden.

Above: **The 98's new era is seen in the person of Willesden's VP 564 (LK04 EKY) at Red Lion Square, Bloomsbury on 16 May 2004.** *Author*

Left: **The need to find stand-ins for the 18's bendies, taken off the road in the fire panic of March 2004, resulted in Metroline helping out its nearest neighbour. Here on the 18 at Euston bus station is Willesden's VPL 187 (Y187 NLK) on 25 March.** *Author*

Metroline 133

Right: **The 240 had now joined the 113 and 204 as a VPL route at Edgware, and seen approaching its terminus on 21 June 2003 is VPL 222 (LK51 XGS).** Author

Below: **VP 499 (LK53 LXR) from the early 2004 topup batch into Holloway has turned in an appearance on the 24 when seen in Charing Cross Road on 26 March 2005.** Author

Metroline as a whole now had just one Routemaster route left. The 390 was nonetheless tendered on the basis of OPO, retained by Metroline London Northern at King's Cross and in April 23 VPLs were ordered to replace its RMLs in time for 4 September, the date of its one-manning. There were more Volvos to come, as the concurrent retention of the 140 and 182 at Harrow Weald and win of the H12 from Sovereign spawned an order for 25 VPs. A little later still the 43 and 134 were kept, and their own intended PVR increase would be furnished by nine more VPLs, after which Alexander Dennis was planning to close the Plaxton factory at Wigan and discontinue President production.

Left: **Holloway's VP 330 (LR52 BNE)** advertises *Thunderbirds* on its way through New Oxford Street on 29 April 2004; unfortunately, the film was a box-office bomb. *Author*

In June Holloway's VP 330 was treated to an all-over ad (barring the front) for the ill-fated *Thunderbirds* live-action movie. Otherwise a revised livery was beckoning, forced by a TfL-mandated increase in the proportion of red; Metroline complied by reducing the height of its blue skirt. The 390's new VPLs, in this revised livery, began delivery in July and started entering service in crew mode on 24 August, though two were allocated to Holloway and King's Cross's allocation was pooled with its parent anyway. The route was converted to OPO on 4 September, the same day as Harrow Weald's new contracts kicked

Left: **Metroline went back to VPLs for the 390's Routemaster replacement fleet, and these wore a new livery with a shorter blue skirt. VPL 582 (LK04 NMA)** in Oxford Street on 10 September 2005 is also equipped with a CrystalEyes advert screen at the front of the upper deck. *Author*

Metroline 135

Right: **Metroline's final batch of VPs comprised the twenty-five for Harrow Weald, principally for the H12 but also to standardise the rest of the garage as a Volvo shed. Brand new VP 620 (LK04 UXC) has arrived at South Harrow on 18 September 2004, two weeks after the takeover.** *Author*

Right: **The rest of Harrow Weald's VP complement was made up of 52-reg examples like VP 317 (LR52 BLK), turning round at Brent Cross on 24 April 2005.** *Author*

Right: ***Mary Poppins** was a rather more successful proposition for West End theatregoers and the ad for it on VP 330 (LR52 BNE) was certainly one of the longest-running, lasting three years. The result is seen at the 24's Hampstead Heath stand on 21 January 2006.* *Author*

in. Only enough VPs had been delivered by then to man the H12 upon its takeover, and immediately prior to that, a shuffle was executed to render Harrow Weald's double-deck complement wholly Volvo B7TL even if that meant cutting the 140's capacity by swapping its TPLs with an equivalent number of 52-reg VPs from Holloway. At Edgware, the 186 had now come in from Harrow Weald and VPL appearances were thus permitted, assisted shortly after by two VPs loaned from Harrow Weald when LLW failures increased beyond the point of acceptability.

In September VP 330 exchanged its *Thunderbirds* ad for one extolling French and Frost and VP 535 gained an ad for Eley Kishimoto. After a month VP 330 gained a third ad to promote the *Mary Poppins* musical. Then came the light blue Back the Bid scheme in aid of London's bid for the 2012 Olympics; VPs 341, 535 and 569 received this livery in October, VPs 319 and 320, which had remained at Holloway, were treated in November and VPs 343 and 558 completed the set in December.

On 1 January 2005 Metroline London Northern vanished from the board, its routes formally reassigned to Metroline and the accompanying discs absorbed by an increase to the main Metroline Travel O-Licence.

Above: **The 43 and 134 had already upgraded from TP to VPL, but fellow Holloway route 17 persisted with the T-reg Tridents. However, 23 May 2006 sees VP 503 (LK53 LXW) in action at the Monument.** *Author*

Left: **On 7 October 2004 in Oxford Street Willesden's VP 535 (LK04 CUJ) is seen sporting this wild all-over ad livery for Eley Kishimoto.** *Author*

Right: **The blue Back the Bid livery was widespread and ultimately successful; here it is on Harrow Weald's VP 320 (LR52 BLX), curtailed to Harrow bus station on 27 December 2004.** Author

Below: **After five years of feverish production at Wigan, the last Plaxton Presidents were built at the start of 2005 and went to Metroline on nine long-wheelbase Volvo B7TLs. Setting off from London Bridge on 30 April 2005 is Holloway's VPL 637 (LK54 FWT), the last of them all.** Author

VPLs 629-637 arrived at the end of January and were put into service on the 43 and 134 in time for their service increase on 5 February. VPL 637 was the last President and the last bus built at the old Northern Counties factory at Wigan. Metroline took no further Volvo B7TLs after this, returning to ALX400 bodywork for one last batch of Tridents and then throwing itself wholesale into the purchase of Alexander Dennis's integral Enviro400 once production got under way at the end of 2005.

For four weekends in February and March double-deck extras (including VPs and VPLs) worked the 214, otherwise the province of DL-class Dart SLFs from Holloway. On 21 May Park Royal closed and the 460 was reallocated to Perivale, taking VPs 482-497 with it; school routes 611 and 643 also came in from Cricklewood. On 26-30 May inclusive, the Back the Bid buses were all loaned to garages operating routes passing Lord's cricket ground for the occasion of the Test Match between England and Bangladesh; Holloway's 341 and 343 guested on the 82 out of Potters Bar while the Willesden trio of VPs 535, 558 and 569 worked on Edgware's 113. VPs 319 and 320 had already regained their fleet colours, and when the Bid was ultimately announced as successful on 6 July, their work was considered done and the livery disappeared.

The terrorist bombings of 7 July prompted extras to be put out on B7TL-operated routes 205 and 390 for a month. Elsewhere two VPs were transferred to Edgware, forming a first allocation of the class there after numerous loans. Thankfully, the rest of 2005 proved peaceful and the next change was not until the start of 2006, when the 24 was converted to TE operation. It was VPLs that left Holloway, heading to Edgware to convert the 186 from LLW. On 21 January 2006, the 643 was reallocated from Perivale back to Cricklewood.

At the start of 2006 VPs 519 (Harrow Weald) and 535 (Willesden) gained a red-based advert for the NSPCC; the former's front remained in fleet colours. Metroline's VPs and VPLs, the early examples of the latter class now commencing a refurbishment cycle, otherwise managed to dodge mass application of the abortive ComfortDelgro livery with sickly light blue skirt. In February a new scheme bowed in the shape of the Oyster Card livery, first applied to Harrow Weald's VP 320 and in this case lasting until December. Several Willesden VPs were fitted with GPS-activated advert panelling which changed the illuminated scrolling aspect when a particular point on the 6 was passed.

Left: **Metroline experimented with a new colour combination to underscore its corporate ownership, but plain white logos soon replaced light blue and orange.** *Author*

Below: **The 186's LLWs had had enough after twelve years and were replaced by VPLs; Brent Cross is where VPL 165 (Y165 NLK) is sighted on 26 October 2005.** *Author*

Above: Pastel blue proved too much of a colour clash with traditional red, despite the white tape separator, and the few unfortunate vehicles to gain this skirt colour were quickly amended. Willesden's VPL 172 (Y172 NLK) is coming into Ladbroke Grove Sainsbury's on 3 March 2007. *Author*

From 13 May 2006 for two months, Kilburn High Road was closed to traffic, necessitating extras on the 16, 98 and 316, which were diverted away from the area. They were provided by temporarily converting the 240 to DLD and releasing its VPLs. For Notting Hill Carnival, Holloway gained a share of the 390, using its own VPLs.

In June VP 507 received an ad celebrating the achievements of London schools; its inspiration was 15-year-old mathematician Menelik Collymore. In October it exchanged this vinyl for a scheme advertising the musical adaptation of *Dirty Dancing*, and spent January on the 390 on loan to King's Cross.

Right: On 31 August 2006 at Edgware, two local B7TLs pass, VPL 156 (X656 LLX) with the shallower skirt and VPL 148 (X648 LLX) with the original depth. The latter has also been fitted with a KM blind panel, which just about fits and provides more information than the DDA version can. *Author*

Tendering during 2006 affected the 204, which was announced as retained in August but with the promise of new buses to displace its VPLs. The 24 was also offered out again, and a smaller win was of an extra journey on what was otherwise Sullivan Buses' school route 606; this commenced on 2 December with an Edgware VPL. Reductions to the 52 on the same date freed three VPLs to serve as refurbishment cover, although their berth at Edgware was under threat with the announcement of an order for more TEs (Enviro400s) for the 204.

During February 2007 the announcement was made that Metroline had lost the 24 to London General after just the one five-year hitch. A new school route 605 was awarded for September takeup, however. In March a bout of vehicle standardisation saw Perivale swap most of the 460's VPs with an equivalent number of Holloway TPs, leaving just four to assist on the 297 until June. Occasionally the odd VPL was loaned from Willesden. In April fifteen new TEs took over Edgware's 204 in advance of its 28 April contract renewal date; the VPLs displaced went to Holloway to allow TPLs to top up Potters Bar, which thus released some of its existing TPLs to Cricklewood.

Metroline suffered its first Volvo B7TL loss when VPL 212 caught fire on 11 June while in the Edgware Road on the N5; it was declared unrepairable the following February and struck off strength.

Left: **On 3 June 2007, just before Perivale's conversion to a Trident shed was completed, VP 484 (LK03 GMF) brings a 297 down the home stretch to Ealing Broadway.** *Author*

Left: **Bringing a modern look to the 4 on 20 May 2007 is Holloway's VP 502 (LK53 LXV) at Highbury & Islington.** *Author*

Right: **VP 507 (LK53 LXV) out of Holloway is wearing a** *Dirty Dancing* **wrap when seen at the foot of Highgate Hill on 25 July 2008.** Author

VP 319 lost its NSPCC ad in August. On 1 September the 605 commenced with an Edgware TE or VPL and any chance of VPs still appearing on the 24 was lost on 10 November with its loss to London General. Twenty-five VPs moved to Harrow Weald to see off all TA support, while the 55-reg TE batch stayed at Holloway to consolidate on the 134 and the 56-reg batch passed to Edgware to convert the 186 from VPL to TE operation. That brought VPLs back to Holloway in force, where their official role was to cover refurbishments. The higher-numbered of the Y- and 51-reg batch of VPLs went through this process during 2008, after which iBus fitment was carried out, though Metroline supplied buses to other operators to cover this rather than taking loans.

Right: **Another Holloway route capable of fielding VPs was the C2, which had otherwise replaced its DNL-class Darts with TPs. On 25 July 2008 VP 499 (LK53 LXR) makes the right-hand swing towards Camden Town on its way south.** Author

Left: **The conversion of the 186 to TE operation released VPLs to Holloway, and still carrying its Edgware code as it rounds Marble Arch on 23 June is VPL 235 (Y235 NLK).** Author

VP 330 lost its *Mary Poppins* ad in December, but NSPCC-liveried VP 319 lasted all the way to August 2008. Between February and April VP 518 gained an advert for the *101 Dalmatians* box set. June saw VP 547 touting the *Prince Caspian* film, and in August VPs 494 and 496 gained dark blue-based ads for Visa. All these latter three resumed red in October. Between September and November VP 518 wore an ad for Burlington.

In August VPLs 207-209 went to Harrow Weald to see off three AVs from Watford-area school contracts, followed by five VPs that ejected the ET-class Tridents that had been acquired from Metrobus but ended up lasting longer than anticipated. Sometimes the three VPLs turned out on the 182.

Now that iBus installation was complete, there had arisen a surplus of VPLs. On 3 January 2009 they were put into Edgware

Left: **The back of the President body had an offset rear window to hide various mechanical items protruding upward from the engine bay; it wasn't particularly attractive and Alexander's ALX400 competitor went for a full-width rear window instead, concealing the offending innards behind a pillar. VP 469 (LK03 GKJ), now of Harrow Weald, finds itself at Harrow & Wealdstone on 22 November 2008.** Author

Above: By 25 May 2009, the paintwork on Willesden's VP 537 (LK04 CUW), seen in Oxford Street, was fading, but it wouldn't be long before a new contract for the 6 and 98 prompted a cycle of repaints. *Author*

to convert the 107 from DLD. Then came the partial conversion to double-deck of Willesden's 302 on 14 February, using VPs.

Tendering over the cusp of 2008-2009 retained the 107 (albeit with new buses) and all of the 606 (the Sullivan Buses half to come off) but lost the 640 to Arriva the Shires. The 260 and 302 were offered out later in the year and the 6 and 98 by the end of 2009.

As 2009 progressed, the order went out by TfL to repaint everything allover red; thus Metroline's characteristic blue skirt in place since 1996 began to disappear, VPL 595 being the first Volvo B7TL to lose it upon repaint in June. Where full repaints were not practicable, just the skirts were gone over in red. VP 507 had worn its *Dirty Dancing* ad for three years now but lost it in the same month.

Right: When repaints did commence, however, you almost wished they hadn't bothered, as the inevitable result was unrelieved allover red. Willesden's VPL 170 (Y196 NLK) demonstrates at Victoria on 14 November 2009. *Author*

Left: **An all-capitals NN blind has found its way onto Edgware's VPL 212 (LK51 XGM) on 21 November 2009, and so has a numberplate with the old size of characters. The location is Harrow & Wealdstone station.** Author

Below: **The 302 was one of those routes that suffered under Dart SLFs due to these being the only low-floor vehicles available until the development of Tridents and Volvo B7TLs. However, its upper deck was restored in 2010 and here at Mill Hill Broadway on 29 August of that year we see Willesden's VP 499 (LK53 LXR), freshly transferred from Holloway and refurbished.** Ian Jordan

On 5 September the 640 departed for Arriva the Shires and the Sullivan Buses share of the 606 was absorbed. The 107's new contract commenced on 10 October but the VPLs stayed put for the moment. Also at Edgware, the 113 was withdrawn between Marble Arch and Oxford Circus on 7 November, the same day as the 186, still capable of fielding VPLs, was rerouted to serve Grahame Park.

Both the 260 and 302 were announced as retained on the basis of new buses, but the deepening recession forced purchasing plans to be put on hold system-wide as well as at Metroline. That put the finishers on the 107's planned upgrade as well, although the 302 would be converted to full double-deck with existing VPs. This took place between March and May 2010, accomplished by putting

Above: **On top of two replacement wings in more blue than was Metroline's standard by now, years of hauling back and forth on the 390 has seen the paintwork on Holloway's VPL 582 (LK04 NMA) fade itself when encountered at Warren Street on 7 November 2010, but the route was retained and repaints began. Metroline was suffering some paint quality problems at the time that led to some of its buses going around in various shades of red faded almost to pink.** Author

new Volvo B9TLs (VWs) into Brentford, the former Armchair garage, which released TPs to Holloway to make spare the VPs required.

The 6 and 98 were announced in May as staying with Metroline with their existing VPs, though with PVR drops on each. At the same time Harrow Weald's VP-operated spread of 140, 182 and H12 and King's Cross's 390 were tendered again.

On 10 July Metroline opened a new King's Cross (KC) to replace the existing facility (KX), but it couldn't accommodate double-deckers, so the 390 and its VPLs passed to Holloway in exchange for the 214. VPLs could not appear on the 186 during the period it was outstationed to Cricklewood with its TEs due to repairs on the approach road to Edgware garage. This applied from 28 August to 18 December 2010.

Refurbishment was carried out to Willesden's 04-reg VPs as 2010 wound down; this was in time for the 6 and 98's contract renewal on 11 December. On this date the 460 regained VP operation with a move from Perivale to Willesden. Finally, 2011 ended with the clean sweep of the 140, 182 and H12, all with their incumbent VPs. This prompted a refurbishment programme for both the 52-reg and 04-reg contingent and the transfer to Harrow Weald of TPLs to stand in for them. The 390 was also kept hold of and its VPLs refurbished later in 2011.

The 43 and 134, which could still field a large quantity of VPLs amid Holloway's thoroughly mixed fleet, were out to tender as 2011 opened, and later in the year VPL-operated 52, 113 and 240 were also offered out, plus the VP-capable 4, 271 and C2 at Holloway.

In February 2011 VP 522 gained an ad for G-Star Raw, carrying it till June, when VP 534 gained one for Capital One's Click card (carrying it until October). August (until November) saw VP 542 adorned with a Google Maps ad and September gave VP 580 its own G-Star Raw ad, which lasted two months. Otherwise, quiet descended over the Volvo B7TL family, none of which was threatened in the short term, unlike the corresponding Tridents, many of which had already departed off lease after just seven years. The 186's and 204's VPLs would be staying when those awards were made in August, but the 240 was awarded with new buses and the C2 lost to Abellio. One-bus school route 605 was also lost, to Sovereign.

Left: **Not only has VP 503 (LK53 LXW) gained a new coat of red paint when seen in Oxford Street on 13 April 2011, but it's carrying a new blind set with just two via points. This bus was new to Holloway but was transferred to Willesden in October 2010 when the 302 was double-decked.** Author

By the autumn, confidence had returned sufficient for Metroline to bid on the basis of new buses again, and this strategy kept them the 4, 43, 82, 113 and W7 when their rounds were announced in October; the 134 would have a mix of new and existing and the 271 keep its incumbents.

3 September saw the 140, 182 and H12 at Harrow Weald and the 390 at Holloway renewed; the 43 and 134 followed on 4 February 2012, the 113 on 31 March (at which point a new N113 joined it, bouncing out the N16 to Cricklewood) and the 240 on 28 April. All of VPs 317-347 and 604-628 plus VPLs

Left: **A red repaint also adorns Harrow Weald's VP 605 (LK04 UWL) from Metroline's final batch of short Volvo B7TLs. It is seen on 19 November 2011 at Harrow & Wealdstone.** Author

Metroline – 147

Above: Now running out of Holloway and looking smart after a repaint, VPL 224 (LK51 XGU) at King's Cross on 18 April 2012 is also carrying a new blind set, but with the intermediate revision that enlarged the route number. *Author*

with new buses, a proportion of which would be hybrids, to replace its Y-registered VPLs.

Route C2 departed for Abellio on 28 April, though not before two VPLs had sneaked out on it. As VW-class Volvo B9TLs arrived in strength and took over Holloway's 43, 134 and W7 during the spring and summer, the early TPs, TAs and then the TALs were withdrawn, leaving the VP class intact.

The Olympics were now beckoning, and in July VPLs 168-170 became the first of their now ageing class to gain ads, Samsung being the beneficiary. The 52 needed extras during the Games as it was, which came in the form of four VPLs loaned from Holloway in July. VP 542 gained an ad for Visa at the same time, lasting three months in it. Then, during the Olympics themselves, recently-refurbished VPLs 629-637 formed part of the support fleet, though without identifying information as per Games rules. Outstationed to Stagecoach, they remained based locally for the duration of the Paralympics and then returned to Holloway in September.

581-603 had been refurbished by the spring of 2012, and the balance of VPs 466-580 hadn't long before they too were completed. VP 469 had its upper deck destroyed by fire on 2 February and was refitted with a new roof. Next up for refurbishment by H&D Trim were VPLs 629-637.

In February VP 542 was given an ad for China Tourism (lasting until June) and in March VP 574 received a month-long ad for the film *The Pirates*. The 52's award was announced in April; back to Metroline but

On 1 September Sovereign took over the 605 and the 29th saw the 4 and 271 renewed; as it turned out, the 4 would be stiffed out of its intended new buses, making do with a mix of whatever Holloway could field, which, to be fair, did end up including a consolation order for four VWs. Nonetheless, 12-reg TEs returning from Olympics duty into Cricklewood displaced 08-registered examples to Edgware to replace the VPLs from the 107 and 240 in September.

Right: Back and front as both of the major Harrow Weald VP batches are represented in this Hayes & Harlington shot of 9 June 2012; VP 317 (LR52 BLK), first of its batch, is heading north on the 140 while VP 628 (LK54 FWG), last of its own batch, heads south. *Author*

Left: **As the VPLs approached their second decade, they began to be eased off their original routes. The 107 was converted to TE in September 2012, so this shot of VPL 199 (Y199 NLK) approaching Edgware on 28 July would not be repeated for much longer. VPL 199 itself lasted another year.** *Author*

On 10 November the 24 came back to Holloway under contract to Metroline again, but with new VWs and VWHs on order, the contribution to it by existing VPs and VPLs was indirect, the B7TLs standing in on the 134 to allow the newest VWs so far to start it off. The 43 at this point had ceded its VWs to the 134 and W7, sharing its VPLs with the 4; VPs stayed on the 17 and 271. Also awaiting a VW/VWH mix was the 52, whose new contract started on 8 December. TEs and TEHs were due for the 189, which would cascade its existing TEs to the 113; in both cases 2013 would see the first VPLs cast out of the fleet. One to go first, albeit on a long-term loan, was VPL 220, which joined Sovereign in October for the 605 that this company had just taken off Metroline. In November eight VPLs were withdrawn and two more sold; the end was beginning for the class.

Left: **The 240 also gained TEs to replace its VPLs; here at Golders Green on 18 August 2012 is VPL 198 (Y148 NLK), looking smart but even so, with only ten more months in service ahead of it.** *Author*

Below: **VPLs came and went at Harrow Weald, and then came and went again. VPL 208 (Y208 NLK) is in Harrow town centre on 28 July 2012 but was about to transfer to WIllesden.** *Author*

Ads to Metroline B7TLs as 2012 wound down were for *Skyfall* (VP 553 between September and October), while VPLs 168-170 lost their Visa schemes in October. November saw a big push by Apple that saw multiple London buses liveried for its otherwise moribund iPod; VPs 520, 542, 546 and 552 were Metroline's contribution and all lasted until January 2013.

A third spell of VPL operation at Harrow Weald saw three appear in January 2013, but sales now commenced in earnest and ramped up when the 52 was converted from VPL to VW and VWH from 5 February. Willesden sent seven VPs to Harrow Weald for boosts to the 140 and 182, but two more, VPs 485 and 608, fell out for the moment through fire and accident respectively.

Right: **The 390's batch of 04- and 54-reg VPLs stayed at Holloway after the 390 was converted to Borismaster, congregating on the 4 and 43 with more regular forays to the 17 than hitherto. On 30 November 2013 VPL 589 (LK04 NMX) is at Archway.** *Author*

Left: **Metroline took to Wrightbus bodywork much later than other London companies, ignoring the combination on the B7TL but falling in love with it on the B9TL and ending up taking that combination exclusively for some years. On the other side of town, First had grown a VNW class and bequeathed eleven of them to what became Metroline West on 22 June 2013. Setting off from White City on 20 November 2014 is Uxbridge's VW 1570 (LK55 ABF), which was new as VNW 32668.** *Author*

New TEHs into Cricklewood for the 189 during May allowed the route's earlier TEs to pass to Edgware for the 113 and finish off the VPL class there.

22 June 2013 was a banner day for Metroline; as well as introducing the first production LT-class Borismasters on the 24, there was spawned a new offshoot called Metroline West, carved out of what FirstGroup had sold to ComfortDelgro. The other new organisation to appear on that date, Tower Transit, took the majority of First's Wright-bodied VNW-class Volvo B7TLs but Metroline West inherited eleven, based at Uxbridge for the 607 alongside some Enviro400s (and occasionally visiting the U1 and U3). VNWs 32658-32668 were renumbered VW 1560-1570.

Below: **Repaints to First's VNWs even before the end of First London exposed the formerly black-painted parts at the back of the Wrightbus Gemini design. VW 1570 (LK55 ABF) is leaving Uxbridge on 9 September 2014.** *Author*

In June VP 543 gained an ad for *Despicable Me 2* and VP 515 for Lycamobile. VP 543's ad lasted a month and VP 515's a year. Then, in August VP 544 was treated to a scheme for Nike and wore it for five months. In November VP 542 gained a fifth ad, this time for Puerto Vallarta in Mexico, losing it in January.

On 7 December the 390 became Holloway's second NBfL route, releasing VPLs to general population at the garage and allowing TEs to displace TPs from Potters Bar and get rid of a few more TPLs from Holloway itself; the long Tridents of roughly the same age as the early VPLs were leaving the fleet at the same time. Even so, VPLs remained available at both Edgware and Willesden into 2014.

Buses from VP 317 and newer received modifications allowing them to accept the Adblue emissions-cleaning ingredient.

Edgware's last VPL was VPL 213, which operated the 240 on 28 April and then passed to Willesden for six more weeks. Including this transfer, Willesden and Harrow Weald could still field five each, but Willesden now whittled its fleet down and VPL 217 ran for the last time on the 460 on 13 June. Harrow Weald had just two by then, but at the end of July sent VPL 207 to Willesden! This bus spent only six days there, however, last working on 5 August. VPL 184 was now Harrow Weald's last, and it lingered on and on, finishing out 2014 on the 140 and 182 and continuing well into 2015.

Below: **The 4 had always been rather forgotten, stealing as it did round the back of most of the population points on its way from Waterloo to Archway. Since OPO conversion on 2 February 1985 it hadn't had a full batch of new buses to call its own, and on 27 October 2014 VPL 591 (LK04 NMZ) at Waterloo represents the newest type that Holloway was willing to put out on it.** *Author*

Right: **In January 2014 VPL 203 (Y203 NLK) was transferred from Edgware to Willesden and on 1 April is seen at Golders Green on a visit to the 260, not by any means a regular pitch for longer buses.** *Author*

152 – Volvo B7TL

Left: **Cheerful polkadots adorn a white background in the service of City of Westminster College on this ad carried by VP 571 (LK04 ELW). It is seen at Edgware Road station on 10 October 2015.** *Author*

Left: **On 2 November 2014 Willesden's VP 537 (LK04 CUW) is seen at Charing Cross wearing an ad for the Philippine island of Camiguin.** *Author*

In May 2014 VPs 568 and 571 received all-over ads for City of Westminster College and in September VP 565 spent a month advertising Rimmel cosmetics. That October saw VPL 594 join 2014's Poppy Appeal contingent and VPs 515 and 537 hustle for Philippines tourism.

2014 saw Arriva the Shires' 640 tendered and awarded to Metroline, and on 30 August it was taken up by Harrow Weald with VPs plus six 12-reg VWs sent in; these also added a modern element to the 140 from the same date.

2015 began with VP 515 swapping its Philippines ad in February for one extolling Pepsi Max. VP 561 followed suit in March, and in April VP 537 lost its Philippines ad and gained one for Crocs instead. The two Pepsi Max ads came off in June and a month later VP 537 acquired a Sunglass Hut scheme. It carried this until October, in which month VP 505 gained a three-month ad for *Mockingjay*.

In the battle of the hybrids, the Volvo B5LH came out very much the winner at Metroline, who bought just one batch of Enviro400 MMCs. The 245 and 460 were due a 33-strong batch of the resulting Wright-bodied VWHs, but in the usual manner it was decided to place them on the 6 and 98 instead. However, it wasn't considered that there weren't enough for both routes and when they did enter service in June, the 6 was prioritised. The destination for the VPs released was unusual; Uxbridge, acquired

Above: **VPs replaced TPs on Uxbridge's U4 in July 2015, and seen on that route on 25 November is VP 481 (LK03 GLY).** *Author*

Below: **Hayes's short period with VPs is personified at Uxbridge by VP 604 (LK04 UWJ) visiting the U5 on 20 January 2007.** *Author*

with First London and now under Metroline West's banner. From July they took over the U4 from what were now TPs, and visits to the U1, U3 and U5 quickly followed. The 607's VWs also saw their first appearance on the U5 at this point.

The VP class was still unscathed by the end of 2015, but that was when the 140 and 182 were awarded to their incumbent Metroline on the basis of new buses. TPs and TPLs suffered heavy withdrawals at this point, with former Willesden VPs moving into Holloway to replace them. That process was complete by the end of February 2016.

On 20 August, to make space for the 114 incoming from Sovereign, Metroline West reallocated the U4 from Uxbridge to Hayes, its Volvo B7TL complement now constituting VPs 604-611 made spare from Harrow Weald by the entry into service of the first VWHs for the 140 and 182 even before their contract dates on 3 September. The H12 had been extended for two years and would thus be holding onto its VPs, letting the 52-reg examples go off lease. The U5 had also moved over to Hayes and thus saw continued VP visits. Still, the first VPs were withdrawn in October and examples began leaving the fleet. VP-operated routes to be out for tender as 2015 wound down were the 4, 17, 260 and 302 as well as the U4. As well as the H12, the 43 had two more years added to its current deal, buying time for its VPLs. At the end of 2015 all four were awarded to their incumbent Metroline with new vehicles. Accordingly, the clock was set ticking on the VPs with the placement at the beginning of 2017 for an order for 79 more VWHs against the 17, 260 and 302. Finally the 6 and 98 completed their extra two years and were retendered themselves, again coming back victorious and with an order for 70 VWHs of their own.

Left: **Now with the unattractive and uninformative blind set with two via points, Harrow Weald's VP 317 (LR52 BLK) comes round the one-way system into Harrow bus station on 10 April 2016. This bus was sold in June.** *Author*

On 11 February 2017 the U4 was reallocated back to Uxbridge, in advance of Hayes's closure on 29 April. The U4 began a new contract on that date, but the U5's departure for Abellio ended the possibility of VPs.

It was late in the day for all-over ads for VPs, but in April VP 539 received one for the University of Westminster. It lasted until August, when the other two still carrying it (VPs 568 and 571) were also returned to red,

and these were the last ad-liveried Metroline B7TLs. Withdrawals over the first half of 2017 concentrated on the 03-reg Willesden contingent and then started on the 52-reg examples during May.

Emissions concerns in central London tended to get in the way of orderly contract requirements, and instead of deploying new VWHs to the 17 as planned, the new buses were put to work on Perivale's 7 from 27 July

Left: **Just having come off a 640 school duty at South Harrow on 13 May 2016 is VP 607 (LK04 UWN).** *Author*

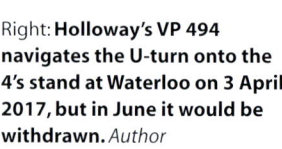

Above: **On 3 March 2017 in Oxford Street, the 98 is still VP-operated, as proven by VP 564 (LK04 EKY), but the 6 has received Volvo B5LHs like VWH 2110 (LK15 CXJ).** *Author*

and cascaded earlier members of the class to Holloway so that the 53-reg VPs could begin standing down. Similar tinkering affected the intended new fleet for Willesden, which were allocated to the 52 instead so that earlier examples could remain based for the 260 and 302. And then there was the 4, which yet again was done out of new buses, but this time because there was a clearance along the route that was fouled by the length of the new VWHs. The VPL class, itself beginning to lose members as the autumn loomed, had gathered here for the most part. Others had become trainers, but while in this mode VPL 632 was deroofed under Old Oak Common bridge in November.

After running in on the 222 acquired from London United and put into Uxbridge,

Right: **Holloway's VP 494 navigates the U-turn onto the 4's stand at Waterloo on 3 April 2017, but in June it would be withdrawn.** *Author*

Left: **Willesden withdrew most of its VPs in 2017 but a handful remained in service. VP 515 (LK04 CRJ) is on final approach to its base on 1 September, and would be withdrawn the following February.** *Author*

further new VWHs were sent to Willesden to prepare to ease out the 98's earlier examples and those still visiting the 6. The 222's full-time VWH batch released some TEs that had been standing in at Uxbridge to replace the U4's VPs by 22 November (VP 604 being the last). Uxbridge could still field its eleven VWs, and would be able to do so for two more years with the 607's extension.

2017 ended with just the H12 operated wholly by Volvo B7TLs, but this had been tendered during the year and in December the announcement was made of its loss to Sovereign from the following September. Willesden's VP complement was sharply reduced and Holloway could field only VPs 490 and 496 against an almost intact fleet of 04- and 54-reg VPLs still running on the 43.

Left: **The 43 operated VPLs into 2018; on 13 August 2017 VPL 595 (LK04 NND) is seen heading south past Moorgate, with fourteen months to go.** *Author*

Right: **The 607 had been spun off from the 207 specifically as a prestige route that warranted two generations of purpose-built high-spec buses, but its latest combination of VWs and TEs were allowed to grow very tired from the extra slogging they did up and down the Uxbridge Road. VW 1560 (LK55 ACU) is coming up to Uxbridge station on 28 August 2017, now with Metroline-pattern seating which doesn't clash too badly with the FirstGroup turquoise handrails that were left alone upon refurbishment.** *Author*

Below: **The last wholly-VP route at Metroline was the H12, which kept them until its departure for Sovereign on 1 September 2018. On 8 June at South Harrow we see Harrow Weald's VP 625 (LK04 UXH), whose last day in service was actually on the 182.** *Author*

January 2018 saw a rush of VWH licensings and the effective completion of the 6 and 98 at Willesden, though a hard core of five VPs (534, 536, 544, 545 and 549) remained doggedly in service. Holloway's two VPs were withdrawn after operation on 12 January (VP 490 on the 43) and 18 January (VP 496 on the 271). Sales thus tore through the 04-reg VP block, most going to Ensign with a number passing directly to Southdown PSV. By the end of the year rather more than hitherto were scrapped on site, being of little resale value now despite only being 14-15 years of age.

A limited route-branding exercise was applied to buses on routes serving Hillingdon from 22 January 2018; five of them were Uxbridge-based VWs 1566-1570, whose themed colour for the 607 on front window and side vinyls was off-yellow.

Left: **By 31 August 2018 the H12's VPs had almost all been replaced by new VWHs that would move to the H14 the next day. Seen opposite its home garage at Harrow Weald, VP 628 (LK54 FWG) was one of three spared, lasting two more weeks in service.** Author

It was another world for buses now; June 2018 saw the 43 awarded to and retained by Metroline but with the promise of electric double-deckers. Its mix of diesel-engined VPLs and TEs suddenly seemed very old-fashioned.

The H12 passed to Sovereign on 1 September and all but three VPs still at Harrow Weald were withdrawn. Of these, VP 620 continued until 12 September and VP 628 the 13th, but VP 614 dug its heels in on the 140 and 640 and lasted out 2018 and into 2019! Willesden's stay-behinds similarly clung to the 460 and would not be dislodged.

That left Holloway's VPLs. Dissatisfied with Wrightbus's build quality and delivery times, Metroline switched its allegiance to MCV with a resulting slew of VMH-class B5LHs. The second batch of these in 2018 took over Edgware's 113 in September,

Left: **Withdrawals tore through the remaining VPLs between September and November 2018, but two of them were retained at Holloway and continued to turn out on the 43 into 2019. On 8 November 2018 VPL 631 (LK54 FWL) is coming up to Highbury Corner.** Author

Right: **By far the oldest buses to be included in the Hillingdon-area branding exercise, Uxbridge-based VWs 1566-1570 were still going into 2019, with the exception of VW 1568. Late on 1 April, VW 1566 (LK55 AAV) comes into Uxbridge, just avoiding an Addison Lee on its way out.** Author

releasing TEs to Holloway and beginning the closedown of VPL operation. Within two months they were all gone – barring a pair of similarly obstinate stragglers in the shape of VPLs 591 and 631, which fought on into the New Year, though the 43 began its new contract on 2 February 2019. Those eight buses (VPs 534, 536, 544, 545 and 549 at Willesden, VP 614 at Harrow Weald and VPLs 591 and 631 at Holloway) were all that remained of Metroline's Volvo B7TL era, barring nine remaining VWs on the 607 at Uxbridge; VWs 1565 and 1568 had been withdrawn in October 2018 and the 607

Right: **One problem with this particular incarnation of route branding was that there really wasn't the physical space available on a Gemini body to display it; a huge vent on the rear has forced a smaller route 607 diagram to be carried offset to the nearside, while the obliteration of the entire downstairs rear window by another sticker is inexcusable. This shot of Uxbridge's VW 1569 (LK55 AAZ), leaving its home base on 1 April 2019, also shows the need to have chopped multiple aeration holes into the bodies' engine cover and sidewalls.** Author

was also due new VMHs after its successful tender retention announced in August. Just once each, one VW appeared on the 222 and 114 on Boxing Day.

In sympathy, and in parallel, Metroline had also held on to five Tridents (TAs) at Cricklewood, long after their compatriots had departed; which type would blink first?

It was the introduction of the ULEZ (Ultra-Low Emission Zone) on 8 April 2019 that did for Volvo B7TLs going into central London. The only two qualifying by then were the Holloway pair of VPLs, and on Friday 5 April both turned out on the 43, VPL 631 coming off at 11:12 and VPL 591 at 13:05. On the following day, the 607's VWs came off as its new contract loomed under an intended mix of B9TL VWs and new VMHs. VW 1570 was the last branded bus and the last 607 on 5 April, because at nine o'clock VW 1564 was switched onto Greenford's 207, which departed for Abellio on the 6th, and finished its day on that route.

With the 6 April changes, four VWs were transferred from Holloway to Willesden to replace the four remaining VPs (VP 545 not having worked after 5 February), but the B7TLs lingered as long as they could. VP 536 fell out after 14 May, but VPs 534, 544 and 549 continued to work intermittently, sometimes taking long spells off and looking done for, only to be resuscitated repeatedly. Meanwhile, VP 614, totally overlooked at Harrow Weald, sidestepped the loss to Sullivan Buses on 1 September of school route 640, against which it was held, and continued on, marking a year since its fellows departed.

And still they wouldn't go; even a cut to the PVRs of the 6 and 98 on 26 October 2019, that would normally have released existing VWHs, couldn't prise loose Willesden's VPs.

Above: **The withdrawal of Greenford's VWs and Holloway's VPLs after 5 April 2019 left just five VPs as the last examples of Metroline's Volvo B7TL in service. Four were Willesden's, and, since neither the 302 nor 460 went anywhere near central London with its ULEZ restrictions, weren't immediately troubled. However, one by one the VP fleet was whittled down. On 5 April VP 549 (LK04 CVL) is coming up to Golders Green on its way north.** Author

Left: **Otherwise history after the H12 was lost to Sovereign on 1 September 2018, the VP class at Harrow Weald survived in the person of one member, VP 614 (LK04 UWW), which just kept going, and going! Over a year later and with no sign of replacement, it is seen at Harrow on 18 September 2019, by which time A4 sheets in the windscreen were serving as running numbers. It even managed to outlast the small band of VPs at Willesden, finishing on a since-curtailed route 140 on 23 December.** Author

Above: **No measures to replace the stalwart VPs really took hold until the inevitable expedient of creeping cuts, imposed by snipping one or two buses off other routes and hoping that passengers didn't notice. Availability itself dwindled steadily, and finally, the remaining two Willesden examples were ceremonially retired on 13 December 2019. That midday sees VP 534 (LK04 CUH) arriving at Kensal Rise as AC354 on the 302.** *Author*

Right: **VP 549 (LK04 CVL) takes a breather in the garage at lunchtime on 13 December before taking up running number AC7 and then AC5 to see out the rest of the day, outlasting VP 534 simultaneously finishing on the 302. A commemorative plaque was carried in the windscreen of each bus to pay tribute to the Volvo B7TLs' nearly nineteen years of service at Metroline.** *Author*

With the 140's curtailment at Hayes & Harlington looming, a running day was held over the route's historic entirety on Saturday 23 November. Alongside eight RTs, four RMs, an RCL and two Ms running free of charge, VP 614, something of a heritage vehicle itself by now, was put out in service. And it just kept on going, even weathering the cutting in half of the 140 on 7 December.

Metroline's VPs outlived the TAs, the latter pair coming off finally after 19 November. VP 544 last worked on 6 December on the 460, and at last an end date of Friday 13th was set for Willesden's Volvo B7TLs. On this day VP 534 performed as AC354 on the 302 until 21:30, while VP 549 started on the 460 as AC3 before switching to AC7 at lunchtime and finally to AC5, the last journey of which finished at North Finchley at 00:19 on the 14th.

Just VP 614 was left now, its incredible survival having stretched into its fifteenth month, and its historical significance was recognised by Metroline with its own gala send-off on Monday 23 December. Not that it happened to plan by any means; its intended roster on HD121 fell through when the new driver scheduled to take it out proved not to be type trained, so it left Harrow Weald garage at 06:45 as HD113 instead, only to break down at Yeading on its second trip south! The problem identified as leaking coolant, VP 614 was fixed, topped up and returned home dead, but the dedicated staff were determined not to let it slip away, working doggedly on this by now elderly bus's coolant and oil issues until it was ready to venture out again, which it did at 14:55, now as HD117. Heavy Christmas traffic obliged it to switch once again to HD119 and skip to Northolt to begin its last northbound run, but finally it slogged its way back to Harrow Weald at 20:10, not just completing the nearly nineteen-year career of the Volvo B7TL with Metroline but seeing off the last Plaxton President body to operate in London.

Above: **Tally Ho Corner at North Finchley had changed substantially in the service period of Metroline's VPLs and VPs, with a multi-storey residential block springing up and the bus station relocated underneath it. Dank and gloomy, its only outflow was on the western edge, from which VP 549 (LK04 CVL) is emerging as AC7 at five to four on 13 December 2019.** Author

Left: **Harrow Weald's epic holdout VP 614 (LK04 UWW) wasn't going to let the assembled enthusiast throngs have it all their own way on its last day, 23 December 2019; all of a sudden, it was feeling every one of its fifteen years, with persistent rust and panels threatening to come away if not guarded carefully. Demob happy, it sprung a coolant leak just past ten o'clock and got no further south than Yeading, White Hart. After valiant work repairing its coolant line and topping up the tank with viscous pink fluid before a jet wash of its rear quarters back at Harrow Weald, Metroline's last Volvo B7TL was ready to take to the 140 once again and at five to three, now plated as HD117, is turning out of the garage's gateway.** Author

Registrations
VPL 135-161	X635-639, 664, 641-649, 663, 651-654, 665, 656-659, 662, 661 LLX
VPL 162-236	Y162-169, 196, 171-174, 195, 176-179, 197, 181-189, 198, 191-194, 144, 146-148, 199, 149, 201-204 NLK, LK51 XGD, Y246, 207-209, 143 NLK, LK51 XGE-H/J/L-P/R-Z, XHA/B, Y232-236 NLK
VP 317-347	LR52 BLK/N/V/X/Z, BMO/U/V/Y/Z, BNA/B/D-F/J-L/N/O/U/V/X-Z, BOF/H/J/U/V, BPE
VP 466-494	LK03 GKE-G/J/L/N/P/U/V/X-Z, GLF/J/V/Y/Z, GME/F/G/U/V/X-Z, GNF/J/N/P
VP 495-511	LK53 LXM-P/R/T-Z, LYA/C/D/F/G
VP 512-580	LK04 CPY/Z, CRF/J/U/V/Z, CSF/U/V/X-Z, CTE/F/U/V/X/Z, CUA/C/G/H/J/U/W-Y, CVA-H/J/L-N/P/R-X, EKU-Z, ELC/H/J/U-X, EMF/J/V/X, ENE/F/H/J
VPL 581-603	LK04 NLZ, NMA/E/F/J/M/U/V/X-Z, NNA-H/J/L/M/P
VP 604-628	LK04 UWJ/L/M/N/P/R-Z, UXA-H, LK54 FWE-G
VPL 629-637	LK54 FWH/J/L/M-P/R/T

Date	Deliveries	Licensed for Service
12.00	VPL 139, 146, 148	
01.01	VPL 135-138, 140-145, 147, 149-161	VPL 135-161 (**HT**)
02.01	VPL 163	
03.01	VPL 162, 164-186	VPL 162-167 (**HT**), VPL 168-183 (**AC**)
04.01	VPL 187-194	VPL 184-194 (**AC**)
07.01	VPL 195-201	VPL 195-200 (**PB**)
08.01	VPL 202-204, 206-210, 232-236	VPL 201-204, 206-210, 232-236 (**PB**)
09.01	VPL 205, 211, 216-223, 225, 226, 229-231	VPL 205, 211 (**PB**), VPL 216-223, 225, 226, 229-231 (**EW**)
10.01	VPL 212-217, 222, 224, 227, 228, 230	VPL 213, 215 (**PB**), VPL 214, 222, 224, 227 (**EW**)
10.02	VP 317-320, 322, 325	
11.02	VP 321, 323, 324, 326-347	VP 317-347 (**HT**)
07.03	VP 466-485, 487-494	VP 466-482 (**AC**), VP 483-485, 487-494 (**PR**)
08.03	VP 486	VP 486 (**PR**)
12.03	VP 495-511	VP 495-507 (**HT**)
01.04		VP 508-511 (**HT**)
02.04	VP 512-533	
03.04	VP 534-580	VP 512-580 (**AC**)
07.04	VPL 581-594	
08.04	VPL 595-603, VP 604-610	VPL 581-588, 591-603 (**KX**), VPL 589, 590 (**HT**)
09.04	VP 611, 612, 616, 618-622, 624, 625	VP 604-616, 618-622, 624, 625 (**HD**)
10.04	VP 617, 623, 626-628	VP 617, 623, 626-628 (**HD**)
01.05	VPL 629-637	VPL 629-637 (**HT**)

Acquired from First London, 22.06.13
VW 1560-1570 (LK55 ACU, AAE/F/J/N/U/V/X-Z, ABF)

Disposals
02.08	VPL 212
11.12	VPL 136, 138
01.13	VPL 135, 137, 139, 145, 148, 150, 154, 158, 166
02.13	VPL 146, 159-161
03.13	VPL 140, 142, 152, 153, 156, 164, 167, 170, 172, 174, 176, 179, 182, 190, 194, 202, 204, 206, 209
06.13	VPL 141, 147, 162, 178, 180, 189, 192, 193, 197, 198, 208, 223, 227, 228, 230
08.13	VPL 143, 149, 163, 175, 177, 185, 188, 196, 199, 201, 216, 236
09.13	VPL 157, 168, 169, 187, 211, 215, 219
03.14	VPL 220, 224, 226, 229, 234
06.14	VPL 210, 222
12.14	VPL 218
01.15	VPL 191, 203, 213, 217, 221, 231, 233, 235

Disposals

02.15	VPL 205
05.15	VPL 207
07.15	VPL 184, 214
10.15	VP 473, 498
12.15	VP 467
2016	VPL 186
01.17	VP 484, 487, 488
02.17	VP 470, 472
03.17	VP 475, 476, 481, 482, 493
04.17	VP 468, 477
05.17	VP 326, 330, 338, 343, 344
06.17	VP 317-319, 327-329, 339
07.17	VP 497
08.17	VP 494
09.17	VP 324, 332, 333, 341, 345
10.17	VP 321, 322, 331, 334
12.17	VP 325, 514
01.18	VP 558
02.18	VP 490, 496, 528, 543, 546, 550, 553, 562, 565, 574, 576, 578
03.18	VP 512, 516, 520, 531-533, 537, 566
04.18	VP 337, 495, 521, 530, 547
05.18	VP 606
	VPL 637
06.18	VP 320, 323, 342, 346, 347, 503, 527, 529
07.18	VP 478, 489, 491, 498, 499, 509, 511, 513, 526, 554, 556, 561, 568, 569, 575, 577, 579
08.18	VP 335, 336, 340, 466, 479, 483, 502, 504, 508, 510, 515, 519, 523-525, 538, 542, 555, 557, 559, 560, 563, 567, 580, 605, 610, 611, 619, 626
	VPL 629
09.18	VP 505, 551, 571, 624
	VPL 633, 636
10.18	VP 507, 612, 613, 615-618, 620-623, 625, 627, 628
11.18	VP 469, 474, 485, 500, 506, 517, 518, 522, 529, 541, 572, 573, 607, 609
01.19	VP 501
02.19	VP 471, 540
	VW 1565, 1568
04.19	VW 1560-1564, 1566, 1567, 1569, 1570
10.19	VP 486
	VPL 581, 586, 595, 600, 603
11.19	VP 492, 548, 604, 608
	VPL 632
12.19	VP 536, 545
01.20	VP 534, 549, 549, 564
	VPL 602
02.20	VPL 583, 591, 598
03.20	VPL 586, 587
04.20	VP 614
06.20	VP 535, 552, 570
	VPL 582, 592
07.20	VPL 584, 585, 590, 593, 596, 597, 599, 601, 634
09.20	VPL 588, 594, 631
10.20	VPL 635
02.21	VPL 630

Arriva

VLW and VLA classes

Otherwise wedded to the DAF DB250RS(LF), Arriva in December 2000 became the launch customer for Wrightbus's first double-deck body, the Eclipse Gemini for the Volvo B7TL, ordering the minimum fifty needed to secure production. These were against the contracts for the 121 and 141, renewed on 3 February 2001, plus the 102, which had long awaited DLAs but couldn't field them due to a clearance problem affecting the left turn from the North Circular Road into Brownlow Road, resulting in its intended buses being apportioned instead to other Palmers Green routes and Ms remaining in charge.

As yet unregistered, VLW 2 was displayed at the UITP Congress and Exhibition at Earl's Court between 21-25 May, prior to the delivery of VLWs 1 and 2 at the end of July. These retained their Y-registrations, the rest coming after 1 September and thus gaining new 51-registrations.

This page: **VLW 2 (Y102 TGH)** was displayed at the UITP Congress at Earl's Court and this montage taken on 24 May 2001 shows the advanced and adventurous design cues by comparison with the straight-up, straight-down nature that double-deckers had followed even into the low-floor era.
All: *Author*

Service entry was on 3 September, though on Wood Green's 29 and 221 at this point due to a shortage of vehicles; the pooled nature of Wood Green and Palmers Green meant that blinds were carried for each garage's routes and both codes adorned vehicle sides. Thus were the 141 and 144 visited before the 102, which finally began to field VLWs on the 20th before the six buses in stock by that time clustered on that route as planned two days later. Wanderings to other Palmers Green routes commenced straight away, beginning with the 125 and then spreading to the 121 and 329.

Above: **On 29 September 2001 Palmers Green's VLW 5 (LJ51 DJO) passes through Bounds Green, heralding the new era on the 102, which would last only six years on this route but another decade for Arriva in general.** Author

Left: **The new registration system introduced on 1 September 2001 ruined forever the ability to book registrations to match fleetnumbers, so, to maintain some sense of recognisability, Arriva added the stock number on the front, as seen on VLW 7 (LJ51 DFL) at Turnpike Lane on 2 June 2002. Later deliveries repeated the whole fleetnumber and every other company followed suit.** Author

Arriva — 167

Right: **During 2000 the W3 had already been restocked with short-wheelbase DLAs, but when VLWs started arriving for the 141 at Wood Green, the new Volvos inevitably wandered. Here at Alexandra Palace station on 2 March 2002 is VLW 1 (Y581 UGC), the first of the class and one of just two to retain Y-registrations; further examples booked in the Y-UGC and Y-TGH series were replaced by 51-marks after 1 September 2001.** *Author*

Right: **The 141 was the Wood Green contribution to the introduction of the first VLWs, and in the High Road on 13 July 2002 we see VLW 31 (LJ51 DHL).** *Author*

Right: **On 3 March 2002 VLW 28 (LJ51 DHF) reposes at Turnpike Lane, terminus of the 329. This route had been carved out of the northern end of the 29 in 1992 and remained a straightforward but well-used route ever after.** *Author*

Left: The 29 had retained M operation until the autumn of 2001, when DLPs took over, but VLWs soon appeared and here at Wood Green on 30 November 2002 is VLW 37 (LJ51 DHY), carrying an original all-capitals NN-depth blind in its destination box. *Author*

Below: The 221 had been the original DLA route at Wood Green, kicking off low-floor double-deck operations there, but Arriva's favours had turned to the Volvo B7TL and any subsequent increases, such as one implemented in 2002, had to be accomplished with VLWs. VLW 57 (LF02 PTO), coming into Edgware station on 22 December 2002, was meant to be taking over the 20 but entered service at Wood Green instead and spent its whole career there. *Author*

From VLW 9 upwards, Euro 3 engines were fitted, but deliveries were slow. Even so, the type had proven successful and in December 2001 nineteen more VLWs were ordered, twelve to double-deck the 20 and seven more for Palmers Green and Wood Green.

The original fifty were all in stock by March 2002, covering Palmers Green's 102 and 121 and Wood Green's 141; the W3 was a new venture for the latter, and a little later still, Dart-operated and DWL-intended 184 and 298. More than a few of the new VLWs had side blinds fitted erroneously in the front destination box.

Shortly before their delivery in July 2002, VLWs 51-69 were diverted from the 20 to furnish PVR increases on the existing 102 and 221 to go with their retention on tender; the 141 had already been boosted. At the same time fifteen more VLWs were ordered, and further added to by 32 in August as new tendering announcements threw up future requirements that were also being furnished by resumed DLA orders as well as DLPs.

On 31 August part of the 121 was reallocated from Palmers Green to Enfield, the former keeping hold of its VLWs to provide the PVR increases mentioned earlier.

Of the second batch of Geminis, VLW 69 was earmarked for Leaside Travel and entered service from Edmonton on 30 September, usually on the schoolday double-deck augmentation of the 184. Other than

Above: The end of 2002 saw VLW numbers at Palmers Green and Wood Green increase to 84. Just leaving the latter garage on the morning of 4 August 2003 is VLW 74 (LF52 UTM). Author

the fleetname, there was no difference in specification from the main batch. Then came VLWs 70-84 in November and December, once again for the Wood Green/Palmers Green combine and intended to cascade DLAs to Brixton for the 59. Three more VLW orders followed over the end of the year and into 2003; 25 in November, 38 in January and finally 20 10.6m versions in February. With so much pressure on Wrights and a particularly big tranche of tenders won at that point in the Croydon area, Arriva reached out to Alexanders again and ordered 55 ALX400-bodied Volvo B7TLs to 10.6m length, which would inaugurate a new VLA class.

VLWs 85-96 and 117-129 were built concurrently and formed a new allocation at Tottenham, where the 76 was due to be regained on 1 February 2003; until then, they were run in alongside new DLPs and existing

Right: After five years with First Capital, the 76 came back to Tottenham as an Arriva London North win and new VLWs took over. Here in Tottenham on the first day, 1 February 2003, is VLW 88 (LF52 UPY). Author

Left: **As well as the 76, Tottenham's new VLWs could also be seen on the 243, otherwise converted to DLA operation during mid-2000. VLW 90 (LF52 URA) is just coming up to the Wood Green stand on 20 June 2003.** Author

Below: **Double-deckers on the 20, busier than its semi-rural nature suggests, had been lost on 4 September 1982 with the move away of Loughton's Titans; Eastern National had only used VRs on a proportion of the route and Grey-Green not at all other than a schools diagram. But in March 2003 new VLWs arrived at Barking to replace the 20's ALX200-bodied Dart SLFs, and here at Walthamstow Central on 12 April is VLW 109 (LJ03 MHZ).** Author

VAs (Volvo Citybuses) on the 41, 168 and 243 plus the 73 on Sundays. The VAs and then the DLPs were seen off by the full VLW allocation up to VLW 139, following which the 20 was treated at last with the input into Barking of VLWs 105-116 commencing on 13 March.

Right: **After an earlier proposal to split the already overlapping 253 into two separate routes was cancelled, the tender issued in 2002 formalised this and the resulting contracts commencing on 31 May 2003 introduced new route 254 as the southern section. Allocated to Stamford Hill, VLWs were delivered to replace its Alexander-bodied Ls and on the first day VLW 145 (LJ03 MFF) is seen at Hackney Central.** *Author*

Below: **The last two batches of VLWs were put into Tottenham to free DLAs for use at Norwood. At Camden Town on 18 July 2003, VLW 172 (LJ03 MOV) is working the 168.** *Author*

Stamford Hill was allocated VLWs 140-168 for new route 254, an offshoot of the 253 planned to start on 31 May 2003, but from 30 April they replaced the Ls on its existing route 253 allocation while Clapton was receiving new DLAs to do the same. Stamford Hill's 149 also saw appearances by the new VLWs.

The deployment of the long-wheelbase VLWs was now changed; instead of going to Arriva London South they would concentrate at Tottenham with VLWs 169-179 and cascade DLAs to Norwood. DAF was now attracting Arriva's attention away with the new DW class, fifty of which would complete requirements at Croydon and Beddington Farm, and while VLAs would continue to be ordered, there would be no further VLWs after VLW 199.

Above: **Where the RML's extra length had been distinguishable through its short bay amidships, the 10.6m Wrightbus Gemini body on the Volvo B7TL was the opposite, and VLW 194 (LJ03 MMX), seen in Bruce Grove on 23 February 2004, has all symmetrical windows.** Author

The last eleven short VLWs entered service at Tottenham in July, followed over the next couple of months by the twenty long ones. At the same time, the VLAs started arriving and, after a period of training at Norwood, the first were put into service on the X68 on 18 August. Their main employ was to be on the 2 and 176 as L replacements, and the conversion was treated in that general order. While they tentatively tried out the 417 by the end of 2003, appearances on the still L-operated 249 and 432 were not forthcoming.

In January 2004 Arriva was awarded the 337, currently with London United, and an order was placed for eighteen more VLAs, fourteen of which would work it out of London Coaches' Wandsworth garage. The other four would top up Norwood.

Left: **Arriva was swayed away from the Wrightbus Gemini by the rather cheaper and more basic-looking ALX400, producing the VLA class that also ended up being taken in both available lengths. The first 55 VLAs were for Arriva London South's Norwood to replace Ls from the 2 and 176, and here at Victoria on 22 October 2003 is VLA 24 (LJ53 BFN). Points off for the thin, almost unreadable fleetnumber transfers, and the omission of the livery's customary accompanying yellow stripe over the front bumper.** Author

Right: **The Oyster card was the Holy Grail of fare collection, finally a success after decades of experiments that never quite could be made to work. It still needed plugging as hard as possible so that passengers would get out of the habit of paying cash fares, and to that effect Norwood's VLA 20 (LJ03 MXP) was given this all-over ad in March 2004. It is seen crossing Waterloo Bridge on 31 May.** *Author*

During March, VLA 20, back from accident damage, was the first Arriva B7TL to receive an all-over ad, donning light blue for TfL's Oyster promotion.

On 24 April 2004 the 149 was converted to MA artic, though on the first day Stamford Hill VLWs could be seen while simultaneously transferring their capacity for strange visits to the new 349 introduced on the same day.

The 337's new VLAs fell foul of the administrative problems at TransBus, and bodying fell far behind. While production resumed under the new title of Alexander Dennis, it was decided to assume the 337 on 29 May 2004, its intended takeover date, but with the DWs intended for the one-manning of the 137 on 10 July. This was accomplished on time, with the first VLAs entering service

Right: **The 149 was Arriva's first stab at artic operation, going over on 24 April 2004, but the first day saw a couple of Stamford Hill's VLWs kept on just in case the conversion didn't go smoothly; here at Stamford Hill Broadway VLW 147 (LJ03 MBF) has just been taken out of service so that MA 27 (BX04 MYC) behind it can continue onwards into town. The Citaro artics were all based at Edmonton but shuttles brought their drivers from Stamford Hill.** *Author*

Left: **Closer to line of route than any garage Arriva London South could muster, Wandsworth, then in use by Arriva's London Coaches touring arm, was restored as a bus-operating garage when the 337 was assumed from London General. After a period with DWs, the first thing that arrived on time, the route received its intended fourteen VLAs, as exemplified on 14 August 2014 by VLA 67 (LJ04 YWW), passing Putney station.** *Author*

at Wandsworth on 2 July. Then came the four for Norwood, VLAs 70-73.

As the 137's RMs left service in June their valuable registrations were retained by Arriva and one modern vehicle to be allotted one was Leaside Travel's VLW 69, but someone made a mistake and allocated VLT 25 to VLW 169 instead! This was cleared up in July.

In July the 123 was won from First Capital and an order was placed for thirty VLAs, but to the shorter length this time. Then in September 25 more were ordered to replace Ls from Norwood's 249 and 432, where they had been holding out doggedly.

September saw VLA 20 exchange its Oyster livery for one for Betty Jackson, while VLWs 19 and 52 donned Back the Bid blue

Left: **Leaside Travel's VLW 69 (VLT 25, ex-LF02 USE), was no different from its peers, but coach seats might not have fared well against schoolchildren on the route 184 diagram for which it was intended. On Christmas Eve 2004 at Wood Green it is running strike cover for the northern end of the Piccadilly Line, which manifested as extras to the 29.** *Author*

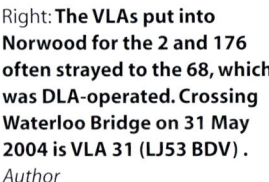

Above: Resplendent in all-over Back the Bid blue at Waterloo's new bus stand on 23 May 2005 is Tottenham's VLW 198 (LJ53 BFE). *Author*

to tout for the 2012 Olympics. This latter became VLA's third livery in October. Then, in November VLWs 198 and 199 and VLA 21 took on Back the Bid colours.

VLAs 74-103 arrived in December and January and their first order of business at Tottenham was to begin displacing VLWs to replace Ls from Barking's 275 in accordance with that retained route's new contract terms. VLWs from the 20 had already visited on and off, as well as wandering to the 103. 15 January 2005, when two more buses were needed for a PVR increase on the 168, was the VLAs' first day in service at Tottenham.

Right: **The VLAs put into Norwood for the 2 and 176 often strayed to the 68, which was DLA-operated. Crossing Waterloo Bridge on 31 May 2004 is VLA 31 (LJ53 BDV).** *Author*

Left: **Short-wheelbase VLAs were chosen for the 123 at Tottenham, and before and after they entered service on that awarded route, they appeared on the 41 and 168. On 25 April 2005 VLA 84 (LJ54 BFO) is coming into the bus station carved out of the wide approach to Waterloo roundabout.** *Author*

Left: **The 41 was also a regular pitch for the 123's intended new VLAs going into Tottenham at the start of 2005. VLA 75 (LJ54 BEO) is seen at Archway on 5 February.** *Author*

Left: **Enough VLWs were released from Tottenham by the new VLAs to convert the 275 at Barking from L operation in accordance with the ongoing directive to remove step-entrance buses by the end of 2005. On 7 May VLW 87 (LF52 UPX) is between Bell Corner and Walthamstow Central.** *Author*

Right: **Tottenham's VLA 77 (LJ54 BFA) is on the route for which it was purchased at Wood Green on 20 March 2005.** Author

Below: **The 19's conversion to OPO was accomplished predominantly with early-arriving VLAs meant for Leyland Olympian replacement at Norwood. On 26 March 2005 at Cambridge Circus VLA 114 (LJ05 BKD) is on attachment to Battersea and is carrying a conductor.** Author

As DWs had filled in for late-arriving VLAs, it was now time for the opposite as it became clear that the DWs on the way wouldn't all be there in time to one-man the 19, especially since its OPO conversion had been brought forward four weeks to 2 April. The VLAs meant to oust Ls at Norwood would be, however. And even before the 19 had been converted to OPO, 10 December 2005 was set as the date when Routemaster operation would finish with the 159, replacing Brixton's mixed RM and RML fleet with an order for 36 new VLAs. These would follow fifteen VLAs for the October takeover of the 128, won in January from East Thames Buses.

The 123 was commenced out of Tottenham on 5 March 2005 and on the 24th the 19 at Battersea began to convert to crew VLA. After a gala finish on 1 April, OPO was executed the following day with a mix of

Left: **Once the 19's intended DWs had arrived, the VLAs temporarily at Battersea could now be sluiced south to eject Norwood's long-established fleet of Ls, which had settled in their last year on second-tier routes 249 and 432. Setting off from the Brixton start of the latter on 21 May 2005 is VLA 127 (LJ05 BJO).** *Author*

VLAs and DWs, plus VLAs plucked from Tottenham's existing allocation, meaning that the 275's conversion from L to VLW couldn't be completed just yet. Norwood helped out by loaning VLAs of its own as well. By May all the DWs were in place and the temporary VLAs headed to Norwood, where they both displaced DLAs to refurbishment and saw off the majority of the Ls; the 249 and 432 were now regular VLA pitches.

The successful conclusion of the Olympics bid meant that the Back the Bid buses' work was done, so they regained their red liveries in July and August. VLA 20 was the first to go into all-over red without the cream front or yellow band.

The new VLAs for the 128, lacking the cream cow horn affectation to the Arriva livery, arrived in August, two months before they were needed, and operated on Barking's

Left: **Like the 432, the 249 was a withered extremity of a much longer route that had been pared back over the years, and as such fielded older buses for a lot longer than its parent. On 21 May 2005 Norwood's VLA 108 (LJ05 BLN) passes the old Streatham garage, which originally operated this incarnation of the 249 when introduced in 1991.** *Author*

Right: **Almost forgotten amid the twin spectacles of the wind-down of the Routemasters and the last examples of step-entrance OPO double-deckers in 2005 was the fact that the last Leyland bus to operate in London did so on the 103. As well as L 319, the Olympian in question, Barking on 8 October had put out VLA 136 (LJ05 GRK), one of the Volvo B7TLs intended for the assumption of the 128 a week later. With these vehicles, the Arriva cow horn was deleted from the livery specification, though the yellow tape skirt band is still there.** Author

20 and 275 before the 128 was assumed on 15 October; the loss of the 103 to Stagecoach East London the same day ensured no further VLW appearances.

VLA 57 was deroofed under Norbiton station's low bridge on 9 October when on a rail replacement; VLA 30 was loaned from Norwood while it was repaired.

October saw the 159's VLAs commence delivery, but they were stored at Brixton Hill overflow depot until the last day of Routemaster operation, 9 December, when they took over from the outgoing RMs and RMLs one-by-one during the morning. These turned out to be the last Volvo B7TLs into Arriva, and indeed the company ignored Volvo's subsequent B9TL entirely, only coming back to the brand when the B5LH hybrid was developed. Brixton's VLAs could soon be seen on the 59, 137 and 319.

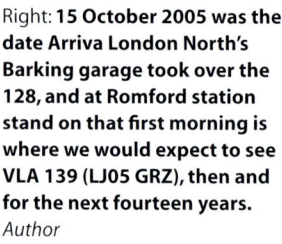

Right: **15 October 2005 was the date Arriva London North's Barking garage took over the 128, and at Romford station stand on that first morning is where we would expect to see VLA 139 (LJ05 GRZ), then and for the next fourteen years.** Author

Left: **The Volvo B7TL was more than adequate and reliable for modern sensibilities, but nobody would seriously prefer the last batch of VLAs over the Routemasters they replaced on 9 December 2005, especially when fitted with the rock-hard and uncomfortably convex Urban 90 seating. At 10:50 VLA 151 (LJ55 BUE) has been taken out of storage at Brixton Hill and would replace RML 2573 on BN141.** *Author*

Leaside Travel was wound up on 14 January 2006, the date of the 29's conversion to artic (thus precluding any further VLWs), and the coaches and four-speed Ls bequeathed their ex-Routemaster registrations to newer buses, seven of which were VLWs. VLW 69, shorn of its own RM mark, moved to Wood Green. In February four further VLWs were re-registered, taking the marks off four outgoing 1961-batch RMLs. The 141 (including an extension from Wood Green to Palmers Green to replace a leg of the 29 abandoned upon conversion to artic) and 329 began new contracts, triggering a refurbishment programme for Palmers Green's earliest VLWs.

On 1 April 2006 Clapton was closed; the move of the 242 and 253 into Stamford Hill now permitted VLW visits from the 254, though that meant the 349 transferred out

Left: **The 1999 incarnation of the 59 followed most of the 59 from Brixton garage towards town before breaking off to reach King's Cross via Waterloo, Aldwych, Holborn and Euston. Operated with its own batch of DLAs, it nonetheless fielded the odd VLA from the 159's allocation, and on 15 July 2006 VLA 146 (LJ55 BTV) is seen circumnavigating the since-deleted one-way system at Brixton.** *Author*

Right: **After carrying Oyster livery, Norwood's VLA 20 (LJ03 MXP) was repainted, losing its cow horns and the usual black accompaniment under the windscreen. The result was unattractively bare and stark, but the remaining individuality, held in the yellow tape band, would also be ordered deleted shortly. On 24 September 2005 it is seen at Aldwych paying a visit to the 68.** *Author*

Right: **Arriva London's two companies had a particular yen for re-registering successive generations of modern buses with ex-RM marks held on to long after their Routemaster hosts had departed. On 15 July 2006 at Golders Green VLW 51 (WLT 751, ex-LF02 PRZ) is seen carrying the registration last on Leyland Olympian L 351.** *Author*

Right: **VLW 27 (VLT 27, ex-LJ51 DHE) was another cusp-of-2005/06 recipient of an RM registration, taking it off Leaside Travel coach DVH 6. As well as that, this Edgware view of 31 August 2006 sees it repainted and without its cow horns. The overpainting of the Wrightbus 'W' indentation where a radiator grille would usually be, plus the black panel between the front upper-deck and lower-deck windscreens, was an aesthetic mistake.** *Author*

Left: **The 159's VLA contingent was also able to turn out on the 137, which had been one-manned on 10 July 2004 with DWs. In the evening rush hour of 16 June 2007, VLA 175 (LJ55 BVG) serves Hyde Park Corner.** Author

to Enfield and lost the chance of VLWs. The 125, on the other hand, was transferred from Enfield back to Palmers Green, restoring the possibility of VLWs. The first refurbishments meted out to early members of the VLW class during the year unfortunately spoiled it by including an all-red repaint that went over the silver- or black-accented pieces.

Tendered during 2006, the 20 was retained in June; fellow Barking route 173 was seeing VLWs and VLAs by this time to bolster its scheduled 10.8m Dart SLFs, though VLW appearances on the 128 were rarer.

The 20 began a new contract on 24 March 2007, but one of the side-effects was its reallocation from Barking to Edmonton and resulting conversion from VLW to DLA operation. That also included school route 657. The DLAs came from Stamford Hill, whose 253 took in VLWs 86-96 in exchange. The 20 wouldn't be the only route to lose VLWs, as the award of the 102's contract was made and the incumbent Arriva would be specifying new Alexander Dennis Enviro400s.

Running as they did in the busiest parts of central and inner London, the VLWs and VLAs suffered more than their fair share of casualties, many of which were repaired by the acclaimed engineering operation at Enfield garage, but VLW 191's accident in Holborn on 27 May 2006 caused two fatalities and thus the bus was impounded by the Metropolitan Police as part of the inquest; they had hold of it for an entire year before it was released for repair.

Left: **Another repaint in 2006, VLW 8 (LJ51 DFN) is demonstrating the layout of the new bus station at Edmonton Green on 27 January 2007. No longer would the 102 have to cross over the flyover, now demolished, to creep round the back, only to get in the way of buses running through to the south.** Author

The fitting of iBus equipment to Arriva buses did not involve the hire of other operators' buses, cover being carried out by an existing pool of twelve spare DLAs. iBus went some way towards restoring the balance of on-bus information removed when blind panels were redesigned to incorporate just two via points.

In advance of the 102's contract renewal a night service was introduced on 1 September 2007, and on 6 October the 128 gained one of its own.

2008 was also quiet. The 102's new Ts (as Arriva classified these new Enviro400s) entered service between late March and April while new route 415, commenced at Norwood on 8 March, immediately used existing VLAs alongside its scheduled DLAs. On 19 April the night service of the 243 was transferred from Tottenham to Wood Green, Tottenham taking the night 242 from Stamford Hill.

24 May saw the introduction of new route 135 with Barking Ts, but its existing VLWs and VLAs saw fit to appear when needed.

Right: **VLW 8 (LJ51 DFN) is seen again, this time at Southgate on 20 May 2007 where it is making a visit to the 125, otherwise operated with short DLPs. The effect of its repaint can be seen by comparison to VLW 74 (LF52 UTM), which is carrying out a Piccadilly Line rail replacement.** *Author*

Right: **Comparatively few Arriva VLWs and VLAs took advantage of the proliferation of all-over advertisements, but far larger numbers were treated to the simpler and less obtrusive rear ads. When sighted at Waterloo on 26 October 2008, Tottenham's VLW 172 (LJ03 MOV) was carrying an advert for Auto Windscreens.** *Author*

Left: **If the 249 and 432 were vestigial enough, no Norwood route was even more so than the 415, introduced on 8 March 2008 to offset the rerouteing of the 333 via Stockwell rather than via the main drag. The opportunity was taken to print a new set of blinds for Norwood that included this route, and unfortunately all but two via points were deleted, making for a look that managed to be both uninformative and unattractive. VLA 120 (LJ05 BKO) sets off from the Elephant on 25 May 2009.** *Author*

From 3 July 2008 Wood Green and Palmers Green were separated in operation once again and their VLW allocations divided accordingly, with 23 based at Palmers Green and 62 at Wood Green. Those displaced from the 102 allowed early DLAs to be converted to trainers and ease out the last Metrobuses used on this work. However, in August it was decided to standardise allocations still further and Palmers Green lost its VLWs in favour of DLPs from Wood Green. On 2 August the 176 was withdrawn between Tottenham Court Road and Oxford Circus, this temporary feature unfortunately becoming permanent and breaking a long-established link.

Snow brought disruption on 2 February 2009, and none of Arriva's artics on the 29, 38, 73 and 149 could operate, leading to VLWs on the 29, 73 and 149 and VLAs on the 73.

Refurbishments had reached VLAs by this year, and one of the main effects of this process was to reduce their downstairs

Left: **Official perception since the withdrawal of Routemasters was that there were now too many routes serving Oxford Street, so the various links into this most vital of thoroughfares were progressively pegged back. The 176 was one such, removing the link to points south and placing pressure on the already congested stand at Tottenham Court Road. On 25 May 2009 Norwood's VLA 36 (LJ53 BBV) demonstrates at St George's Circus.** *Author*

Right: **Since its appearance four pages and four years earlier, VLA 20 (LJ03 MXP) has suffered distinct degradation in its paint quality. Metroline in particular was the worst example of this, where modern paint jobs were otherwise good enough to last a decade if properly cared for. The date is 14 November 2009 and the location is Victoria. The blinds for the 2 now are an aesthetic and information disaster!** *Author*

seating capacity by one by either locking out or removing the tip-up seat attached to the wheelchair backrest.

Tendering of the 2, 76, 221, 253, 254 and 432 over 2008 and 2009 proved successful for Arriva and the Volvo B7TLs thereon, all six being retained. By the end of 2009 the 159, 168, 176 and 243 were up for grabs again.

The conversion of the 38 back to double-deck on 14 November 2009 allowed the operational reopening of Clapton garage, and on that date the 242 was put in from Stamford Hill with VLWs 86-96 plus eighteen 03-reg DLAs, although the intention was to to convert it to DW once the new buses had arrived.

After an uneventful couple of years, the new decade saw the beginning of concerted Volvo B7TL movement now that the initial contracts for their routes had expired, plus the two years' extra for many of them. And there were new routes to cover, one being the 133, taken over by Arriva London South with T operation from Norwood on 23 January 2010 but immediately visited by VLAs. Night route N133 was also operated

Right: **The full effect of red repaints now began to reach VLWs, as shown on 20 July 2010 by Stamford Hill-based VLW 154 (LJ03 MDK) dodging traffic at Finsbury Park.** *Author*

Left: **VLW 97 (WLT 897, ex-LF52 UPL)** wore the registration originally on RML 897 for six years, and on 20 July 2010 is seen about to make the swing into Turnpike Lane on the 41. *Author*

until 28 August. During March Stamford Hill increased its VLW complement on the 253 and 254, not only seeing its existing examples put through refurbishment (which now included a new design of seat moquette) but acquiring the long-wheelbase examples from Tottenham, whose allocation was reduced in favour of transferred DLAs.

Extensive roadworks in Gants Hill between 10 July and 21 August spawned a temporary 599 with Barking double-deckers to fill the gap across that major junction; the 128 had to run via Ley Street for the duration.

On 31 August the 159 was extended from Marble Arch to Paddington Basin over a section vacated by the 15 and a night element with Brixton VLAs replaced the N159. Seven more buses were needed for the extension and these were VLAs 122-128 transferred from Norwood, which received six DLAs.

The 168 had now been awarded to and retained by Arriva London North and on 25 September began its new term, but on this day it was reallocated from Tottenham to Ash Grove, taking with it 22 VLWs. These were replaced by Ts between 26 October and

Left: **On 9 October 2010 VLW 132 (LJ03 MHE)**, with an all-capitals ultimate blind, heads north through Waterloo. Since 25 October it had been an Ash Grove bus, in a transfer steadily restoring buses to that reopened but underutilised garage. *Author*

Right: **Long-wheelbase VLW 188 (LJ03 MKN) out of Stamford Hill, refurbished, repainted and with Arriva's new seat moquette, works a 253 through Hackney Central on 30 April 2011. One of the refurbishment's features was the replacement of the sidelights/turn signal indicators with an LED unit.** *Author*

November and a number moved to Enfield, beginning a new allocation there meant for the 349 as DLA replacements. Appearances followed on the 121, 279, 307, 313, 317 and N279.

Tendering during 2010 had put up the 337, which was lost to London General, and the 123, 144 and W3, which were kept hold of by their incumbent Arriva London North, though with new vehicles for the last two. The 159 and 176 also stayed put but with an element of new buses. VLA-capable Barking school routes 651 and 673 were both lost, as was the 275 when that was tendered.

The 349 at Enfield was completed in January 2011 by VLWs leaving Tottenham after the conversion of the 76 to HV-class Volvo B5LH hybrids; the last VLW operated there on 5 February. VLAs were still present, however, and could now turn out on the 149 following its double-decking. With DLAs similarly ejected from Tottenham, Wood

Right: **As well as the construction of the new bus station, Edmonton Green had undergone considerable change in the first half of the 2000s, with some additional and rather more upmarket new tower blocks erected for buses like VLW 110 (LJ03 MJE) to serve when seen on 28 July 2012. This was now an Enfield motor, put in to upgrade the very vestigial but still broadly useful 349.** *Author*

Left: **5 June 2012 was an absolutely filthy day, without a trace of summer but torrential rain instead; the results are seen within Crystal Palace bus station where Norwood's VLA 55 (LJ53 BBU) has now added the 417 to its list of regular routes. Yet another short stub of a curtailed trunk route, the 417 was re-equipped with VLAs leaving the 337 as well as Norwood's original examples.** *Author*

Green withdrew VLWs 1-6, which were disposed of to Arriva North West.

The loss of the 337 to London General was implemented on 28 May; VLAs 56-69 were refurbished before passing to Norwood to oust the 417's DLAs ahead of its own contract renewal on 20 August.

During the second half of June the 78 at Ash Grove was double-decked with Ts, but the first VLW made its appearance on the 30th. New DWs into Clapton for the 38 had made possible the exit of these Ts, and the rest ousted earlier DWs to Brixton where they standardised the 159 on the type and allowed VLAs 124-128 to return to Norwood and release DLAs from the 432. The 249 would not be seeing them much longer, however, as it was announced as lost to London General.

Below: **Tottenham's VLA 99 (LJ54 BCF), recently repainted, is getting a route 123 journey under way when seen at the eastern end of Ilford on 25 March 2012.** *Author*

As hybrids increased in number, so were artics disappearing; the 149 had already lost them and the 73 was next. To prepare Stamford Hill to receive that major route, the 254 was transferred to Ash Grove on 20 August with VLWs 138-169. When the 73 came in on 3 September, its mix of DWs and HVs had not all made it in time for the changeover date, so those VLWs that had not transferred to Ash Grove with the 254 turned out in support, plus three loaned from Enfield.

A similar change of garage occurred in advance of the 29's restoration to double-deck; to make sure it would fit into Wood Green, the W3 was pushed out to Lea Valley on 15 October, using DLAs until its new Ts arrived. The 29 duly changed types and garages (though not contracts at this stage) on 29 November, Wood Green's existing VLWs supporting its new DWs.

At the end of 2011 the 29 and 141 were out to tender and the 128 had been retained. One new venture for Volvo B7TLs was beckoning

Right: On **On 20 August 2011 Ash Grove added the 254 and its VLWs to its existing complement on the 168. VLW 146 (LJ03 MFK), wearing the AE code which the garage's Arriva operation had appropriated from the historic Hendon, negotiates the one-way system at Aldgate on 4 May 2015; revamping of this junction followed shortly afterwards.** *Author*

Right: **An unhappy seven years of artic operation on the 73 ended with a flourish on 3 September 2011 when new DWs and a handful of VLWs restored this most important of central London trunk routes to double-deck operation. On that first day Stamford Hill's long VLW 182 (LJ03 MLZ) is coming up to the stand at Stoke Newington.** *Author*

Left: **Paddington Basin was a new development which was initially served by an extension of the 15. From 26 June 2009 this leg was transferred to the 159, and on 8 March 2012 Brixton's VLA 149 (LJ55 BTZ) is performing it when sighted about to make the right turn into Whitehall via the recently-restored bus-only lane.** *Author*

Left: **In March 2012 the 144 was converted from VLW to T operation, but the Volvos continued to turn out for as long as they were based at Wood Green, and on 2 June 2013 we see VLW 52 (PSO) in its last full year of service.** *Author*

with the retention by Arriva Southern Counties of the 370 in and out of Romford; former DLAs gravitated to Grays to work this route and under the terms of this next contract they would be replaced by VLAs.

On 3 March 2012 the 123 began a new term with its incumbent Tottenham VLAs but the 275 passed to Stagecoach East London, releasing VLWs to Enfield and Wood Green. On the 10th school route 667, latterly operated by Barking VLAs, passed to First London and on the 31st the 249 passed to London General, freeing more VLAs for transfer to Grays. The same date saw Beddington Farm garage close, a side-effect being the transfer of the 50 (ex-Croydon) and 109 (ex-Thornton Heath) into Brixton, where they could now host VLAs. School routes 647 and 678, won the previous July, were taken up by Barking.

Ts took over Wood Green's 144 during March, allowing twenty of the earliest remaining VLWs to be seconded to Olympics duty. April saw a big win for Arriva with the retention of the 29 and 141, though their VLWs would be replaced by new buses, leaving some for Tottenham's 41, retained at

Above: **A late rally for adverts plastered five VLWs with schemes conceived by two companies wanting to gain maximum exposure for their products during the Olympics. Samsung was one such, and one of their three rolling ad platforms for the Galaxy S phone is Stamford Hill's VLW 173 (VLT 173, ex-LJ03 MPE), seen in Hackney on 15 July 2012.**
Russell Young

the same time. A second place for unwanted VLAs to go was identified as Arriva the Shires' Garston garage, operator of the 142 in one form since 1986 and now about to keep on doing it with another contract. However, no sooner had fourteen gone than three came back on loan, taking their new numbers (6121-6123) to Barking to furnish a temporary boost to the 135.

In June VLWs 170 and 174 gained all-over adverts for Visa, after a long time for the class without such treatment. VLWs 172, 173 and 175 followed in July for Samsung. VLWs 7-20, taken from service earlier to be prepared for Olympics work but gaining Arriva national blue in the process in preparation for onward cascade to Arriva Midlands, fulfilled that duty during the Games from a base at Poyle. 05-reg DWs had also carried out Olympics work, but when this was over they displaced sixteen of the 159's VLAs, which left Brixton for Arriva the Shires' 142 at Garston.

From 2 September the Sunday services on Enfield's 349 and Norwood's 176 were converted from VLW and VLA respectively to T operation, taking advantage of a weekend surplus of the newer buses. Advert VLWs 170 and 172-175 resumed red by October.

A slew of HVs arrived as 2013 got going; those into Wood Green for the 29 caused the DWs to move over to the 141, releasing a dozen VLWs to Enfield to further displace DLAs and DLPs for sale. Then VLWs 21-49 began coming off service during the summer, those re-registered examples bequeathing their Routemaster marks to newer buses or staff cars. There was a boost for many of the rest, however, TfL announcing a programme to convert the VLW and VLA classes (barring the VLWs at Enfield and Wood Green and the VLAs at Barking and Tottenham) to Euro 5 emissions specification, involving the fitting of an AdBlue tank.

On 1 March Lea Valley was closed and Edmonton reactivated, setting into motion a complicated set of transfers where ferry buses to remote locations would become the norm. In Volvo B7TL terms the 123 found itself reallocated from Tottenham to Edmonton, though its drivers remained based at the former, half its VLAs were outstationed back at Tottenham during the week and on Saturdays and Sundays DWs from Tottenham were the staple. The VLAs thus began visiting the 125 and 629, whose DLAs were also now at Edmonton but with

Left: **On 14 July 2013 Wood Green's VLW 43 (LF02 PKU) comes up to Edgware at the end of another long journey on the 221. This bus was withdrawn in January 2014 and sold to Arriva North East in March.** *Author*

ferried Palmers Green drivers! The W3 was put back into Wood Green but took its Ts along, so VLW visits proved rare.

On 29 March 2014 the 159 was withdrawn once again between Marble Arch and Paddington Basin; that leg was not replaced.

Two Arriva London South VLA possibilities tendered at the end of 2013 were the 109 and 415, and both were announced in March as lost to Abellio for implementation at the start of 2015. In May the 125 was awarded to Metroline and August brought more misery with the award of the 432 to London General. By the summer the 168 and 253 had been offered out again, and both ended up being held onto, albeit with the intent to replace their VLWs with new buses. The 135 was still capable of fielding VLAs, but would not be

Left: **The reallocation of the 109 from Thornton Heath to Brixton on 31 March 2012 brought the possibility of VLAs, and on 4 April 2014 VLA 150 (LJ55 BUA) is seen at the route's Croydon stand. However, Abellio took it over on 31 January 2015.** *Author*

Right: **Photographed for posterity before London General fulfilled the award of the 432 and took it over is Norwood's VLA 26 (LJ53 BCZ), passing through Brixton on 20 September 2013.** *Author*

Below: **More often than not, the short VLAs from the 249 and 432 would turn out on the 176, and with the loss of the 432 this became more frequent. In fact, VLA 74 (LJ54 BGO) had made its way from Tottenham to Norwood and on 10 October 2015 is seen at Waterloo.** *Author*

able to following the implementation in 2015 of its September award to Docklands Buses. Later in the year the 349 was tendered, setting the clock ticking on Enfield's remaining VLWs, followed by the 159 once again.

17 May brought the N133 back to Norwood from Croydon and restored its capacity to field VLAs. June saw DWs displaced from Brixton by newer examples moved into Enfield to begin reducing the proportion of VLWs on the 349 (and 307 and 317), and this process continued in ones and twos into the autumn.

It was now the era of the Borismaster, and the conversion of Brixton's 137 from DW to LT between 2-6 December precluded VLA visits other than out of desperation. Another Brixton route lost the chance of VLAs when the 109 shipped out to Abellio on 31 January 2015, the same day as Palmers Green's 125 was lost to Metroline. On 7 March Norwood's 415 passed to Abellio and the 432 left for London General on 4 April. Heavy inroads

Left: **On 2 September 2014 Clapton's VLW 90 (LF52 URA) operates through Threadneedle Street on the 242, but in six more months would be off the books, damaged by fire.** *Author*

were made into the DLA class, while VLWs continued to be edged out of Enfield. VLW 56, shortly after leaving Enfield for Stamford Hill, became a fire casualty on 25 February and was withdrawn. On 11 March VLW 90 was also fire-damaged beyond further use.

Arriva really wasn't having the best of it where tendering was concerned; the 168 was awarded to Metroline in March, the 307 the same way in May and the loss to Abellio of the 159 that same month was nothing short of disastrous, though VLW-capable routes 78 and 349 were both retained, albeit with new buses. The 173 (including school route 673 won from Docklands Buses) was also kept hold of with an eye to converting it to double-deck operation.

On 23 May the 135, which had continued to field VLAs and VLWs alongside its Ts, passed to Docklands Buses. The conversion of the 73 to LT during the month began displacing HVs to the 253, whose new contract began on 6 June. The twenty long-wheelbase VLWs plus seven short ones transferred to Wood Green for the 221, ejecting VLWs 57-79 and 82-85. Not long after their acquisition by

Left: **Showing off its full 10.6m length by just about managing to wrench itself round the U-turn at the top of Turnpike Lane bus station on 31 July 2015 is VLW 194 (LJ03 MMX), transferred to Wood Green to take over the 221 from departing earlier examples. White-on-black blinds to the latest standard (though still with just two via points) have been fitted, even this late in the VLWs' career.** *Author*

Right: **VLWs had been capable of visiting the 78 since its double-decking with Ts, but the end of 2015 saw the route converted to HA and the other types ceased to appear. On 16 December VLW 129 (LG52 DAA), which lasted two years more, stages through Peckham.** *Author*

Right: **Another unusual deployment of VLWs in their final few years was to the 307 at Enfield as wanderings from the 349, and on 27 February 2015 in a much-revamped Enfield town centre, VLW 111 (LJ03 MJF) is heading west. Nonetheless, the route would be lost to Metroline and depart at the end of the year.** *Author*

Right: **After nearly two decades of single-deck operations, the 173, still with the Arriva direct descendant of the Grey-Green firm which converted it thus, was restored to double-deck operation. Ts were the staple but Barking's existing VLAs could be counted on to turn out, as VLA 138 (LJ05 GRX) is doing when seen coming up to the redesigned Beckton bus station on 10 October 2015.** *Author*

Left: Normally when like-for-like replacements are carried out, the substituting vehicles are newer than their predecessors, but with the 123 at the end of 2015 the opposite was the case. A protected right turn had been instituted in Ilford for northbound buses, and on 29 April 2016 Edmonton-allocated VLA 2 (LJ03 MVR) is performing it. *Author*

Travelmasters of Sheerness, VLWs 69 and 70 were seen in London on 6 July when strike replacement duties took them to the 25!

The departure of the 168 to Metroline on 26 September released Ts to Barking to double-deck the 173 and thus legitimise its frequent VLA and VLW appearances. Ash Grove's VLWs, still undergoing repaints, remained on the 254 with visits to the 78, soon to be converted to HA-class E40H MMC Citys.

October saw a rash of tender announcements, bringing Barking the 368 as a double-deck route and retaining Norwood's 417. The 221 was also now out to tender.

12 December saw the 307's departure for Metroline and the end of VLWs at Enfield. VLAs also finished at Brixton with Abellio's takeover of the 159. AdBlue-equipped Norwood VLAs (displaced from the 417 by Ts leaving Tottenham after the 149's conversion to Borismaster released DWs to replace them from the 341) moved over to Edmonton to replace 54-reg examples one for one, making up for in extended length what they lost by being a year and a half older. One of these, VLA 102, spent December on loan to Arriva the Shires, presaging future plans. VLWs 128 and 129 replaced it at Garston in January 2016, having otherwise spent a month on Barking's 647 and 673 after transfer from Ash Grove. VLA 100 and VLWs 130 and 131 joined them in February.

Left: Under Arriva London South the 133 was operated by Ts from Norwood, but VLAs were capable of appearing and did so regularly. On the afternoon of 30 August 2016 VLA 57 (LJ04 LFM) is working south through Monument. *Author*

Arriva — 197

Above: By 2016 the 142 had been operated by the same undertaking for thirty years, whether named London Country, London Country North West, Luton & District, LDT the Shires (Watford Bus) and finally Arriva the Shires. Now it was Garston that joined Arriva London North and the VLAs sent there earlier regained their fleetnumbers. On 11 September 2016 VLA 175 (LJ55 BVG) is setting off from Brent Cross, but the blinds have been installed in the wrong order; the ultimate should be on the bottom! *Author*

Indeed, Arriva group reorganisation from New Year's Day brought the TfL operations of Arriva the Shires and Arriva Kent Thameside under Arriva London control. The former's Garston reintroduced VLAs 109, 122, 123 and 164-179 to the combined fleet, operating the 142 with visits to the 258, 288, 303, 340, H18 and H19, while Grays (itself novated from Arriva Southend stewardship on 11 March 2014) had VLAs 110-121 for the 370 (and visiting the 66). They had previously been numbered in the 6100s to match their VLA stock numbers. Physical renumbering was effected at Garston during April, Grays taking longer but eventually applying the restored VLA transfers during the summer. The O-Licences identifying Grays and Garston as Arriva London North garages were finally cleared in August, the route registrations went over on 29 October and the

Right: Grays was the other extra-London Arriva garage contracted to operate a TfL route, and like Garston, its holding company was brought under Arriva London North stewardship in 2016. The 370 was the route in question, but on 5 June 2016, what was still labelled as 6120 (LJ05 BKO) is seen at Romford on the 66, before resuming its original identity as VLA 120. *Author*

Left: **The 254 found itself converted to Borismaster operation in June 2017 and VLWs 167 (LJ03 MMU) and 170 (LJ03 MOA) were made redundant. Before that, they stand together at Aldgate on 3 March.** Author

long-drawn-out process finally concluded with TfL's formal transfer of the routes on 12 November!

Although another Volvo B7TL possibility opened up on 30 April with the takeup by Barking of the 368 under Arriva London North, many of the VLW- and VLA-operated contracts with two-year extensions on them were now coming to an end, triggering the retendering over 2015/16 of Wood Green's 221 and Ash Grove's 254 plus VLA-capable 133 at Norwood. In April Norwood's 2, which along with the 176, was a major bastion of VLAs, was tendered, though DWs were now appearing as the 417's intended charges so that the Ts could be transferred elsewhere. In practice the 417 remained VLA and the DWs turned out on the 2 in strength. June and July then saw the 133, 221 and 242 announced as retained, which set the clock ticking on Wood

Left: **The running down of VLW operation at Wood Green over the second half of 2017 saw the end of the last two with Routemaster marks. On 26 May 2016 VLW 173 (VLT 173, ex-LJ03 MPE) crosses Spouter's Corner on the only route still scheduled for VLWs by then; it was re-registered back to its original mark in August 2017 and disposed of in September.** Author

Above: **Resplendent in the winter sun shining over Wood Green on 13 February 2017 is Edmonton's VLA 10 (LJ03 MYA), in what would be its last full year in service.** *Author*

Green's remaining and Clapton's only VLWs respectively.

In April VLAs 99 and 100 were set aside for conversion to VantagePower hybrid propulsion as a trial to see whether retrofitting to this Euro 5 standard would be cheaper than the cost of new buses. Further withdrawn VLAs from Brixton's batch were reactivated during May for rail replacement work over the London Overground.

20 July saw the 647 operate for the last time. At this point Garston's 340 removed itself from consideration for VLAs or VLWs with its conversion to SW-class Wrightbus Streetdecks. Edmonton had never used VLWs until VLW 189 was loaned from Wood Green on 22 July and put out on the 123.

August saw the 2 announced as retained with new buses to replace its VLAs, and then the 176 was tendered in the autumn. While at Norwood, enough refurbished DWs had now gathered to effect the formal conversion of the 417 from T and VLA on 9 September. VLA 123, reclaimed from Garston to become Norwood's dedicated bus for school route 690 this year, had e-leather seating fitted for the purpose. That made up somewhat for the concurrent award of Barking's 678 to Stagecoach East London and Wood Green's 617 to Sullivan Buses.

On 15 October operation of the 123 was standardised under Tottenham and VLAs 1-16 and 101-106 moved in from Edmonton. 5 November saw the 221 begin its new contract, while the 254 was announced as retained with LTs. At the end of the year the 142, 176 and 370 were out, plus VLA-capable 66. The one-bus 375 at Grays was seeing increasing VLA and DW operation due to the transfer away of appropriate single-decks.

2017 began with the 133 and N133's removal from VLA consideration when they moved to Brixton with HVs and HAs. In February Grays's 66 and 370 were announced as retained with the promise of DWs on the latter, and on the 20th of that month Clapton started replacing the 242's VLWs with new HVs in line with the contract beginning on 25 February. Norwood's 2 followed suit on 9 March, again in advance of that route's own contract on 1 April, and the announcement in March that the 176 had been lost to London Central suddenly put the VLA and VLW classes under serious threat. At least the two years added to the 123's current term from 4 March theoretically bought time for that route's VLAs. The Overground-replacement VLAs, latterly moved from Brixton to Barking, were sold in March and the 617 and 678 passed to their new operators on 1 April.

Left: Somehow, by 6 November 2016, Clapton's VLW 94 (LF52 UPH) in New Oxford Street has managed to keep hold of an original route 242 blind with plenty of intermediate information. HVs took over the following February. *Author*

One last adventure remained for the 128's VLAs, as the route was included in a scheme to brand a proportion of buses passing through Barkingside. Each route had a colour, carried in a row of diagonal slashes across each nearside roof dome, and that applied to VLAs 132-143 was purple.

During May the 221's VLWs began departing, their place taken over the next few weeks by DWs leaving store at Norwood. Penny numbers, however, held out for six more months and set a precedent that similar garage stragglers would follow in the wind-down of Arriva Volvo B7TL operation. May

Below: Purple flashes adorn Barking's VLA 142 (LJ55 BTE) in accordance with the standards of the Barkingside-area route branding scheme introduced in 2017. It is captured in Gants Hill on 24 September of that year. *Author*

also saw DWs gravitate to Grays to ease out the 370's VLAs.

The timer was set on Garston's Volvo B7TLs in June with the award of the 142, 258 and 642 to Sovereign for January 2018 implementation, and on the 3rd of the same month the 254 began a new term, with LTs coming to Ash Grove to replace its VLWs by 14 July. Seven of those VLWs headed to Garston to replace DWs from the 258, while Clapton's VLW 155 ran for the last time on 29 July, having lasted long enough to witness the 242's unfortunate withdrawal between St Paul's and Tottenham Court Road on 17 June.

Vantage Power VLA 99 entered service on the 123 on 17 July, but its service (and that of partner VLA 100) proved almost laughably brief, in concert with the unhappy revival of two London General VLWs and two Sovereign VLPs at the same time.

Notting Hill Carnival express route 2X had been been a Norwood perennial for some years, but 2017, specifically Sunday 27 August, was to be its last year with VLAs.

VLWs 92 and 173 were the last to carry ex-Routemaster registrations, but turned them in during August in preparation for sale. VLWs and VLAs flooded out of the company in large numbers that month as Arriva cut a deal with BASE Coach Sales to shift them. Twenty-seven more VLWs departed in September.

Grays' last five VLAs operated on 29 September, replaced by DWs. The following day saw Garston's 258 taken over by Sovereign and nine VLWs withdrawn, but at Barking on 14 October two years were added to the 128's contract, effectively prolonging its VLAs' lifespan well into 2019. On 14 October Grays reactivated three VLAs so that the 370's DWs could join additional numbers brought in to take over the 103 and 175.

Right: **On 25 May 2017 in Hackney Ash Grove's VLW 167 (LJ03 MMU) ushers out the Volvo B7TL era on this corridor; Borismasters would be the fare from shortly after.** *Author*

Right: **11 November 2017 saw the end of VLAs at Norwood when the 176 passed to London Central. Prior to that, VLA 73 (LJ04 YWE) with white-on-black blinds serves the reconstructed Elephant & Castle roadway on 9 March.** *Author*

Left: **VLA 115 (LJ05 BKF) found itself the last representative of its type at Grays and on 2 December 2017 is seen laying over at the 370's Lakeside stand, otherwise host to Ensignbus's running day that year.** Author

VLW 181 was Wood Green's last there, running on the 144 on 10 November. The 176's takeover by London Central the following day stripped Norwood of all but three VLAs, of which VLA 53 fell out within a fortnight, but VLAs 56 and 57 continued gamely on the 690 during school hours. Grays was now down to just VLA 115 and there were only four VLWs left, all based at Garston.

Even with the two Vantage Power VLAs in service, Arriva was intent on replacing the 123's ageing VLAs with anything it could muster; in October Tottenham collected six DWs to do half the job, while Arriva went so far as to take a type it had never operated in the form of ten B9TLs returned off lease by Tower Transit, which did not suspect that they would be immediately scooped up and returned to service by competitors. Thus bowed a second VLW class and the ten 61-reg examples, which didn't even need a repaint, ejected the remaining VLAs from Tottenham beginning on 2 January 2018. VLA 100 hadn't even made it into the New Year. Even so, a

Left: **A handful of VLWs were put into Garston for its last year as an Arriva London North garage, to add a little variety as well as expelling DWs. Here in Wealdstone High Street on 20 September 2017 is VLW 131 (LJ03 MHA), though the 258 would pass to Sovereign before the end.** Author

Right: **On 8 September 2016, Garston's VLA 167 (LJ55 BVV) has served Edgware bus station and is heading south towards the 142's Brent Cross terminus. The route was up for tender and would find itself lost to Sovereign.** *Author*

late change put the 123 back into Edmonton and VLAs 1, 2, 6, 8, 15 and 101-103 lasted long enough to go with it.

On 6 January the 142 and associated school route 642 left Garston for Sovereign, and in theory that should have finished off the VLW and VLA classes there. As it turned out, there was to be a protracted goodbye for the garage, all of whose remaining routes were lost to Sovereign when their awards were announced. All of the 55-reg VLAs were withdrawn, while the simultaneous exit of VLWs 138, 144 and 149 left just VLW 95 as the last of its class in service. Aided by the small cohort of surviving VLAs plus one of each length added from Edmonton as an end was finally put to the 123's B7TL fleet, this last Gemini would dig in its heels and continue on alone, month after month, working on the 288, 303, 305 and H18/H19, plus the 340

Right: **The 303 had originated as a minibus route and had graduated to Dart-sized buses, but under Garston's stewardship its DWL-class DAF SB120s were frequently supported by double-deckers. On 8 June 2018 VLA 116 (LJ05 BKG) is seen coming out of Edgware bus station.** *Author*

before its transfer to Palmers Green on 9 June. VLA 115 was the equivalent at Grays, lasting there until 25 April, while retro-hybrid VLA 99 transferred from Tottenham to Barking, spending until 22 April on the 128.

By April Garston was slowly amassing stray VLAs unwanted elsewhere, even in the knowledge that 31 August would be its last day. VLAs 8 and 122 came off in the first week of June, but the fleet of two long ones (VLAs 2 and 15) and two short (VLAs 103 and 116) held out until the last day, on which VLAs 15 and 103 and VLW 95 (as GR256) operated the 303, VLA 116 as GR245 seeing out the 288 and VLA 2 bringing the Garston era to a close on the H18 at eleven o'clock sharp. Even then

Above: 31 August 2018 was the last day of Garston operations, the garage site proving more valuable than the operations therein, which had all been lost on tender anyway. VLA 116 (LJ05 BKG) spent the day on the 288, another single-deck route perfectly capable of fielding double-deckers, and is seen at the bottom of Edgwarebury Lane, never having got around to having its Grays codes removed from its time on the 370. *Author*

Left: And then there was VLW 95 (LF52 UPJ, ex-WLT 895, ex-LF52 UPJ), the last of what was once a class of 199 buses. Having worked alone for several months, on 31 August 2018 it worked GR256 on the 303 and at ten to five is seen leaving Edgware bus station, with a little less than three hours to go. *Author*

Right: The last two 10.6m VLAs found themselves given a new lease of life when transferred from their cushy gig on Norwood school work back into the daily maelstrom at Barking. On 5 April 2019 VLA 56 (LJ04 LFL) negotiates the 173's double-run at Chadwell Heath. *Author*

VLA 116 escaped and six days later was back in service at Barking, where it joined VLAs 126-143 as the last representatives of the class on an everyday route. After working the 690 on 18 September, VLAs 56 and 57 were added from Norwood and all nineteen continued into 2019. With the 128 tendered since the summer of 2018 and announced on 13 February 2019 as lost to Stagecoach East London for 12 October implementation, the clock started ticking for the Volvo B7TL in Arriva London service. VLA 56 last worked

Right: The 128 ended up as Arriva's last Volvo B7TL route, and on 1 March 2019 it is seen in the hands of Barking's VLA 135 (LJ05 GRF), coming through Ilford. However, on 12 October 2019 it was transferred on tender to Stagecoach East London, who were due even a small victory after some years of ignominious defeat in the London tendering game. *Author*

on 8 April, but VLA 57 was revived just as withdrawals started to hit the 2005-vintage batch. 11 October duly saw the last day of the 128 with Barking, VLA 139 being the last in, but the following day dawned with VLAs on the 150, 173 and 368! After a few days, these survivors comprised the unbranded examples, and of these, VLAs 128, 130 and 131 were still running in November, plus VLA 57. VLA 128 last worked on 3 December, which left three to make it into the new decade, splitting their time between

Above: **The 129's little stand at Claybury Broadway, just a hundred yards from the choke point into the Eastern Avenue where through buses might have proved a better option than just terminating more or less in the middle of nowhere, was taken over by the 128 in 2004 and on Arriva's last day on this route, 11 October 2019, was occupied by VLAs 132 (LJ05 GPX) and 142 (LJ55 BTE). Both these branded buses were withdrawn and sold soon after.** *Author*

Left: **VLA 131 (LJ05 GMF) was one of just three survivors of the loss of the 128, continuing beyond the end of 2019 on the 173 and 368. On 2 February 2020 it is seen coming up to Becontree Heath. Two buses behind it was VLA 130, pictured overleaf.** *Author*

Arriva — 207

Above: **On 2 February 2020 Barking's VLA 130 (LJ05 GME) rests at the King George Hospital terminus of the 173, as one of two VLAs on the route that Sunday.** Author

the 150, 173 and 368. Even the onset of the coronavirus pandemic, which locked society down altogether from the second half of March 2020, didn't initially deter VLAs 57 and 131 from lingering into April, though VLA 130 last operated on 20 March.

In the end, however, it was the older vehicles among London bus fleets that found themselves mothballed or put on SORN, and pollution conditions were the better for it. VLA 131 worked a full day on the 173 on Tuesday 21 April, leaving just VLA 57, the oldest one and most unlikely survivor of the 179-strong class. It spent Friday 24 April on the 173, coming off for the last time at 20:54 hours.

Right: **The three VLA survivors dug in their heels at Barking and refused to budge until their last possible mainstream service, the 173, was taken away from them by the vicissitudes of tendering, or, as it turned out, being unexpectedly struck down by disease. They turned out to be some of the last London buses with both traditional blind boxes and inward-opening exit doors, and as the coronavirus lockdown drove away their custom, were stood down just after their Go-Ahead WVL counterparts. After it was all over, they are pictured in Barking garage as disposal stock on 6 May; the full line-up is VLA 128 (LJ05 BJU), VLA 131 (LJ05 GMF), VLA 57 (LJ04 LFM), VLA 130 (LJ05 GME), VLA 116 (LJ05 BKG) and VLA 56 (LJ04 LFL).** Mark McWalter

208 – Volvo B7TL

Registrations

VLW 1, 2	Y581 UGC, Y102 TGH
VLW 3-40	LJ51 DJF/K/O, DFK/L/N-P/U/V/X-Z, DGE/F/O/U/V/X-Z, DHA/C-G/K/L/N/O/P/V/X-Z, DJD/E
VLW 41-66	LF02 PKO/U/V/X-Z, PLJ/N/O, PRZ, PSO/U/X-Z, PTO/U/X/Z, PVE/J/K/L/N/O
VLW 67-104	LF52 UTC/E, USE, UTG/H/J/L/M, USM-O/S-Y, UPV-Z, URA, UPD/E/G/H/J-M, LG52 DDA/E/F/J-L
VLW 105-116	LJ03 MHU/V/X-Z, MJE/F/K/U/V, MGX, MGY
VLW 117-129	LF52 UPN/O, UOS-Y, UPA-C, LG52 DAA
VLW 130-199	LJ03 MGZ, MHA/E/F/K-N, MFN/P/U/V, MEV, MFA/E/F/K, MBF/U/V/X/Y, MDE/F/K/N/U, MPX-Z, MRU/V/X/Y, MSU/V/X, MMU/V/X, MOA/F/V, MPE/F/V, MLL/N/V/X-Z, MMA/E/F/K, MKM/N, MYN, MXR-U, MWX, LJ53 BEU/Y, BFA/E/F
VLA 1-55	LJ03 MYP/R-T, MXV-Z, MYA-D/F/H/K/L-N/P, LJ53 BFK-O, BCZ, BDE/F/O/U/V/X-Z, BEO, BBV/X/Z, BCF/K/O/U/V/X/Y, BAA/O/U/V, BBE/F/K/N/O/U
VLA 56-73	LJ04 LFL-N/P/R-T, YWS-Z, YXA/B, YWE
VLA 74-103	LJ54 BGO, BEO/U, BFA/E/F/K-O, BCY/Z, BDE/F/O/U/V/X-Z, BBV/X/Z, BCE/F/K/O/U/V
VLA 104-128	LJ05 BKY/Z, BLF/K/N/V/X/Y, BMO/U, BKD/F/G/K/L/N/O/U/V/X, BJE/F/K/O/U
VLA 129-141	LJ05 GLZ, GME/F, GPX-Z, GRF/K/U/X/Z, GSO/U
VLA 142-179	LJ55 BTE/F/O/U/V/X-Z, BUA/E, BPZ, BRV/X/Z, BSO/U/V/X-Z, BVP/R-Z/D-H/K-M

Date	Deliveries	Licensed for Service
07.01	VLW 1, 2	
08.01	VLW 3, 4	
09.01	VLW 5-9, 11	VLW 1-9, 11 (**WN**)
10.01	VLW 10, 12, 14-17	VLW 10, 12, 14-17 (**WN**)
11.01	VLW 13, 18-22	VLW 18, 19 (**WN**)
12.01	VLW 23-29, 31	VLW 13, 20-28 (**WN**)
01.02	VLW 30, 32-34	VLW 29-34 (**WN**)
02.02	VLW 35-41	VLW 35-41 (**WN**)
03.02	VLW 42-50	VLW 42-50 (**WN**)
07.02	VLW 51-60	VLW 51-60 (**WN**)
08.02	VLW 61-68	VLW 61-66 (**WN**)
09.02	VLW 69	VLW 67, 68 (**WN**), VLW 69 (**EC**)
11.02	VLW 70-75	VLW 71-75 (**WN**)
12.02	VLW 76-84, 117-119	VLW 70, 76-82 (**WN**)
01.03	VLW 85-94, 120-123	VLW 83, 84 (**WN**), VLW 85-94, 117-123 (**AR**)
02.03	VLW 95-100, 102-104, 124-128	VLW 95-100, 102-104, 124-128 (**AR**)
03.03	VLW 101, 105-116, 129-135	VLW 101, 129-135 (**AR**), VLW 105-116 (**DX**)
04.03	VLW 136-140, 143-148, 151, 152, 156, 159	VLW 136-139 (**AR**), VLW 136-140, 143-148, 151, 152, 156, 159 (**SF**)
05.03	VLW 141, 142, 149, 150, 153-155, 157, 158, 160-170	VLW 141, 142, 149, 150, 153-155, 157, 158, 160-168 (**SF**), VLW 169, 170 (**AR**)
06.03	VLW 171-179	VLW 171-179 (**AR**)
07.03	VLA 1-4	
08.03	VLA 5-20 VLW 180-189	VLA 1-20 (**N**) VLW 180-189 (**AR**)
09.03	VLA 21, 23-29, 31-50, 52, 53 VLW 190-199	VLA 21, 23-29, 31-50, 52, 53 (**N**) VLW 190-199 (**AR**)
10.03	VLA 22, 51, 54	VLA 22, 51, 54 (**N**)
11.03	VLA 55	VLA 55 (**N**)
06.04	VLA 56-68, 70, 72	VLA 56-68 (**WD**)
07.04	VLA 69, 73	VLA 69 (**WD**), VLA 70-73 (**N**)
12.04	VLA 74-78, 82, 83	

Date	Deliveries	Licensed for Service
01.05	VLA 79-81, 84-93, 95-97	VLA 74-86 (**AR**)
02.05	VLA 94, 98-103	VLA 87, 89-103 (**AR**)
03.05	VLA 104-114, 119, 120, 122, 124	VLA 104-114, 119, 120, 122, 124 (**BA**)
04.05	VLA 115-118, 121, 123, 125-128	VLA 88, 115-118, 121, 123, 125-128 (**BA**)
08.05	VLA 129-138	VLA 129-138 (**DX**)
09.05	VLA 139-143	VLA 139-141 (**DX**), VLA 142, 143 (**AR**)
10.05	VLA 144-148	
11.05	VLA 149-169	
12.05	VLA 170-179	VLA 144-179 (**BN**)

Re-registrations
06.04   VLW 169 from LJ03 MMX to VLT 25
07.04   VLW 169 from VLT 25 to LJ03 MMX
07.04   VLW 69 from LF02 USE to VLT 25
10.05   VLW 32 from LJ51 DHN to VLT 32
12.05   VLW 12 from LJ51 DFV to VLT 12
12.05   VLW 27 from LJ51 DHE to VLT 27
12.05   VLW 47 from LF02 PKZ to VLT 47
01.06   VLW 51 from LF02 PRZ to WLT 751
01.06   VLW 54 from LF02 PSX to WLT 554
01.06   VLW 69 from VLT 25 to LF52 USE
01.06   VLW 72 from LF52 UTJ to WLT 372
01.06   VLW 173 from LJ03 MPE to VLT 173
02.06   VLW 88 from LF52 UPY to WLT 888
02.06   VLW 92 from LF52 UPE to WLT 892
02.06   VLW 95 from LF52 UPJ to WLT 895
02.06   VLW 97 from LF52 UPL to WLT 897
06.11   VLW 12 from VLT 12 to LJ51 DFV
10.11   VLW 27 from VLT 27 to LJ51 DHE
02.12   VLW 95 from WLT 895 to LF52 UPJ
05.12   VLW 97 from WLT 897 to LF52 UPL
09.12   VLW 47 from VLT 47 to LF02 PKZ
06.13   VLW 32 from VLT 32 to LJ51 DHN
09.13   VLW 51 from WLT 751 to LF02 PRZ
08.14   VLW 88 from WLT 888 to LF52 UPY
06.15   VLW 54 from WLT 554 to LF02 PSX
06.15   VLW 72 from WLT 372 to LF52 UTJ
08.17   VLW 92 from WLT 892 to LF52 UPE
08.17   VLW 173 from VLT 173 to LJ03 MPE

Loaned from Arriva Southern Counties, 06.12-09.12
6121-6123 (LJ05 BKU/V/X)

Acquired from Arriva Southern Counties, 01.01.16
From Arriva the Shires: VLA 109, 122, 123, 164-179, VLW 128, 129
From Arriva Kent Thameside: VLA 110-121

Disposals
02.11   VLW 1-6
04.12   VLA 110-122
06.12   VLA 123
07.12   VLA 109
08.12   VLW 7-20
10.12   VLA 164-179
08.13   VLW 25, 27, 29-33
01.14   VLW 28, 46
02.14   VLW 22, 24, 26, 35-37, 40, 42, 47
03.14   VLW 21, 23, 34, 38, 39, 41, 43, 45, 48, 51

Disposals

04.14	VLW 44
07.14	VLW 52
08.14	VLW 49, 50, 106
10.14	VLW 107, 110, 112
12.14	VLW 53
06.15	VLW 54, 55, 57-79, 82-85, 90, 97, 98
08.15	VLW 99, 100
09.15	VLW 102, 103, 123
10.15	VLW 56, 101, 104, 108, 114-116, 119, 120
11.15	VLW 105, 111, 118, 124, 125
12.15	VLA 78, 83, 85, 86, 88, 90, 91, 93, 97, 98
	VLW 109, 113, 121, 122
01.16	VLA 80-82, 84, 87, 89, 92, 94, 144-155
	VLW 117
	Re-acquired: VLA 109-123, 164-179
02.16	VLA 95
04.16	VLA 79
03.17	VLA 50, 96, 156-163
04.17	VLA 20, 33
05.17	VLA 17, 22-24, 26, 27, 29, 34-36, 38, 107
06.17	VLA 18, 19, 31, 32, 108, 130, 139, 185
07.17	VLA 28, 37
	VLW 80, 87, 94, 126, 174-177, 179, 180, 182, 184, 186-198
08.17	VLA 39-42, 106, 114, 117, 120, 124, 125
	VLW 91-93
09.17	VLW 132-137, 140-143, 145, 148, 150, 152-155, 157-162, 165, 167, 169, 172, 173, 178
10.17	VLA 12, 72
	VLW 81, 86, 88, 89, 96, 127-129, 131, 147, 151, 156, 163, 164, 166, 170, 171
11.17	VLA 3-5, 9, 11, 14, 46, 49, 53-55, 73, 74, 76, 77, 104, 105, 109
	VLW 178, 181, 183, 199
12.17	VLA 47, 48, 51, 52, 70, 71, 75
01.18	VLA 16, 21, 25, 30
02.18	VLA 7, 10, 13, 43 45
	VLW 138, 144, 149
06.18	VLA 1, 6, 101, 102
07.18	VLA 8, 122
09.18	VLA 15
	VLW 95
10.18	VLA 2
12.18	VLA 103
06.19	VLA 68
07.19	VLA 59, 61, 63, 66, 69, 110, 119
08.19	VLA 62
09.19	VLA 136
10.19	VLA 129, 132-135, 137-140
11.19	VLA 141-143
02.20	VLA 127
03.20	VLA 126
05.20	VLA 56, 57, 128, 130
08.20	VLA 131
10.20	VLA 116
02.21	VLA 58, 60, 65, 111-113, 115, 118, 121, 164, 165, 167, 169, 175, 177
03.21	VLA 123, 170, 176, 179

Arriva the Shires and Arriva Southend

6109-6123, 6164-6179

Arriva Southend, part of the Arriva Southern Counties subset of the group, received thirteen former Arriva London South ALX400-bodied Volvo B7TLs on 26 April 2012 with the intent to put them onto TfL route 370 in replacement of Dennis Dart SLFs. VLAs 110-122 were renumbered 6110-6122 and began undergoing refurbishment prior to allocation to Grays. 6123 followed in June, only to be loaned back to Arriva London North with 6121 and 6122. Otherwise the first was seen on 9 July. That same month Arriva the Shires received VLA 109, renumbered it 6109 and put it into service on the 142 from Garston. This route had been renewed and required newer buses than its DLA-lookalike DAFs.

The 370's 'VLAs' were all in service by September, when they were joined by the three loaned to Barking, but on the 21st 6123 headed onward to Garston to join a band of other VLAs released from Olympics work. These were 6164-6179, ex-VLA 164-179, and were also refurbished by H&D Trim before re-entering service. While at Garston they visited the 340 and 642 plus single-deck 288, 303, 305, H18 and H19. 6123 was formally taken into stock there in October. Those at Grays, meanwhile, visited the 66.

Reorganisation within Arriva deleted Arriva Southend at the end of 2013 and brought its operations (including Grays and the 370) under Arriva Kent Thameside within Arriva Southern Counties.

Right: **On 31 October 2015 Grays' 6115 (LJ05 BKF) has just served Upminster station on its way to Hornchurch.** *Author*

Left: 30 November 2013 sees Garston's 6173 (LJ55 BVE) setting off from Brent Cross. As VLA 173 it served six and a half years at Brixton, and it would become VLA 173 again in 2016 when Garston's TfL operations were put under Arriva London North. *Author*

On 27 May 2014 Garston's 6123 suffered fire damage that kept it off the road for a year. Then on 27 June Grays' 6118 was incapacitated in an accident and to cover it, VLW 52 was hired from Arriva London between 10 July and 27 August. Other VLWs had been acquired for non-TfL operations but this one, despite gaining the number 6136, retained red livery and both doors.

6122 was transferred from Grays to Garston in October 2014. On 12 March 2015 6119 turned out on the 499, of all things, and 6114 followed it two days later. When 6123 came back from repair on 26 September it had been fitted with leather seats.

Further Arriva rationalisation involved moving the TfL operations of Grays and Garston to London control. In December VLA 102 came on loan from there and joined the 142's contingent at Garston. The transfer took effect on New Year's Day 2016 but the issue of the appropriate licences took seven more months, during which the VLAs' original fleetnumbers were restored.

Arriva Southend (Arriva Kent Thameside from 12.13)

Acquired from Arriva London South
04.12   **6110-6122** (LJ05 BLX/Y, BMO/U, BKD/F/G/K/L/N/O/U)
10.12   **6123** (LJ05 BKX)

Hired from Arriva London North, 07.14-08.14
6136 (LF02 PSO)

Arriva the Shires

Acquired from Arriva London South, 07.12
07.12   **6109** (LJ05 BLV)
10.12   **6164-6179** (LJ55 BVS-Z/D-H/K-M)

Acquired from Arriva Southend
09.12   **6123** (LJ05 BKX)

Hired from Arriva London North, 12.15
VLA 102 (LJ54 BCU)

Both Arriva the Shires and Arriva Kent Thameside regrouped under Arriva London, 2016

London Easylink

VP and VPL classes

May 2000 brought a surprise tendering victory for Durham Travel Services, a National Express contractor with roots in United Automobile Services. This was the 185, then operated by Stagecoach Selkent with Catford Titans. With the aim of establishing a 70-vehicle London bus operation within two years, a site was taken at the Transco premises off the Old Kent Road and twenty Plaxton President-bodied Volvo B7TLs were ordered. The trading name would be London Easylink, adapting a moniker used briefly in York.

On 6 September Volvo B7TL demonstrator X157 JOP was borrowed to run out along the 185; this bus would later be more closely associated with the route. The intended fleet arrived at Volvo's Beddington premises during December, spanning multiple gaps in the registration block booked for them and thus omitting those matching fleetnumbers.

However, when the time came to take up the 185's contract on 20 January 2001, it was realised that the application for an Operators' Licence had not gone through, having been lost in the post during a series of postal disputes over Christmas, and LBSL had to issue three short-term contracts to Stagecoach Selkent, Blue Triangle and London General, which would apply until the paperwork was cleared with the Traffic Commissioner. London Easylink drivers drove the Selkent Titans (the same ones made redundant from the 185) and London General Metrobuses, though Blue Triangle manned its own Metrobuses and Trident. The replacement O-Licence needed three weeks to clear, but once it did, VP 149 was the first into service on 12 February, followed that afternoon and the next day by the rest.

Things settled down thereafter; in January 2002 X157 JOP was taken into stock, repainted

Right: **In full London Easylink livery complete with two side fleetnames, route branding and a diagonal bank of company logos stamped up each side like footprints, VP 173 (X173 FBB), the last of twenty Plaxton President-bodied Volvo B7TLs delivered to this new company, stands at Lewisham on 17 March 2002.**
Author

and christened VPL 174 to reflect its 10.6m chassis. The 19th of that month saw the 42 commenced on behalf of Connex Bus, with VPs quickly in evidence alongside the hired Dart SLFs that were standing in until the delivery of new Scania OmniCitys. 20 April saw the formal takeup of the route.

Unfortunately, disaster struck, all of it of the MD's own making. When it became clear quite how much was being haemorrhaged out of the company and to whom, the accountants struck back. On the afternoon of 21 August 2002 drivers were ordered to take their buses back to base and leave them there; the Volvo B7TLs were locked up pending repossession by KPMG, the official receivers.

As it turned out, the VPs would gravitate back to the 185 under East Thames Buses, under whose account their story continues; and they were to live out a full lifespan (in the modern interpretation of that term) under a third operator, London Central.

Above: **On 20 April 2002, one day after the assumption of the 42, VP 173 (X173 FBB) is seen at Aldgate, and by now it has a new numberplate with the narrower, 51mm-width characters which sit so uneasily on registrations of the original system.** Author

Left: **VPL 174 (X157 JOP) climbs out of Lewisham bus station on 13 July 2002, showing off its Lothian-spec blinds albeit out of service. The diagonal logo stamps were never applied to this bus and the company collapsed anyway shortly after.** Author

Registrations
VP 149, 151-154, 157-159, 161-169, 171-173

X149, 151-154, 157-159, 161-169, 171-173 FBB

Date Deliveries
01.01   VP 149, 151-154, 157-159, 161-169, 171-173

Licensed for Service
VP 149, 151-154, 157-159, 161-169, 171-173 (**DR**)

Acquired from dealer stock, 01.02
VPL 174 (X157 JOP)

Repossessed upon company's collapse, 21.08.02
08.02   VP 149, 151-154, 157-159, 161-169, 171-173, VPL 174

London Easylink — 215

East Thames Buses

VWL and VP classes

The former Harris Bus had settled down following its purchase in 2000 by TfL, but the ongoing imperative towards all low-floor operations prompted the outlay of money upon the appropriate number of new buses to replace the existing Volvo Olympians and DAF DB250s on the 128, 129 and 180. June 2002 saw this order formalised as 31 Wrightbus Gemini-bodied Volvo B7TLs on the 10.6m chassis. They began appearing in mid-July and the first of the resulting VWL class was deployed to Belvedere for the 180, entering service from 22 August. Appearances soon followed on the 132 to the extent that most of the route was VWL-operated before long. Fleetnames and fleetnumbers were slower to appear, however, not coming until the beginning of 2003.

Ash Grove then followed, putting out its first VWL on the 128 on 19 October and phasing in the rest on this route and the 129 from 11 November, with visits to the 150. Belvedere's VWLs soon found themselves turning out on the 42 and 185, each taken over on a temporary basis from the collapsed London Easylink. VWLs 30 and 31 were late arriving but completed the set in December.

The batches of VWLs at each garage became mixed in practice due to maintenance work being carried out at Ash Grove and the buses then subsequently entering service from there; in any case blinds for all routes were carried. On 23 November access to Belvedere depot was made easier with the extension there of the 180 from Thamesmead East.

Right: **After four years of Volvo Olympian operation on the 180 initiated by Harris Bus, its successor East Thames Buses put into service their replacement Wright-bodied Volvo B7TLs in the summer of 2002. Unfortunately without any identifying information, not to mention blinds, at Lewisham on 24 August is VWL 4 (LB02 YXA).** *Author*

Above: **VWL 23 (LF52 THG) out of Ash Grove is covering the 128 on 15 March 2003 at Ilford, not long after delivery to replace a Volvo Olympian.** Author

On 25 January 2003 Arriva Kent Thameside gave up its schoolday double-deck journeys on the 132, since the bulk of the route was now VWL-operated.

East Thames Buses' help on the 42 and 185 was rewarded in January 2003 through the award of the contracts on both routes, and for the latter the former London Easylink Volvo B7TLs were taken on from their lessors, who had dispersed them to various storage sites. 5 April was the commencement date, but it wasn't until the 22nd that the first VPs (now numbered VP 1-20 in registration number order) started entering service

Left: **The London Easylink VPs were too new to let go to waste despite the grotesque circumstances of their original operator's fall. Their lease, plus the 185, was taken over by East Thames Buses and they were returned to service under new fleetnumbers and without the Easylink branding. Accordingly, on 19 June 2003 at Dulwich we see VP 12 (X164 FBB), formerly VP 164.** Author

East Thames Buses 217

Right: **The 132 had become used to single-deckers since Harris Bus Optare Excels replaced the miscellany of Volvo and Scania double-decks operated by Kentish Bus, but when the occasion warranted, East Thames Buses put its VWLs out on the route in strength. VWLs 17 (LF52 TGO) and 19 (LF52 TGV) demonstrate at Eltham on 1 October 2002.** Author

on the 185. The Arriva (TOLST) Metrobus allocation remained until 5 October. The VPs, meanwhile, popped up on the 132 and 180 at Belvedere and on the 150 at Ash Grove off and on, though without blinds. All twenty were in service by July, allowing Belvedere to take off its last Olympians. Still, an element remained with the company and in January 2004 a second order for VWLs was placed. There were thirteen, VWLs 32-44 being taken into stock in April and featuring changes specified since the last intake, like single-line blinds, white roofs, tinted windows and fire suppression kits. Nominally Olympian replacements based at Ash Grove, in practice they were shared out and tended to concentrate on the 185.

On 26 June some structural changes came to East Thames Buses' VWL-operated routes, principally to free stand space in Ilford for

Right: **The second batch of Volvo B7TLs into East Thames Buses wore Birmingham registrations, as exemplified on 16 July 2004 at Lewisham by Belvedere-allocated VWL 43 (BX04 BKK). The single-piece blinds were a step backwards in information provision, and the heavy window tinting was rather excessive for a region of the world which would only need it for two or three months out of every year.** Author

Left: **The 129 gave way to the 128 when stand space considerations at Ilford, Clements Road forced the throwing out of every terminating route so that the 25's new bendies could stand there. On 12 April 2004 the 129, in the hands of VWL 18 (LF52 TGU) at Barkingside, has less than a fortnight left.** Author

the 25 upon its conversion to artic operation. The long-standing 129 was withdrawn and its Claybury Broadway leg replaced by an extension of the 128 from Ilford, while the 150 was extended beyond Ilford to Becontree Heath.

Quiet followed, now that all East Thames Buses routes were low-floor. However, upheaval beckoned when the company developed plans to move from Ash Grove to a projected new site at Mandela Way and in the process offered the 128 and 150 to open tender, which awarded them in January 2005 to Arriva London North and First London respectively. In exchange the 1, which was coming to the end of a term with First Capital, would be transferred to East Thames Buses on 15 October and assume its VWLs.

Arsonists torched VWL 5 when it was stood at Chigwell Row on the 150 on 10

Below: **Well bedded in on the 185 at Lewisham on 27 August 2005 is VP 19 (X172 FBB). This bus station was to prove as short-lived as its previous incarnation.** Author

Right: **East Thames Buses's VWLs moved off the 128 and 150 on 15 October 2005 to make the 1 their mainstay at the expense of First Capital. Seen at the route's New Oxford Street stand on the first day of such operations is VWL 17 (LF52 TGO), newly transferred to Mandela Way.** *Author*

Below: **The VWLs were also regulars on the 185 alongside the allocated VPs, as made plain by VWL 28 (LF52 THX) at Vauxhall on 13 May 2006.** *Author*

January, but what was left of the bus had a more auspicious future when it was set up in the London Transport Museum as a working sample in the tradition of the old DM 963 and Metrorider mockup 'MRL 242'.

Ash Grove was duly vacated by East Thames Buses on 15 October and Mandela Way (MA) assumed the 1 and N1 as well as the 42, allowing it VWL appearances; the 128 and 150 passed to their new operators.

Left: **2006 saw loans out and loans in. Coming in to sit on the 132 while its usual DWLs were sent to man the 201 were twelve PVLs from London General, which assumed East Thames Buses VP identities. Thus coming round Eltham bus station on its way to stand on 23 May 2006 is VP 28 (X596 EGK), otherwise known as PVL 196.** Author

With a lot of spare buses now available, East Thames Buses was in a position to loan VPs 3, 9, 12, 17, 19 and 20 to First London following the fire at Westbourne Park garage on 22 January 2006.

On 20 May the assumption of the 201 from the collapsed Centra was carried out with DWL-class DAF SB120s (or Volvo Merits) from Mandela Way, released from Belvedere by the full double-decking of the 132. This produced a shortfall which was filled by hiring twelve PVL-class Volvo B7TLs from London General, which had previously loaned them to Metrobus. Similar to the existing VPs, they gained numbers in that series as VP 21-31 and worked the 132, 180 and 185 as fit.

25 May saw six of the nineteen buses on the 185 reallocated from Belvedere to the much closer Mandela Way. This being a sensible

Left: **Although the route that London General had lost to make buses available for loan was the 188, its Stockwell PVLs released Merton examples to first man the 127 out of Metrobus and then pass to East Thames Buses. VP 25 (X705 EGK) was known as 875 when with Metrobus and was new as PVL 205. On 19 August 2006 it is passing through Lewisham.** Author

East Thames Buses – 221

Right: **Long neglected despite crossing tourist-friendly Tower Bridge, the 42 was seen fit for little more than minibuses and then Dart-sized single-deckers, but its turning over to East Thames Buses allowed the appearance of VWLs. Eventually the entire Sunday service was double-decked, as evinced by VWL 4 (LB02 YXA) coming up to Aldgate on 4 February 2007.**
Author

option, plans were made to put the rest in, but were repeatedly postponed.

In August the VPs loaned to First came back, allowing the London Central hires to start moving on; six passed to a third operator in the form of London United. The rest remained into 2007, but on 24 March of that year the loss of the 393 allowed its short DWs to pass to the 201 and thus release DWLs back to the 132 and let the last hired VPs leave. At this point occasional VWLs were visiting the 108 on shortworkings between Lewisham and North Greenwich, usually in connection with events at the O2.

In June 2007 VP 20 left service strength to be converted to open-top as a TfL promotions bus and VPs 18 and 19 were similarly withdrawn to be converted to trainers in replacement of two long-serving Metrobuses. The rest of the VPs began a refurbishment and repaint programme, which was completed by the end of 2008.

Below: **VWL 1 (LB52 YWX) is captured south of Waterloo on 28 September 2008 as talks were entered into about selling off East Thames Buses. The 1's panel was one of the first of the dumbed-down variety with just two via points in a space which could fit four.**
Author

Left: **Going in the northbound direction on 28 September 2008, VWL 14 (LB02 YXM) reveals a rear ad for Cyprus.**
Author

On 25 October the 108's peripatetic post-concert double-deck journeys were increased to a full evening service tying into the N1. In December VWL 1 was treated to an advert (minus the front) in a blue and mauve advert for Bingo.

Clamour had been made for some years for a service linking North Greenwich to points immediately south, and on 24 January 2009 this came in the form of an extension of the 132 from Eltham.

2009 was to be East Thames Buses' last year; as ever, money issues pressed, and on 10 December 2008 TfL announced that this subsidiary was something whose original need had subsided and which could now be privatised. Maintenance worries caused a reduction in the company's discs from 170 to 150 in April as it was.

Unused to Tridents, East Thames Buses nonetheless began operating the type when four First TNs arrived on 14 February to cover on the 1 so that its VWLs could be treated to iBus fitment. They lasted until April.

After consideration of various options, TfL chose to sell East Thames Buses to Go-Ahead and consolidate its route setup into normal contracts. This took place on 3 October 2009.

Registrations
VWL 1-31   LG02 YWX-Z, YXA/C-H/J-N, LF52 TGN/O/U/V/X-Z, THG/K/N/U/V/X/Z, TJO/U
VWL 32-44   BX04 AZW/V/U/Z, BAA/U/V, BBE/F/J, BKL/K/J

Date	Deliveries	Licensed for Service
08.02	VWL 1-15	VWL 1-13 (**BV**)
09.02	VWL 16-22	VWL 14 (**BV**)
10.02	VWL 23-29	VWL 15 (**BV**), VWL 17-20 (**AG**)
11.02		VWL 16, 21-29 (**AG**)
12.02	VWL 30, 31	VWL 30, 31 (**AG**)
04.04	VWL 32-41	VWL 32-41 (**BV**)
06.04	VWL 42-44	VWL 42-44 (**BV**)

Acquired from dealer stock, 04-07.03
VP 1-20 (X149, 151-154, 157-159, 161-169, 171-173 FBB)

Hired from London Central, 05.06-03.07
VP 21-31 (X699, 504, 598, 702, 705, 503, 597, 596, 502, 501, 595 EGK)

Disposals
2007   VWL 5 (front to LT Museum)

Company sold to Go-Ahead, 03.10.09; VP 20 remains with TfL

First London

VE, VN, VTL, VFL, VNL, VNW and VNZ classes

By the time First Capital and Centrewest effectively merged their operations, both companies had extensive experience with Dennis Tridents and had already pooled their fleetnumbering system.

In July 2000 East Lancs unveiled their new Vyking body for Volvo B7TLs and FirstGroup was the launch customer, taking delivery of VE 953 on the 27th and handing it over to Centrewest on 11 October. Plans to operate it from Uxbridge on the 207 alongside the recently-introduced TNLs came to fruition on 29 November, after a period back at Blackburn for modifications. While in service, it was discovered that its air-conditioning system was not up to the rigours of pounding up and down the Uxbridge Road and on one warranty visit it was fitted with opening windows. At least the chassis was considered broadly successful, as it spawned an order for thirteen B7TLs with Plaxton President bodywork to be delivered for the 61 in the spring of 2002, shortly after it began a new contract with Orpington on 1 December.

Below: **First London's debut order for Volvo B7TLs produced the thirteen-strong VT class, which went to Orpington to replace Volvo Olympians from the 61. Coming into the town centre on 4 May 2002 is VT 1105 (LT02 ZCU).** *Author*

VE 953 itself was put into store after its trial period ended and when attempts to sell it fell through, it was formally acquired in March 2002. After training drivers at Westbourne Park and Alperton, it re-entered service on the latter's 79 on 16 April, though continued to suffer reliability problems that kept it out of traffic for prolonged periods.

March 2002 saw an order placed for 29 Volvo B7TLs for the 83 at Alperton; these, VTLs 1200-1228, would be to 10.6m length with Plaxton President bodywork.

VTs 1100-1102 were delivered in April 2002 and the first entered service on the 61 on the 26th, with the requisite visits to the R9 as the outgoing Vs had done.

In July plans were formalised to split the current 10, RML-operated by Metroline London Northern, and its new western section between Hammersmith and King's Cross was awarded to First London, who ordered 28 Alexander ALX400-bodied Volvo B7TLs to 10.6m length. Then came the orders for the retained route 259 and new route 476 tenders out of Northumberland Park – 35 more 10.6m B7TLs but with Plaxton President bodywork. Slotting in around a number of Tridents, these batches would be known as VFLs 1249-1276 and VTLs 1294-1328 respectively.

The 83 had already started re-equipping with new TNs on a temporary basis by the time its new Volvos started arriving in September, and the first two new VTLs delivered were drafted to assist on the 207 during a Tube strike on 2 October. The rest

Left: **After a large quantity of Tridents to bulk out fleetnumbers in the 1100s, Volvo was returned to for the 83's batch at Alperton, which also replaced Volvo Olympians as the push to low-floor went on. Seen at Wembley Park on 27 July 2003 is VTL 1210 (LT52 WTR).** *Author*

Below: **The VTLs into Alperton standardised the 79 and 258 on the type so that their TNs could head elsewhere within Centrewest and First Capital. Edgware is the location for VTL 1226 (LT52 WUL) on 14 December 2002.** *Author*

Above: It wasn't certain what the 'F' in the class code carried by the 10's new ALX400-bodied Volvo B7TLs stood for – perhaps Falkirk, where they were built. In any case, VFL 1262 (LT52 WWH) out of Westbourne Park brings OPO to the 10 as it approaches Tottenham Court Road on 18 April 2003. TfL's enforced specification from this point of DDA-compliant blinds is not only restrictive to the poor passenger after the superb wide KV panels, but unattractive against the original masking of the bodywork's illuminated blind box edges. *Author*

Right: The 10's new VFLs quickly turned out on Westbourne Park's other double-deck routes, and here at Putney Bridge on 28 June 2003 VFL 1253 (LT52 WVY) is investigating the recently-introduced 414. *Author*

began work from the 7th, where, as well as taking over the 83 from VNs, ousted the TNs from the 79 and 258 to render Alperton's double-deck complement 100% Volvo B7TL. They also appeared on DML-operated route 92.

VFLs 1249-1276 arrived in January 2003 and on 1 February went into service on the 10 from Westbourne Park, though in practice an outstation was established for this route at Ariel Way. The 414 was the first route these new buses found themselves wandering to, followed by the 27.

Type training for Northumberland Park's new fleet of VTLs was carried out in April by VTL 1201 on loan from Alperton, soon replaced by VTL 1206. 7 May was their service debut on the 476, whose first three months had seen the 76's Arrows stay on, but these now departed and the 259 and 476 were complete by June. The 91 and 341 were quick to see VTL appearances.

Left: **Two new batches of VTLs took over the 259 and 476 from Dennis Arrows at First Capital's Northumberland Park during the spring of 2003. Seen coming up to Tottenham High Road on 23 February 2004 is VTL 1303 (LK03 NHC).** *Author*

Below: **Northumberland Park's new VTLs also took advantage of other opportunities than their assigned routes, and at Waterloo on 29 May 2004 we see VTL 1304 (LK03 NHD) on the 341, still Volvo Olympian-operated at this point.** *Author*

Above: Upon the FirstGroup renumbering of 2003, VFL 1250 became VNL 32250 (LT52 WVN) and the result is seen at Hyde Park Corner on 5 July 2004, continuing to serve its regular 10. *Author*

On 5 June orders for 119 new buses were announced and included 43 new Volvo B7TLs, but this time with Wrightbus Gemini bodywork. All for Alperton, where part of their remit would be to double-deck the 92, there would be 21 10.6m examples, pencilled in as VWL 1387-1407, and 9.9m VW 1408-1429.

Following on from Stagecoach practice at the beginning of the year, FirstGroup too implemented a fleetwide renumbering system whereby chassis were separated into blocks of thousands. The existing system, which had climbed numerically regardless of chassis, was thus broken up, but First London insisted upon retaining class codes for one-look identification. These, however, were altered so that in terms of Volvo B7TLs, the VT class became VNs (the existing Volvo Olympians of that class becoming VDNs) and the VTLs and VFLs both became VNLs. Complicating matters, the incoming VWs and VWLs would now be VNWs and VNZs! Finally, the lone VE 953 became VNE 32052.

Right: Similarly, VE 953 was renumbered VNE 32052 (X578 RJW), which was as close as it could get to recalling its original number wedged in between two batches of Tridents. The air-cooling system with which this bus was originally fitted repeatedly failed and was soon replaced by opening windows. After a decade's service it was dispersed within FirstGroup to serve as an engineering trainer, but on 22 May 2004 it is seen in Wembley on Alperton's 79. *Author*

Left: **VWL 1399 (LK53 LZA) was one of Alperton's new 10.6m Volvo B7TLs taken early in 2004 to restore the 92's upper deck. It is seen in Wembley on 22 February, and was physically renumbered VNZ 32340 shortly after.** *Author*

Alperton's Wright-bodied B7TLs commenced delivery in December, the first examples coming as VWLs and entering service from 19 January 2004, by which time the accompanying VWs (or VNWs) were arriving. These began on 20 February, at which point sixty more were ordered to finally bring a close to the minibus era on the 28, 31 and 328, announced as retained by Centrewest the previous October.

The destruction of three London Central Citaro G artics by fire over 2003/04 sparked panic, and on 24 March TfL ordered them taken off the road until fire suppression equipment could be fitted. That included the 18's ECAs, which were replaced for a week by existing Westbourne Park double-deckers (including VFLs) plus two new Alperton VNWs awaiting service. Six Metroline VPLs assisted on the 25th and six VPs on the 26th.

Below: **VNZ 32338 (LK53 LYY) was delivered as VWL 1397 but is seen carrying its updated fleetnumber on 27 December 2004 at Golders Green.** *Author*

Above: **Cheerful-looking in their excess of yellow paint, the VNW class rescued the 28, 31 and 428 from a decade of well-intentioned but ultimately impractical small buses. Laying over at Camden Town, which continued to be the 31's northern terminus after the 1999 revamp, Westbourne Park's VNW 32376 (LK04 HZF) is seen on 27 November 2004.** Author

In April eight more VNZs were ordered, with the intention being for them to release VNLs to Northumberland Park for a planned boost to the 259 later in the year; the highest-numbered two VNLs of the first batch were transferred straight away. Westbourne Park's VNWs for the 28, 31 and 328 started arriving in May and service entry there commenced on 3 June, first on the 31, then the 28 and finally the 328, with all three complete by the end of August. The VNWs spread their net to the 10 and 23 and received the odd VNL (ex-VFL) in return. By the end of the year they had achieved the full spread of Westbourne Park double-deck routes, including the 7 and 23 one-manned over the year.

Right: **Westbourne Park also operated the 295, having upgraded it from DM to TN operation halfway through its current term. Now VNWs could join in, and VNW 32413 (LK04 HZP) is doing so at Shepherd's Bush Green on 17 April 2005.** Author

230 – Volvo B7TL

Left: **The 91 at Northumberland Park was another TN-operated route, but in this case its interlopers were VTLs from the 259 and 476. At Charing Cross on 1 September 2004 is VTL 1295 (LK03 NGN), with Blue Triangle's RT 3871 coming up behind on a special working commemorating the 9's outgoing conductors.** Author

Mid-September 2004 saw the delivery of VNZs 32495-32502; their entry into service at Alperton the following month allowed VNLs 32219-32226 to join 32227 and 32228 at Northumberland Park for the 259's increased PVR applying from the 16th.

The Capital half of First London had no experience with Wright bodies, but at the beginning of 2005 the 150 was won from East Thames Buses and an order for twelve VNWs was placed.

Other than rogue visits to the 91, 97 and 357, Northumberland Park VNLs had stayed put on the 259 and 476, but on 22 April 2005 VNL 32317 was loaned to Orpington and put out on the 61. Another loan during September took Westbourne Park's ALX400-bodied VNL 32267 to Alperton.

During the period of coverage to the Piccadilly Line while repairs to the bomb damage of 7 July took place, First Leicester lent five Volvo B7TLs to Rainham to operate

Left: **Eight 54-reg VNZs were the last Volvo B7TLs into the Centrewest portion of First London during October 2004. Here at Ealing Hospital on 2 July 2005 is VNZ 32496 (LK54 FLB).** Author

Right: **Three unusual workings for First Volvo B7TLs in the mid-2000s; this one is of Northumberland Park's VNL 32296 (LK03 NGU) visiting the 357 at Walthamstow Central on 7 May 2005.** *Author*

Right: **Alperton was apt to put its Volvo B7TLs out on the 487, the busier half of the 187 and 487 pair. Seen at Willesden Junction on 5 November 2005 is VNL 32213 (LT52 WTW).** *Author*

Right: **The one-manning of the 23 was accomplished with TNA-class Dennis Tridents, but Westbourne Park occasionally put the 10's ALX400-bodied VNLs out on it, as VNL 32265 (LT52 WWL) is doing in Oxford Street on 21 October 2005.** *Author*

Left: **Out went all the yellow accenting and proper blinds for the final Volvo B7TL intake into a First London component, with the plain result shown by Rainham's VNW 32660 (LK55 AAF) at Ilford on 15 October 2005, the first day of First Capital operation of the 150.** *Author*

the Arnos Grove-Seven Sisters replacement service between 18 July and 3 August. These were 32075, 32077, 32094, 32097 and 32099 (KP51 WAO, WBD, WCR/Y and WDW).

VNWs 32657-32668 arrived in October, having voided their booked 05-registrations for 55-marks, and on the 15th took over the 150 from Rainham. They had single-line destinations to the new coarsened standard, plus white roofs and upper-deck air cooling equipment. On 17 December they transferred, with the rest of Rainham's allocation, to Dagenham (DM). Wanderings to the 179 followed, with TNs and TNLs on the 150 in return.

Quiet ensued, and indeed Volvo B7TL production came to an end in 2006. However, buses were needed to fill in after a teenage arsonist torched the overspill yard at Westbourne Park on 22 January, destroying ten Tridents. Six East Thames Buses VPs were hired, lasting till the end of August.

Left: **The immolation of ten Westbourne Park Tridents on 22 January 2006 necessitated external hires to cover their loss, and VP 3 (X152 FBB), seen at Russell Square during June, was one of six East Thames Buses B7TLs hired for the purpose.** *Haydn Davies*

Right: **Adorned with a vinyl advert for the NSPCC, Alperton's VNZ 32341 (LK53 LZB) reposes at Wisley airfield on the occasion of the 2006 Cobham open day on 2 April of that year.** Author

Then, front-end fire damage to Orpington's VN 32108 on 6 February caused VNLs 32201 and 32207 to come on loan from Alperton. This garage, meanwhile, was no longer able to put VNWs and VNZs onto the 258 with its loss to Arriva the Shires on 4 February 2006, though wanderings of all three B7TL classes to the 487 remained frequent.

In February Alperton's VNZ 32341 was given an all-over advert for the NSPCC, followed in March by the treatment of Orpington's VN 32105 to one for the Oyster card. VNZ 32341's ad lasted eighteen months.

May 2006 saw the announcement of the loss of the 61 to Stagecoach Selkent. Two other routes lost were school routes 697 and 698,

Right: **Orpington's VN 32105 (LT02 ZCU) was another bus to receive an all-over ad in 2006, and when seen at Bromley South on 23 October it was still carrying most of it.** Author

Above: **First London held onto the thirteen VNs after the loss of the 61, transferring them to Westbourne Park. On 16 June 2007 VN 32109 (LT02 ZDH) operates the 414 at Hyde Park Corner.** Author

whose departure on 31 August freed enough TNs to let the loaned East Thames Buses VPs leave. On 2 December the 61 duly departed for Selkent and all thirteen of its VNs moved to Westbourne Park, five to provide stock for the extension of the 31 from Notting Hill Gate to Shepherd's Bush Green and the rest to top up in an era of gradually increasing PVRs.

Red repaints had now begun to eliminate the yellow-accented livery that had made First London's buses so colourful; the first B7TL so treated was former Oyster advert VN 32105 in January 2007. Repairs to fire-damaged VN 32108 at the same time saw red paint applied, but only to the replacement sections! VNZs 32333 and 32340 saw severe accident damage over the year.

Volvo B7TL appearances on the 7 ceased with its loss to Metroline on 23 June 2007. On 7 July three VNWs left Alperton for

Left: **Northumberland Park's VNL 32307 (LK03 NHG) is seen rounding Euston station's war memorial on 5 August 2007.** Author

Right: **On 28 May 2006 at Park Royal station Alperton's VNW 32353 (LK53 LZR) is turning out on the 95, a route gained by First a month previously with DMLs.** *Author*

Right: **The 10 was lost after five years with First plus two more for good performance, and that was that for the 28 ALX-bodied VNLs. On 24 May 2008 Westbourne Park's VNL 32257 (LT52 WWC) is in Oxford Street.** *Author*

Westbourne Park to serve as iBus fitment cover, although that produced a shortage of double-deckers that led to DMLs on the 79 and 92. Over the rest of 2007 and into 2008 we could see Dagenham VNWs on the 165 and 252 and VNL 32217 loaned from Alperton to Westbourne Park. Partial repaints were now under way, affecting the earliest VNLs' lower halves. Otherwise, 2007 and 2008 were untroubled; Alperton VNWs were appearing on the 95 and 245 and Northumberland Park VNLs on the 191. During 2008 the 83 was tendered and retained with new buses, which would be of Volvo's revised B9TL chassis and begin the cascading out of VNLs despite their low age by modern standards.

A second order for the resulting (and third distinctive) VN class came when the 259 and 476, also offered out again during 2008, were announced as retained in March 2009. The big loss for First and Volvo B7TLs was the 10, which was awarded to London United in May.

The exit of B7TLs began in November 2009 when new B9TLs (VNs) began taking over the 83 at Alperton; the first act moved VNZs 32495-32502 to Westbourne Park to eject the ex-Orpington VNs (of which VN 32100 had spent the summer of 2009 at Alperton). Alperton's VNLs were all but cleaned out by year's end, four remaining while the seats were upgraded on the new buses and three of those surviving into March 2010. VNE 32052 was also withdrawn, eventually passing to group ownership as an engineering training bus that returned to the capital on occasion.

The 10 departed for London United on 30 January 2010 and VNLs 32249-32276 were stood down en bloc. The 414 was ceded to Abellio on the same date, thus precluding any more B7TL appearances.

The conversion of the 476 from VNL to VN began on 3 February 2010, displacing VNLs 32313-32327 to Dagenham to man the London Overground rail replacement service beginning on the 20th. The 259's own batch of VNs then followed and by May only VNLs 32306 and 32307 were left in service. However, these stayed put and when the London Overground service finished on 31 May, its fifteen VNLs returned to Northumberland Park and took over the 67 from its previous TNs of Y-reg vintage.

One departure at this time was a little ahead of schedule; this was VNZ 32348, which was readied as a Green Line backup vehicle for First Berkshire. Even newer a B7TL to fall out was VNW 32657, which was withdrawn during 2010 to be converted into

Above: **All-over red repaints were the order of the day by the end of the decade, but partial repaints were also far from uncommon even if it led to bits of old liveries being left behind. Here at Golders Green on 21 October 2009 is Alperton's VNL 32206 (LT52 WTW).** *Author*

Left: **Another bus missing a bit of its original livery is VNL 32317 (LK03 NHY), now redeployed to the 67 after being replaced from the 259 and 476 by VNs. It is seen coming through Shoreditch on 7 August 2010.** *Author*

a community education bus. The 150 had already been awarded to Arriva London North and it made its way there on 16 October, standing down the rest of the 55-reg VNWs, though those not stored continued to turn out on rail replacement work until a new deployment was figured out for them. On 13 December the 92 was reallocated from Alperton to Greenford and took VNZs 32328-32347 with it.

During 2011 the 28 group's VNWs began to undergo refurbishment for their second term on these routes beginning on 30 April, and were stood in for by TNs otherwise on their last legs. The accompanying red repaints to all of these, plus the 92's VNZs without the refurbishment, removed all of the yellow accenting, and the illuminated panels around the blind box were also gone over in opaque black.

The 79, tendered during 2010, was announced in April 2011 as lost to Metroline.

Between 14 July and September otherwise spare VNWs 32663 and 32664 were operated by Willesden Junction (WJ), home of the 18, as MOT/FFD cover. That wasn't the only new First garage to see Volvo B7TLs, as on 1 October Atlas Road (AS) opened to take on the 28, 31 and 328 and allow the overspill area at Westbourne Park to be given over to Crossrail construction for however long that took. In went VNWs 32361-32370 and VNZs 32495-32502 plus ten Tridents and the five WNH-class Wrightbus integrals, though the pooled nature between here and Westbourne Park ensured that B7TL appearances continued on the latter's 23 and 295. Then in November a third new garage saw VNWs when six moved from Atlas Road to Lea Interchange (LI) to operate a service for employees within the

Right: **In their new livery of red with off-white First fleetnames are VNWs 32400 (LK04 HXJ) and 32401 (LK04 HXL), entering the Shepherd's Bush gate of White City bus station on 18 March 2012. The 31, like the fellow VNW-operating 28 and 328, was now run out of Atlas Road, though garage codes were never carried for any of First's bases.** *Author*

Right: **Resplendent in its new coat of red, VNW 32665 (LK55 AAX) is seen outside its new home garage, Uxbridge, on its new route, the 607, on 7 May 2012.** *Author*

Left: **On 17 June 2012 at Ladbroke Grove Sainsbury's, VNW 32425 (LK04 HYC) takes a day away from its customary 28 group at Atlas Road to turn out on the 295 from Westbourne Park. Repanelling has inadvertently taken off almost all its TfL roundel, a new (or restored) aesthetic feature which will need to be replaced.** Author

Left: **The 308 had enough of the old 162's busiest part in it to have outgrown its Dart-sized single-deckers almost immediately, and its temporary conversion to double-deck during the Olympics prompted a decision to specify double-deckers for it permanently. VNW 32355 (LK53 LZU) is in Stratford town centre on 4 August 2012 on attachment to Lea Interchange.** Author

Olympic Park as preparations for the 2012 Games got under way.

On 16 November the 79 passed on tender to Metroline and VNWs 32349-32357, 32359 and 32360 were stored pending refurbishment in order to replace Dagenham's remaining TNs and TNLs still holding out on school routes. Meanwhile, a berth was identified for the former route 150 VNWs after a year in storage; this was the 607, retained by Uxbridge on the basis of existing vehicles. Once refurbished, they would share the express route with ten DN-class Enviro400s made spare from the 23 by more new VNs. The 427 was also fair game for VNW appearances.

VNW 32358 was the last B7TL at Alperton and it continued there up to and including 11 March 2012, moving to Dagenham the next day. Greenford's VNZs now came under threat with the order in January of 20 DN-class E40Ds to replace them by autumn.

Even before the Volvo B7TLs' lifespans had been lived out at First, the group realised it needed money and fast by the time 2012 opened, and on 29 January it made the decision to sell Northumberland Park to Go-Ahead and the transfer took place on 31 March. Going with it were the 67's seventeen VNLs, which were reclassified a second time to become PVNs at London General. They had visited the 191, 231 and 357 and continued to do so under their new ownership.

April 2012 saw the 55-reg VNWs complete refurbishment and move onto Uxbridge's 607 as planned, while the VNWs at Lea Interchange returned to Atlas Road. Nine of Dagenham's VNWs, meanwhile, were seconded to Lea Interchange in July to convert the 308 to double-deck during the period of the Olympics. Once, one got out on the 26 for the first time. They returned to Dagenham in mid-September.

Above: **The majority of First London's surviving Volvo B7TLs passed to Tower Transit on 22 June 2013, retaining their identities rather than having new ones created for them like those buses that went to Metroline on the same day. Leaving Golders Green on 27 May 2012 is VNW 32376 (LK04 HZF).** Author

Between 26 September and 24 October DNs replaced the 92's VNZs, leaving just the eight 54-reg examples still at Atlas Road.

Selling Northumberland Park didn't help FirstGroup's bottom line, and when a particularly cruel tranche lost First London most of Dagenham's runout, it was decided to pull the trigger. Leaving aside Dagenham for the moment, the company was divided into two, half sold to Metroline's owner ComfortDelgro and the rest to Australian-based Transit Holdings. This took place on 22 June 2013, the Volvo B7TL fleet (what was left of it) passing to Metroline West (VNWs 32658-32668, as VW 1560-1570, for the 607 at Uxbridge) and Tower Transit (VNWs 32361-32430 and VNZs 32495-32502, retaining their fleetnumbers, for Atlas Road's 28, 31 and 328).

All that remained of First London now was the First Capital East-flagged rump at Dagenham, which could still field VNWs 32349-32360 for a spread of school routes. Occasionally they worked the 368 when its Enviro200s were needed for rail replacements at weekends, but they were the first to be withdrawn, coming off by 21 June with VNW 32356 turning out one last time on the 179 on the 24th. First Capital East didn't last much longer itself and was wound up after service on 27 September.

Registrations

VE 953	X578 RJW
VT 1100-1112	LT02 ZCJ-L/N/O/U/V/X/Y, ZDH/J-L
VTL 1200-1228	LT52 WTE-G/K-P/R/U-Z, WUA-E/G/H/J-L, XAL/M
VFL 1249-1276	LT52 WVM-P/Y/Z, WWA-H/J-P/R/S/U, WXC-F
VTL 1294-1327	LK03 NGJ/N/U/V/X-Z, NHA-H/J/L-N/P/T/V/X-Z, NJE/F/J/N/V/X-Z, NKA
VWL 1387-1407	LK53 LYH/J/O/P/R/T-Z, LZA-H/L
VNW 32349-32370	LK53 LZM-P/R/T-X, MBF, LK04 HYP/N/M/W/T/X/Y/A/S/U/V
VNW 32371-32430	LK04 HZA-H/J/L-N, JBU, HZS-Z, HXA-H/J/L-N/P/R-X, JBE, HZP, JBV/X-Z, JCJ/U/V/X, HYZ, JCZ, HYB/C/F-H/J/L
VNZ 32495-32502	LK54 FLA-G, JFF
VNW 32657-32668	LX55 ACO/U, AAE/F/J/N/U/V/X-Z, ABF

Re-registrations

10.04	VNW 32397 from LK04 HXF to LK54 FNO
10.04	VNW 32398 from LK04 HXG to LK54 FNP

Date	Deliveries	Licensed for Service
10.00	VE 953	
11.00		VE 953 (**UX**)
04.02	VT 1100-1112	VT 1100-1112 (**Y**)
09.02	VTL 1200, 1202	VTL 1200, 1202 (**ON**)
10.02	VTL 1201, 1203, 1204-1219	VTL 1201, 1203, 1204-1219 (**ON**)
11.02	VTL 1220-1228	VTL 1220-1228 (**ON**)
01.03	VFL 1249-1276	VFL 1249-1276 (**X**)
05.03	VTL 1294-1315	VTL 1294-1315 (**NP**)
06.03	VTL 1316-1327	VTL 1316-1327 (**NP**)
12.03	VWL 1387-1389	
01.04	VWL 1390, 1392-1396, 1398	VWL 1390, 1392 (**ON**)
02.04	VWL 1391, 1397, 1399-1407	VWL 1391, 1393-1407 (**ON**)
	VNW 32349-32359	VNW 32349-32359 (**ON**)
03.04	VNW 32360-32370	VNW 32360-32370 (**ON**)
05.04	VNW 32371-32378	VNW 32371-32378 (**X**)
06.04	VNW 32379-32385, 32399-32401, 32403-32409, 32411, 32412	VNW 32381-32385, 32399-32401, 32403-32409, 32411, 32412 (**X**)
07.04	VNW 32386-32392, 32394, 32410, 32413-32430	VNW 32386-32392, 32394, 32410, 32413-32430 (**X**)
08.04	VNW 32393, 32395-32398, 32402	VNW 32393, 32395-32398, 32402 (**X**)
09.04	VNZ 32495-32502	
10.04		VNZ 32495-32502 (**ON**)
10.05	VNW 32657-32668	VNW 32657-32668 (**R**)

Hired from East Thames Buses, 22.01-30.08.06
VP 3, 9, 12, 17, 19, 20 (X152, 161, 164, 169, 172, 173 FBB)

Renumbered, 01.11.03
VE 953 to VNE 32052
VT 1100-1112 to VN 32100-32112
VTL 1200-1228, 1294-1327 to VNL 32200-32228, 32294-32327
VFL 1249-1276 to VNL 32249-32276
VWL 1387-1407 to VNZ 32328-32348

Disposals
11.09	VN 32100-32107
01.10	VN 32108-32112
	VNL 32200-32213, 32216, 32217, 32219, 32220
	VNE 32052
02.10	VNL 32249, 32250
03.10	VNL 32214, 32215, 32218, 32251-32276
05.10	VNL 32221-32228
06.10	VNL 32294, 32295, 32297-32299, 32308-32312
07.10	VNL 32296, 32300-32305
09.10	VNW 32657
10.10	VNZ 32348
03.12	VNL 32306, 32307, 32313-32327
10.12	VNZ 32338, 32347
11.12	VNZ 32328, 32332-32334, 32337, 32342, 32346
12.12	VNZ 32329-32331, 32336, 32339-32341, 32343, 32344
01.13	VNZ 32335, 32345
06.13	VNW 32658-32668, 32361-32430
	VNZ 32495-32502
08.13	VNW 32349-32360

Tower Transit

VNW and VNZ classes

Upon the split from First on 22 June 2013, Australian-owned Tower Transit inherited seventy-eight Volvo B7TLs, comprising VNWs 32361-32430 and VNZs 32495-32502, all based at Atlas Road for the 28, 31 and 328 and their night counterparts but capable of turning out on the parent Westbourne Park's 23 if needed.

Quiet followed, only the tendering of the 23 distinguishing 2014, followed by the appearance of some ex-Stagecoach Tridents to bolster that route for a while. The 23 was duly retained and then, during 2015, the main three were offered out again. The result of that particular tender was announced in August as a victory, with the 31 and N31 extended for two years, new buses for the 328 and the 28 and N28 gaining the VN-class B9TLs from the 295, which departed for Metroline West on 31 October. Although four of the VNZs and all the remaining Tridents, indigenous and ex-Stagecoach, were stood down on this date, the conversion of the 28 to VN didn't happen straight away, however, as the buses were needed to cover refurbishments elsewhere within Tower Transit.

Below: **The VNWs and VNZs had already lost their distinctive yellow-accented livery before the takeover of First's operations by Tower Transit and Metroline West, and on 25 July 2014 at Westbourne Park, Atlas Road's VNZ 32498 (LK54 FLD) is suitably plain red.** Author

Left: On the opposite side of the road at Westbourne Park we see VNZ 32502 (LK54 FLH) on 10 October 2015. This one lasted until the following August. *Author*

From 21 March 2016 the 328 received its new buses in the form of 25 VH-class Volvo B5LHs; no VNWs left at this point either but stayed to effectively replace the 23's DNs which were removed to go on hire to CT Plus. The new contracts for the 28, 31 and 328 applied from 30 April, and once CT Plus had its own new buses for the 26 the DNs returned and began finally displacing B7TLs. In June the last four VNZs were withdrawn, but VNWs 32429 and 32430 moved to Lea Interchange to serve on the Overground rail

Below: On the first day of Tower Transit operations, 22 June 2013, VNWs 32398 (LK54 FNP) and 32410 (LK04 HXW) are still carrying their First fleetnames as they respectively leave and enter the Shepherd's Bush end of the White City shopping complex. *Author*

Above: **On 9 November 2015 VNW 32410 (LK04 HXW) is seen at Notting Hill Gate. The 328 had been retained by now and new VHs would take it over within six months.** *Author*

replacement on sub-contract to Arriva. VNW 32391 joined them later but all three returned to Atlas Road in April 2017.

2017 was to prove a decisive year for the VNW class; first, with the appearance of further new B5LHs (this time MCV-bodied MVs) in May, DNs were cascaded west to see some more VNWs off the 23 and the VNs intended for the 28 finally took up service on that route. Then, in August, the 31's two years expired but the route was lost to Metroline West.

Right: **The VNWs' place in future plans was cemented by the ordering for them of blinds with white characters; on 3 April 2017 in Regent Street VNW 32367 (LK04 HYA) is serving the 23.** *Author*

On 1 July Atlas Road closed and Westbourne Park took back the 28, 31, 328, N28 and N31 with the vehicles that worked them, which still included 46 VNWs. Even so, the loss of the 266 to Metroline on 29 July didn't prompt the use of its VNs to replace the remainder; instead they were returned off lease. Not long later ten of them pitched up with Arriva London North.

On 30 September the 23, still capable of fielding VNWs, was withdrawn between Aldwych and Liverpool Street. The VNWs had now made it into 2018, but 28 April of that year saw the departure of the 31 for Metroline West as planned, and that on the face of it would seem to have marked the end for the type, but five survived; these were VNWs 32389, 32401, 32421, 32423 and 32429. The first two didn't survive past September but the others soldiered on, continuing into 2019 with no sign of replacement. After the convolution of the 23 back on itself on 24 November to reach Hammersmith, the three survivors were restricted to the 28 and almost never wandered off it. Two more, VNWs 32427 and 32428, served as training buses.

With the onset of the ULEZ, Tower Transit stood down the three remaining VNWs, their last day being 31 March 2019 with VNW 32429 bringing the B7TL era to a close.

Left: **The loss of the 31 to Metroline West and its departure on 28 April 2018 theoretically sealed the fate of the Volvo B7TL at Tower Transit, but a handful survived and continued on into 2019. Here at White City on 22 April 2018 is VNW 32424 (LK04 HYB), which would be withdrawn a week later.** *Author*

Acquired from First London, 22.06.13
VNW 32361-32430 (LK04 HYN/M/W/T/X/Y/A/S/U/V, HZA-H/J/L-N, JBU, HZS-Z, LK54 FNO/P, LK04 HXH/J/L-N/P/R-X, JBE, HZP, JBV-Z, JCJ/U/V/X, HYZ, JCZ, HYB/C/F/G/H/J/L)

VNZ 32495-32502 (LK54 FLA-H)

Disposals
11.15	VNZ 32496, 32497, 32499, 32500
05.16	VNW 32361, 32382
07.16	VNW 32363, 32365, 32368, 32418
08.16	VNW 32370, 32374, 32404
	VNZ 32495, 32498, 32501, 32502
08.17	VNW 32369, 32380, 32381, 32383, 32387, 32388, 32395, 32396, 32399, 32400, 32406, 32410, 32413, 32414, 32420, 32426
11.17	VNW 32378
05.18	VNW 32362, 32364, 32371-32373, 32375-32377, 32394, 32402, 32407
06.18	VNW 32366, 32367, 32379, 32384-32386, 32390-32393, 32397, 32398, 32403, 32405, 32408, 32409, 32411, 32412, 32415, 32416, 32419, 32422, 32425, 32430
11.19	VNW 32401, 32421, 32423, 32429
12.19	VNW 32389

Tower Transit 245

Sovereign

2717-2733, VLP and VLE classes

Long-held plans to convert Dart SLF-operated route 183 back to double-deck operation came to fruition in the autumn of 2001 with the delivery of seventeen 10.6m Volvo B7TLs with Plaxton President bodywork. To accompany the schedule change implemented on 3 November, the buses were put into service beginning on the 29th. In a livery of red with black skirt and gold fleetnames, they were numbered 2717-2733 to follow on from a batch at fellow Transdev-owned Burnley and Pendle. As was customary, they soon appeared on the 114, 292, N13 and the OPO workings of the 13 during the evenings.

On 22 October 2002 Transdev purchased London Sovereign from Blazefield and immediately federated it with London United, and the Volvo B7TLs' adventures thereafter resume in London United's chapter.

That wasn't the end of the story, however; eight years later further corporate wranglings centred around Transdev's own prospective merger with fellow French transport undertaking Veolia, and as part of the deal a third such organisation, the RATP in Paris, withdrew its 25% stake in the form of London United with effect from 3 March 2009. Transdev retained control of Sovereign and

Below: **2721 (LN51 AZF) is seen reposing at Golders Green on Boxing Day 2002, shortly after Sovereign was taken over by Transdev.** *Author*

Left: **Sovereign's sixteen Plaxton President-bodied Volvo B7TLs all had the wider rear number blind, as exemplified at Golders Green by Edgware's 2730 (LN51 AZW) on 22 March 2002.** *Author*

Below: **On 18 May 2002 2720 (LN51 AZD) swings round the Harrow one-way system into the bus station. The gold fleetnames are a nice touch.** *Author*

Above: On 28 July 2012 in Harrow we see VLE 38 (PO54 ACY), now carrying Transdev fleetnames to underscore Sovereign's staying with that particular French organisation. *Author*

inherited back VLE 27-39 as well as the VLP class, which now that the 183's contingent had departed in the interim, comprised the 292's batch, VLP 18-27. A repaint cycle to the VLEs was nearing completion at this point.

Tendering in September 2011 awarded school route 605 to Sovereign for commencement on 1 September 2012, and it was quickly found that a dedicated bus was needed, so in came Metroline's VPL 220 on a year's loan; it was similar enough that no changes to its fleetnumber were made.

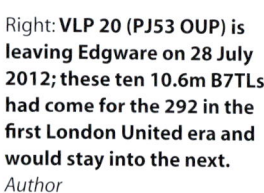

Right: VLP 20 (PJ53 OUP) is leaving Edgware on 28 July 2012; these ten 10.6m B7TLs had come for the 292 in the first London United era and would stay into the next. *Author*

248 – Volvo B7TL

Above: **VLP 25 (PJ53 OUY) pulls into Edgware bus station on 28 July 2012. The 292 received SLEs spare from the 13 the following August but the VLPs managed to stay put and lasted until 2018.** *Author*

Routes 13 and 292 were tendered during 2012 and both were retained, though with new buses to replace the 13's existing SLEs straight away. The 13 (including night route N13) was duly converted to its new VH-class Volvo B5LHs between 10-31 August 2013 and ten of the SLEs stayed behind to see off the 292's VLPs in advance of its own contract renewal date on 7 December. VLP 21 was detached to serve as a trainer and renumbered TV 1.

Still more ownership fluctuations were in the offing, and the latest one was on 20 March 2004 when RATP purchased Sovereign from Transdev and once again reunified it with London United with effect from 28 April. As before, the Volvo B7TLs' fates are continued under London United's heading.

Registrations
2717-2733   LN51 AZA-D/F/G/J/L/P/R/T-Z

Date	Deliveries	Licensed for Service
11.01	2718-2721, 2723-2725, 2727, 2729, 2731, 2733	2718-2721, 2723-2725, 2727, 2729, 2731, 2733 (**BT**)
12.01	2717, 2722, 2726, 2728, 2730, 2732	2717, 2722, 2726, 2728, 2730, 2732 (**BT**)

Acquired upon demerger from London United, 03.03.11
VLP 1-27 (LN51 AZA-D/F/G/J/L/P/R/T-Z , PJ53 OUN/P/U-Y, OVA/B)

Loaned from Metroline, 10.02-09.03
VPL 220 (LJ51 XGK)

Company purchased by Transdev and federated with London United, 22.10.02
Company demerged from London United under Transdev, 03.03.11
Company purchased by RATP and federated again with London United, 20.03.14

Travel London/Abellio

V 1-73

Below: **The 381 had come a long way from the minibus-operated P11 which preceded it. Travel London won it and on 9 October 2004 put into service the first of what would be 73 members of the V class of Wrightbus Gemini-bodied Volvo B7TLs to what was basically Travel West Midlands specification other than London blinds and dual doors. Here at Peckham on 28 December is Walworth's V 10 (BX54 DHZ).** *Author*

With every takeover of a London bus company in the post-privatisation era, the companies acquired tended to take on the characteristics of their new parents, and so it was with Travel London, which discarded its Connex antecedents and taste for Tridents and rebranded as a subsidiary of Travel West Midlands with the according predilection for long-wheelbase Volvo B7TLs with Wrightbus Gemini bodywork. Twenty of these was what was ordered when Travel London scooped the 381 and N381 from London Central in March 2004, and general expansion would see them operate from a reactivated Walworth garage.

The V class began gathering as early as August and as delivery commenced, training was accomplished by loaning Vs 1-3 to Battersea for use on the 344 before the 381's commencement date on 9 October, and the process continued thereafter with V 20. Vs then began visiting Beddington Cross's 3 when driven by a loaned driver, and by the end of 2004 the 156 followed as a spot for the Vs to visit. Much more unusual was the 196.

Above: Sporting the new and straitened blind standard on 3 December 2005 is V 40 (BX55 XMP), coming round Surrey Quays shopping centre on the first day of Travel London operation of the 188 with a second V in view behind. *Author*

Two more routes were won from Go-Ahead in the form of the 188 and 343, awarded in March 2005. Expansion during the year saw the takeover of Tellings-Golden Miller on 17 June and one of the routes it operated, the H50, was designated for conversion to double-deck to go with its new contract.

July saw 45 more Vs ordered for the 188 and 343, and of the first delivered, Vs 24-26 made their debut on a Diwali service on 2 November. Otherwise the 188 was taken over on 3 December with Vs 21-44 and the 343 (including night bus N343) followed on 4 February 2006 with Vs 45-65, both out of Walworth. There were some London registrations mixed in with the usual Birmingham marks, and all had single-line blind boxes and white roofs.

Left: A handful of the batch of Vs for the 188 and 343 had their Birmingham registrations voided and replaced by London marks; only fitting since they were after all, London buses! Walworth's V 52 (LF55 CYV) is at the Elephant & Castle on 7 October 2006. *Author*

Above: **Otherwise concentrated in inner south-east London, the V class of Travel London opened an outpost far to the north-west in the shape of the H50, a route inherited with the purchase of Wing's Buses. Here at Hayes & Harlington during May 2006 is V 66 (BX55 XNV), one of the four new Volvo B7TLs assigned to the route.** *Haydn Davies*

Right: **The 3 was Connex London's flagship route, but time had marched on and by the time Travel London took over Connex it was just one of many and its buses were approaching the end of one contract term. In the event, the need to add resources to the 344 took precedence and in June 2006 V 73 (LF06 YRC) is seen passing through Vauxhall bus station. This was to be the highest-numbered Volvo B7TL in the fleet, as purchases thereafter were of Enviro400s.** *Haydn Davies*

The H50 was renewed on 14 January 2006 and four more Vs ordered for it. Arriving at Hayes in February, Vs 66-69 took over the route on the 28th. In April another four Vs were ordered against a PVR increase applying to the 344 from 3 June, but in the event they turned out just as often on the 188 and 343 from Walworth, which was wholly V where Battersea had standardised on TAs. In any case Vs 70-73 were the last Volvo B7TLs ordered by Travel London, which had discovered the Alexander Dennis Enviro400.

The 350's Vs moved on 9 September from Hayes to the former Wing's garage, which took on the Hayes name. On 11 November the 344 gained a night service.

The introduction of new route 452 prompted some movements occasioned by its conversion to Enviro400. Five of the new ED class took over the V element on the 344

252 – Volvo B7TL

Left: **The first and second batches of Vs mixed freely, bringing each blind box configuration to the other's route as seen on V 14 (BX54 DJJ) at the Elephant on 4 February 2007.** Author

and released the highest-numbered Volvos to Beddington Cross for an increase to the 3 implemented on 10 February 2007. Once there, they soon began to visit the 157.

A renumbering scheme was undertaken on 3 March 2007, which unfortunately removed the class codes in favour of monolithic number blocks fitting in adjacent to series used by Travel West Midlands and Dundee. In this way the Vs became plain 9001-9073.

The 188 received a night service on 28 July 2007, after a couple of postponements. 8 October saw the 3's 'Vs' at Beddington Cross moved over to the 157, and over the cusp of 2007/08 loaned Metroline TAs joined the 'Vs' on the 381 to help out during the closure of the East London Line for reconfiguration into the new London Overground. Replacement services were otherwise entrusted to temporary routes ELC and ELP, which failed

Left: **London buses have had class codes since time immemorial, even before London Transport, but some of that body's independent successors dropped the practice, making it harder to identify buses in general. Walworth's 9023 (BX55 XLU) is seen on 25 May 2009 at St George's Circus, after having been renumbered from V 23.** Author

Travel London – 253

to attract custom more used to the 381. These were operated with Tridents, though one 'V' made it to the ELC. A similar new venture for Volvo B7TLs was the 152 at Beddington Cross, visited once at least.

On 22 March 2008 new route 350 to Heathrow Terminal 5 began as a replacement for the H50, awarded to Travel London and, other than a schoolday double-deck journey, replacing its 'Vs' with nine new Enviro200s. Just 9066 remained at Hayes for this purpose. Accident damage accrued to 9015 and 9063 during the year, but both were repaired.

By 2009 National Express was eyeing its debt with some wariness and shopping Travel London round to potential buyers to raise cash quickly. On 21 May the sale took place to NedRailways and was formalised on 9 June.

New ventures for 'V' visits by this time were the 40, taken up by Walworth on 2 May with new Enviro400s, and once 9012 even got out on the C1, with cards in the windscreen. The 381 was tendered and retained with its existing 'Vs'.

NedRailways lost no time subjecting its new acquisition to rebranding, and from 30 October 2009 the new name for operations was Abellio London. Buses kept their numeric fleetnumbers and a new plain grey seat moquette was phased in on refurbishments, which began to affect the earliest 'Vs' as 2010 got going, even though their routes 188 and 343 were both out to tender by that point. The parent company followed suit, dropping its NedRailways moniker for Abellio itself.

In May 2010 both the 188 and 343 were announced as retained, though the former would be replacing its 'Vs' with new hybrids during the term of its new contract. On 12 June the removal of the long-standing augmentations to the 381 freed three 'Vs' for a boost to the 343, overriding plans to transfer them to the 3 at Beddington Cross.

4 December saw the 188 renewed but one of its 'Vs' transferred to Beddington Cross, while the 343 was set going anew on 5 February 2011. The 157 was tendered at this time and announced as renewed in March, just as an order was announced for

Below: **After the renumbering came the renaming, when Travel London's new Dutch owners gave the body an auto-generated handle that endeavoured to offend nobody in a host of European languages. The resulting Abellio 9065 (BX55 XNU) is at Canada Water on 20 July 2010.**
Author

Left: Only one 'V' ever carried an all-over ad in Travel London or Abellio days, but the type was just as subject to rear ads as any other London bus. Here at Waterloo on 24 September 2011 9064 (BX55 XNT) is carrying one for Tunisia. *Author*

Left: The 35 and 40 had been exclusively associated with Camberwell, latterly of London Central, for two decades before Abellio won them both. Although the scheduled type was Enviro400s, Walworth sometimes put its Volvo B7TLs into action on the 40, as proven by 9057 (BX55 XNL) just south of London Bridge on 28 August 2011. At that time Battersea operated the 35 but would later cede it to Waterloo and bring it too into the realms of possibility for 'Vs'. *Author*

Left: Beddington Cross carved out a solid placement for Volvo B7TLs with the conversion of the 157 from 'TA' at the end of 2007. Passing through West Croydon on 8 September 2012 is 9072 (LF06 YRE). *Author*

Above: **White-on-black blinds now began to appear, and on 1 April 2014 at Waterloo 9070 (LF06 YRC) is taking them to the 172. Garage codes were now carried.** *Author*

thirteen E40Hs to take over part of the 188; the rest would retain 'Vs', now undergoing refurbishment. Of these, the later repaints went over the black trim carried when new, producing a rather different appearance.

2011 ended with the renewal of the 157 on 3 December. The 3's own contract renewal on 11 February 2012 prompted its transfer from Beddington Cross to Battersea, removing the likelihood of 'V' appearances. When the new E40Hs started taking over the 188 they displaced 'Vs' to Beddington Cross to complete the 157 and see off Tridents from this route, with the expected wanderings to the 3. 31 March saw the 350 double-decked with some of these spare Tridents and Hayes's solitary 9066 was transferred to Beddington Cross.

The transfer of the 35 from Battersea to Walworth on 23 June permitted Volvo appearances. Refurbishments had reached the end of the series over 2013 and into 2014 as the 'Vs' approached their second decade. November 2014 wasn't so good for the type, however, 9066 suffering fire damage on the 4th and 9031 on the 6th. 9031 was repaired but 9066 was written off the following May.

Abellio's 'Vs' could still visit new routes away from their usual 157, 188, 343 and 381, when on 31 January 2015 the 109 was taken over from Arriva London South with E40H MMCs from Walworth; late deliveries of the intended new buses forced Volvos to deputise on the route then and ever since. Beddington Cross was also apt to put a Volvo out on the 3, 152 and the schoolday double-deck journey of the 407 introduced with its latest Abellio contract.

October 2014 saw the first all-over ad applied to an Abellio B7TL in the form of 9061, which touted Mexico until December.

Right: **The 35 and 40 had been allocated to separate garages when assumed by Travel London, but in the Abellio era they were reunited at Walworth, permitting Volvo B7TL appearances like that of 9048 (LF55 CYZ) at Liverpool Street on 24 February 2014.** *Author*

The 381 was out for tender during 2015 and while announced as retained, the decision to put newer vehicles onto it set the clock ticking on the former V class, just as refurbishments were completed. However, the 343 had two years added to its current term on 6 February 2016, ensuring the type's survival until 2018 at least. It was the conversion of the 3 to Borismaster (LT) operation in February 2016 that released E40Hs to the 381, and in turn its 'Vs' replaced large numbers of Tridents still in service.

The loss of routes 35 and 40 back to London Central on 30 April removed them from consideration for 'V' operation. Tendering in May saw the 157 announced as lost to Arriva

Left: Another Walworth 'V' visitor to the 35, 9070 (LF06 YRC) at Clapham Junction on 22 November 2015, shows off the differences in repainting styles; in this case all the black trim has been gone over, even that surrounding the blind box, to make for an awkwardly stark appearance. *Author*

Left: The 381 was the first of the core three Volvo B7TL routes to lose its 'Vs', E40Hs taking their place in February 2016. On 31 May 2014 9052 (LF55 CYV) comes round the old Bullring at Waterloo. *Author*

Below: **The planners saw fit to demote the busy Wallington-Croydon corridor of the 407 to single-deck operation, but passenger numbers remained sufficient to need one double-decker to augment the Enviro200s of Abellio's contract. Even after the 157 was lost to Arriva London South, two Volvo B7TLs remained behind at Beddington Cross to fulfil this task, and on 8 January 2016 9067 (BX55 XNW) is heading south through Sutton town centre.** Author

London South and the 152, often a pitch for 'Vs', would similarly be passing to London General. Each departed on 3 December, the 157's 'Vs' being redeployed to Walworth to replace the 172's band of second-hand Tridents and thus the last of that chassis in Abellio service by the following March.

The 211 had never seen 'Vs' and by 2017 was LT-operated, but four Beddington Cross expellees came to help on 9 January when the Tube was on strike. Both remaining B7TL-operated Abellio routes, the 188 and 343, were now out to tender again, as was more recent candidate the 172. The latter service

Right: **On 8 May 2016 Beddington Cross's 9030 (BX55 XMC) comes into Morden after a typically long journey on the important suburban route 157.** Author

was rerouted in central London on 17 June to terminate at Clerkenwell Green rather than St Paul's.

On 21 February 9026, just transferred from Beddington Cross to Walworth, was destroyed by fire at Aspen Way after a runout on a rail replacement service. But it was to be tendering that would knock out Abellio's 'Vs' in a one-two-three punch that saw all of the 188 (March), 172 (June) and 343 (June) awarded to Go-Ahead.

Beddington Cross had kept hold of 9067 and 9068 for the 407 school journey but the garage's spell with the BTL ended in July

Above: **Abellio's acquisition of the 109 saw the first E40H MMCs put into service. Their backups were usually 'classic' Enviro400s, but the two 'Vs' held in reserve for the 407 often turned out themselves, as 9067 (BX55 XNW) is doing when seen at West Croydon on 25 April 2017.** Author

Left: **Repainted and refurbished with the latest, shouty red style of Abellio moquette combined with yellow handrails, Walworth's 9072 (LF06 YRE) works its last full year on the 343 when seen at Peckham Rye on 23 February 2017.** Author

Right: **It probably wasn't the designers' intent that the revamping of the roundabout at St George's Circus would improve matters immeasurably for bus photographers, but so it has proved, with many pixels expended here. Walworth's 9044 (BX55 XMU) is heading south towards the Elephant on 9 March 2017, in the last full year of Volvo B7TL operation on the 188 and by Abellio London in general.** *Author*

Below: **Similarly, the Elephant & Castle has been upgraded from a dirty, threatening warren of subterranean tunnels to a bright and open vista with easy photographic opportunities from any angle; so long as cyclists don't roar across your lens, that is. Two-line blind boxes were becoming very thin on the ground by the time 9011 (BX54 DJD) was captured on 9 March 2017, and this bus was withdrawn when the 343 passed to London Central the following 3 February.** *Author*

upon their transfer to Walworth. Outright disposals began in earnest, even before the exodus began with the loss of the 188 on 11 November, and many of these were for scrap despite their comparatively young age.

2018, then, was the Abellio B7TLs' last year. The 343 passed to London Central on 3 February, leaving just twenty 'Vs' for the 172 until 17 March when it too would leave for Go-Ahead. In service on the last day, Friday 16 March, were 9018, 9022, 9029, 9039, 9047, 9050, 9052, 9053, 9060, 9062, 9065 and 9067, of which 9053, running in at 00:55 on the 17th, brought down the curtain on stage Volvo B7TL operation at Abellio London. Nineteen units remained for rail replacement work in the short term and 9001 became a heritage vehicle within the company.

Left: **Abellio London's last Volvo B7TL-operated route** was a recent entry to the company, coming in from London Central and serving a single term at Walworth before being awarded back there. Its unlucky cohort of ex-Armchair Dennis Tridents were replaced by 'Vs' coming off the 381 and here at Waterloo on 4 January 2018 is 9029 (BX55 XMB), which was in service on the final day, 16 March. *Author*

Registrations
V 1-20	BX54 DHJ-P/V/Y/Z, DJD-F/J/K/O/U/V/Y/Z
V 21-69	BX55 XLS-W/Y/Z, XMA-E/G/H/J-M/P/R-V, LF55 CZA, BX55 XMW/Z, LF55 CYZ/Y/X/W/V, CZB, BX55 XNG/J-P/R-U/V/W/Y/Z
V 70-73	LF06 YRC-E/G

Date	Deliveries	Licensed for Service
09.04	V 1-17	V 1-17 (**WL**)
10.04	V 18-20	V 18-20 (**WL**)
10.05	V 22, 24-26, 29	
11.05	V 21, 23, 27, 28, 30-44	
12.05	V 48, 49	V 21-44 (**WL**)
01.06	V 45-47, 51-65	V 25-65 (**WL**)
02.06	V 66-69	V 66-69 (**TM**)
05.06	V 70-73	V 70-73 (**QB**)

V 1-73 renumbered 9001-9073, 03.03.07

Disposals
05.15	9066
02.17	9026
06.17	9008
08.17	9020, 9025
09.17	9013, 9023, 9032, 9033, 9043
10.17	9004, 9036
12.17	9011, 9014, 9024, 9028, 9031, 9035, 9038
01.18	9002, 9003, 9006, 9007, 9009, 9010, 9012, 9015-9017
02.18	9019, 9030, 9037, 9044-9046, 9049
03.18	9005, 9021, 9034, 9036, 9040, 9041, 9051, 9057-9059, 9061, 9063, 9064, 9069-9073
12.18	9042, 9053, 9055
04.19	9034, 9040, 9049, 9061
05.19	9009, 9024, 9044
06.19	9013, 9018, 9019, 9027, 9029, 9033, 9039, 9047, 9048, 9050, 9052, 9054, 9056, 9057, 9062, 9067
08.19	9050, 9052
09.19	9027, 9047
02.20	9001

Sullivan Buses

ELV 1

Below: **Almost ideally positioned for a picture postcard on 3 December 2005 but for the cones on Westminster Bridge is ELV 1 (EL04 SUL).** *Author*

June 2004 saw the delivery to Sullivan Buses of the company's first Volvo B7TL, ELV 1. On an 11m chassis, it had East Lancs Myllennium Vyking bodywork seating 80 (H47/33F).

VPL 174 (X157 JOP), ex-London Easylink and new as a Lothian-spec demonstrator, had already found its way here, but the ELV remained the only B7TL purchased new. Both were for private hire with only limited forays to service on the company's local 398 and TfL school route 606.

In October 2008 Wrightbus Gemini-bodied WVL 1 (GD52 SYC) was acquired; it had been new to Morton's in Dublin and came via Circle Line. ELV 1 was repainted early in 2009. July of that year saw two more Myllenniums added, former London General EVLs 31 and 35 which became ELVs 2 and 3 (PN02 XCR, XBY). ELV 3 was quickly renumbered ELV 4 to make room for a second ELV 3 (PL51 LGD), which came with ELV 6 (PL51 LGG); these were formerly London General EVLs 3 and 6.

The 606 was lost after 9 October 2009, this being Sullivan Buses' only TfL contract for the moment. ELV 4 was given an anniversary livery with an additional red midriff to celebrate ten years of operation.

In August 2010 two ex-London United Volvo B7TLs with Plaxton President bodywork were taken to start Volvo Olympian replacement; VPs 113 and 116 (W459, 463 BCW) retained their London United class codes and centre doors. VP 116 was soon exchanged for VP 119 (W466 BCW).

Sullivan Buses marked their return to TfL tendering in 2012 with the award of school routes 628, 653, 683 and 688 plus the more regular 298. The former added three Volvo B9TLs (covered in the volume on that type) and diverted ELVs 2 and 4, and the 298 soon saw very occasional double-deckers alongside its scheduled Enviro200s. Buses for TfL routes omitted the white relief and yellow doors or lost them upon repaint.

Despite having taken second-hand Tridents in recent years, Sullivan acquired five more B7TLs in April 2013 in advance of the takeover of the 626 from Metroline on 4

Left: **On 9 August 2015 WVL 1 (GD52 SYC) negotiates the new layout of Tottenham's one-way system while on a rail replacement covering the top end of the Victoria line.** *Author*

Left: **Fourteen years after delivery, ELV 1 (EL04 SUL) looks as good as new when sighted coming around Loughton station on a Central Line rail replacement service on 9 September 2018, thanks to its reupholstering with the most attractive maroon moquette based on that used in the Borismaster.** *Author*

September. Formerly London United VLEs 25, 40 and 43-45, they became ELVs 5 and 7-10 (PA04 CYH, PO54 ADU, OOE-G).

Up to 150 extra buses were added to the Night Bus network on 14/15 June 2014 to meet expected extra patronage during the World Cup, and Sullivan Volvo B7TLs featured on the N15 and N55.

In May 2015 VPs 113 and 119 were sold to Action Cars at Pinewood Studios, but in July came three more Volvo B7TLs; WVLs 5-7 (LF52 UPV/L/M) were ex-Arriva VLWs 85, 97 and 98. VLW 123 followed in September as WVL 8 (LF52 UOW), and in October came WVLs 9 and 10 (LF52 UOS/T), ex-VLWs 119 and 120.

VPL 174 was withdrawn in June 2017 and sold to Ripley in November. WVL 6 suffered roof damage under the low bridge at Staines on 29 May 2018.

When 230 extra buses were added to school services post-COVID lockdown, ELV 8 found itself recommissioned and put out on the 653 from 4 September to 16 December 2020.

Registration
ELV 1   EL04 SUL

Date   Deliveries
06.04   ELV 1

Licensed for Service
ELV 1 (**SM**)

Metrobus

865-875

Although Metrobus of Orpington had been brought into the Go-Ahead fold in 1999, it remained a self-standing operation with its own numbering system and its own distinct taste in vehicles, namely Scania chassis. Even so, when the company was called upon to step in to take the 127 from the failing Centra on 10 December 2005, there was no choice but to pull existing vehicles that happened to be spare at the same time. Thus were PVLs 195-205, Plaxton President-bodied Volvo B7TLs otherwise allocated to Merton, borrowed and renumbered 865-875 for the occasion, though in loose registration number order so that PVLs 200 and 202 were transposed. They operated from Croydon on Mondays to Saturdays, with the Sunday service the responsibility of Godstone. The latter occasionally borrowed the 'PVLs' for its own ends, with 865 popping up on the 166 on 9 January 2006. Darts from Godstone's route T33 batch deputised in return.

When the 127's intended batch of new Scanias arrived and entered service, the 'PVLs' were returned to London General on 11 April and from there formed a group that would rove to two more companies as cover for various enhancements.

Loaned from London General, 10.12.05-11.04.06
865-875 (X595-598, 699, 702, 501-504, 705 EGK)

Below: **Labelled with Metrobus's own logos in silver, 865 (X595 EGK) looks smart against brilliant winter sunshine on the 127's incongruous but pleasing rural section during January 2006.**
Haydn Davies

TfL

VP 20

During June 2007 Transport for London, as distinct from its operating arm East Thames Buses, took back in-house a Volvo B7TL surplus to the 185's complement. It was converted to open-top and began a new life as a roving ambassador.

Kept at Mandela Way, even after the sale of East Thames Buses to Go-Ahead on 3 October 2009, VP 20 remained in sporadic use, mostly on Pride events and once on the 2018 iteration of Imberbus, before sale to Alpine Travel in October 2019.

Left: **On 26 September 2010 VP 20 (X173 FBB) poses at Birchanger Green services, a long way from the 150's patch but close enough to that year's Showbus rally to refuel.** *Russell Young*

Left: **Five and a half years on from the previous photo, VP 20 (X173 FBB) was taken to Brooklands on 17 April 2016 and shows off not only posters suitable for any occasion, but a towbar as well.** *Author*

Other London-area Volvo B7TL operators

Several non-TfL companies in the London area operated Volvo B7TLs, some of them in sizeable numbers. The most prolific was Arriva Kent Thameside, whose order for 49 ALX400-bodied 10.6m versions in 2004 revitalised the Medway Towns.

When the terrorist bombings of 7 July 2005 severed the Piccadilly Line, First Leicester supplied Volvo B7TLs as replacement buses. To the immediate west of London, First Beeline's Green Line-themed 702 route to Windsor and Legoland employed three Volvo B9TLs but added B7TL VNZ 32348 in 2010 to support them.

As Volvo B7TLs came out of frontline service, some after relatively curtailed lifespans, their second operators in the London periphery put them out on rail replacement services where contracted for. Just one such deployment was by Ensignbus, which used seven ex-Arriva VLAs on Overground service T in 2016-17. For that particular occasion they donned a splendid red and silver variant of company livery.

Below: **When Arriva Kent Thameside ordered 49 ALX400-bodied Volvo B7TLs for the Medway Towns, the group was rebranding; 6401 (GN04 UDM) was carrying the six-year-old Arriva livery when displayed at North Weald on 27 June 2004.** Author

Left: Arriva's general rebranding of the mid-2000s added a dark skirt and relegated the front stone cap to more of a bonnet, as seen on 6443 (GN04 UFM) leaving Bluewater on 2 December 2016. *Author*

Left: On 20 July 2005 First Leicester's 32077 (KP51 WBD) is seen at Seven Sisters station on a rail replacement which allowed passengers otherwise needing the stricken Piccadilly Line to board the Victoria Line into town instead. *Author*

Left: Green Line had long since withered and died, a victim of London's unbearable traffic, but the brand was still solid and was re-used by Bee Line for its service to Legoland, which proved so popular that Volvo B7TL VNZ 32348 (LK53 LZL) was detached from First London and added to Bracknell's VNX-class Volvo B9TLs. Slough bus station, where this bus is pictured on 12 May 2013, was a similarly moribund (if not outright toxic) brand and also benefited from being brought up to date. *Author*

Other B7TLs – 267

Right: **Despite the colourful livery and eclectic set of cherished registrations, Buses Excetera had endemic structural troubles and eventually foundered in its Surrey home region, a frequent killer of bus operators large and small. Former London Central PVL 175 (S25 ETC, ex-X575 EGK) came via Ensign in March 2013 and on 8 May 2016 was performing a rail replacement through Staines.** Author

Below: **Go-Ahead sold PVL 93 (W493 WGH) to Plymouth Citybus in January 2013, but in February 2016 this bus passed to Go-Coachhire as their number 8303. It is seen on 13 February 2017 working a Tramlink replacement through Wimbledon; this was to cover track and signal replacement on the northernmost leg of the line.** Author

268 – Volvo B7TL

Above: Naturally, Ensignbus applied to its acquired former Arriva London North VLAs a splendid, yet simple livery that would have done them proud in their London service days. Allocated to London Overground replacement service T, 903 (LJ54 BDF), formerly VLA 88, is really flourishing when seen on 23 November 2016 at Walthamstow Central. *Mark McWalter*

Left: And then there is preservation, though fifteen years is barely middle age in old money. Still, London General WVL 1 (LG02 KGP) was acquired by the London Bus Museum at Brooklands and is seen beside a similarly prematurely retired transport fixture during the Spring Gala held on 9 April 2017. *Author*

Other B7TLs – 269

London Tour Operators
London City Tour

During 2014 Top of Town Tours of Willesden (later Bedfont) applied to run a 15-minute open-top tourist route, and after some months getting it together, changed their name to London City Tour Ltd and commenced operations on 23 March 2015.

Plaxton President-bodied Volvo B7TLs ex-Metroline and acquired through Ensign were the preferred stock, London City Tour amassing the former VPLs 163, 164, 171, 175, 185, 187, 191-193, 197, 198, 200, 201, 203, 204, 207-210 and 232 over 2016 in either full- or part-open-top form before the supply ran dry and Tridents started appearing.

During 2017 the operation moved to Hounslow and then back to Willesden, and as 2018 bowed, the B7TLs started giving way to B9TLs ex-Metroline and London Central, though the process was interrupted by the closedown of the company on 10 August and the transfer of its branded tours to the OLST.

Below: **Full open-top Y183 NLK, formerly Metroline's VPL 183, comes off Westminster Bridge towards Parliament Square on 17 August 2016.** Author

Above: **Y143 NLK was formerly Metroline VPL 210, and on 25 May 2017 is seen at the Hyde Park Corner end of Piccadilly in partial open-top format.** *Author*

Left: **Swinging its way round Parliament Square on 1 July 2018 is Y179 NLK, another of the large contingent of London City Tour acquisitions that had spent their service lives on the 52 out of Metroline's Willesden garage.** *Author*

London City Tour 271

Totals

Company	Total	Fleetnumbers
Go-Ahead	790	**AVL** 1-46, **PVL** 1-419, **EVL** 1-52, **WVL** 1-273
London United	148	**VA** 60-104, **VP** 105-130, **VR** 226-228, **VA** 293-311, **VLP** 18-27, **VE** 1-10, **VLE** 1-45
Metroline	305	**VPL** 135-236, **VP** 317-347, 466-580, **VPL** 581-603, **VP** 604-628, **VPL** 629-637
Arriva	378	**VLW** 1-199, **VLA** 1-179
London Easylink	20	**VP** 149, 151-154, 157-159, 161-169, 171-173
East Thames Buses	44	**VWL** 1-44
First	228	**VE** 953, **VT** 1100-1112, **VTL** 1200-1228, **VFL** 1249-1276, **VTL** 1294-1327, **VWL** 1387-1407, **VNW** 32349-32430, **VNZ** 32495-32502, **VNW** 32657-32668
Sovereign	27	2717-2733
Travel London	73	V 1-73
Sullivan	1	**ELV** 1
TOTAL	**2014**	

Totals are for buses bought or leased new for LBSL/TfL services, 2000-2006.

Bibliography

Books
The London Enviro400, Matthew Wharmby, Pen and Sword 2016.
The London Volvo B9TL and B5LH, Matthew Wharmby, Pen and Sword 2019.

Magazines, Supplements, Articles and Periodicals
The London Bus (TLB), LOTS, monthly
London Bus Magazine (LBM), LOTS, quarterly
BUSES magazine, Ian Allan (to 2012), Key Publishing (2012-present), monthly
The Londoner, Visions, bi-monthly

Websites and Groups
London Bus Routes by Ian Armstrong (www.londonbuses.co.uk)
Bus Lists on the Web (www.buslistsontheweb.co.uk)
London Vehicle Finder (www.lvf.io)